Constitutional Law

Edited by
R Hughes LLB, CQSW
and
S Migdal Barrister (Midland and Oxford Circuit)

HLT Publications

HLT PUBLICATIONS
200 Greyhound Road, London W14 9RY

First Edition 1995

© The HLT Group Ltd 1995

All HLT publications enjoy copyright protection and the copyright belongs to The HLT Group Ltd.

All rights reserved. No part of this publication may be reproduced or transmitted in any form or by any means, electronic, mechanical, photocopying, recording or otherwise, or stored in any retrieval system of any nature without either the written permission of the copyright holder, application for which should be made to The HLT Group Ltd, or a licence permitting restricted copying in the United Kingdom issued by the Copyright Licensing Agency.

Any person who infringes the above in relation to this publication may be liable to criminal prosecution and civil claims for damages.

ISBN 0 7510 0599 1

British Library Cataloguing-in-Publication.

A CIP Catalogue record for this book is available from the British Library.

Printed and bound in Great Britain.

CONTENTS

Acknowledgements	v
Introduction	vii
How to Study Constitutional Law	ix
Revision and Examination Technique	xi
Table of Cases	xv
Table of Statutes	xxi
1 The Nature of Constitutional Law	1
2 The Characteristics of the British Constitution	3
3 Sovereignty of Parliament	24
4 Sovereignty of Parliament and the European Union	33
5 The Electoral System	47
6 Legislature I – the House of Commons	59
7 Legislature II – the House of Lords	74
8 Parliamentary Privilege	85
9 The Executive	103
10 The European Convention and a Bill of Rights	120
11 Public Order	140
12 Freedom of Expression	154
13 Police Powers	172
14 University of London LLB (External) 1994 Questions and Suggested Solutions	179

ACKNOWLEDGEMENTS

Some questions used are taken or adapted from past University of London LLB (External) Degree and the University of Wolverhampton examination papers and our thanks are extended to the universities of London and Wolverhampton for their kind permission to use and publish the questions.

Caveat

The LLB answers given are not approved or sanctioned by the University of London or the University of Wolverhampton and are entirely our responsibility.

They are not intended as 'Model Answers', but rather as Suggested Solutions.

The answers have two fundamental purposes, namely:

a) To provide a detailed example of a suggested solution to an examination question, and

b) To assist students with their research into the subject and to further their understanding and appreciation of the subject of Law.

INTRODUCTION

This Revision WorkBook is aimed to be of help to those studying constitutional law. Its coverage is not restricted to any one syllabus but embraces all the core topics which can be found in university level examinations.

Students will hopefully find it useful not only at examination time but also as a helpful summary of and introduction to the subject when studying it for the first time.

The WorkBook has been designed specifically to address common problems suffered by students when studying any legal subject. All examination based courses consist of four main processes, all of which may cause problems for some students. The WorkBook can be of help with each of these processes.

a) *Acquisition of knowledge*

This is achieved by individual work – attending lectures and reading the relevant textbooks and source materials such as cases and articles. The WorkBook is not intended to be a textbook and is in no way a substitute for one. However, the 'key points' and 'recent cases and statutes' sections will help students to direct their study to the important areas within each topic.

b) *Understanding*

Whilst difficulties in understanding a topic or particular point are best solved by a teacher's explanation. The WorkBook offers a summary of the essential points together with cases. This is the key to understanding for many students.

c) *Learning*

The process of learning is also a highly individual one. As a rule, however, students find it much easier to learn within a clear structure. The WorkBook will be an aid to those who find learning a problem.

d) *Applying the knowledge to the question*

This is, perhaps, the most common problem of all. The WorkBook includes examination questions and answers covering many possible question variations within each topic.

In this revised 1995 edition the final chapter contains the complete June 1994 University of London LLB (External) Constitutional Law question paper, followed by suggested solutions to each question. Thus the student will have the opportunity to review a recent examination paper in its entirety, and can, if desired, use this chapter as a mock examination – referring to the suggested solutions only after first having attempted the questions. Note that some questions will be on administrative law, and for these reference should be made to the *Administrative Law Revision WorkBook* published by HLT Publications and available in early 1996. For the June 1994 paper the relevant questions are 5, 6 and 8.

HOW TO STUDY CONSTITUTIONAL LAW

Constitutional law is a vast subject covering a variety of topics ranging from the structure and organisation of government to civil liberties. Examiners must be selective in the areas they choose to examine and students should pay regard to their particular syllabus and the emphasis placed on each topic. By and large however the subject divides into two areas – the characteristics of the British Constitution and civil liberties. If your syllabus includes judicial review of administrative action you should also refer to the *Administrative Law Revision WorkBook*, published by HLT Publications and available in early 1996.

The first part of any syllabus – usually the characteristics of the British Constitution – demands a background knowledge of British history and politics. This can cause problems for students who do not have any interest or knowledge of this area and overseas students in particular can experience difficulty here. To place the subject in its proper context requires some background reading – Maitland's *A Constitutional History of England* is authoritative – and knowledge gleaned from keeping abreast of current affairs is vital. In addition there are several good introductory works which help students. In terms of the examination this area can unsettle students simply because there is an absence of legal authority for the points they make. The questions are often discursive demanding the discussion of an issue and the presentation of a point of view. A well-read student who can present the salient points with authority will achieve good marks – the student who 'waffles' will not. Examples are important eg answer to a question on conventions demands an explanation of the part played by convention in our constitution backed by examples of conventions in operation.

The second part of the syllabus will deal with civil liberties. Again this is an extensive area and examiners are often selective. Police powers may appear in some syllabuses, citizenship and immigration in others. It is important to appreciate that what liberties are enjoyed in the United Kingdom are residual and the part played by the European Convention on Human Rights must be understood. The subject matter is topical, statute and case law are important. Questions can be either essay or problem – for example an essay on a Bill of Rights for the United Kingdom is frequently examined and demands that students present the argument both for and against the adoption in the United Kingdom of a written Bill of Rights. Problem questions, for example on public order or police powers, require students to apply the relevant statute and case law to the facts given, remembering again to take care to advise the client.

In essence constitutional law, like all legal subjects, requires students to present arguments in a precise, reasoned and authoritative manner.

REVISION AND EXAMINATION TECHNIQUE

(A) REVISION TECHNIQUE

Planning a revision timetable

In planning your revision timetable make sure you don't finish the syllabus too early. You should avoid leaving revision so late that you have to 'cram' – but constant revision of the same topic leads to stagnation.

Plan ahead, however, and try to make your plans increasingly detailed as you approach the examination date.

Allocate enough time for each topic to be studied. But note that it is better to devise a realistic timetable, to which you have a reasonable chance of keeping, rather than a wildly optimistic schedule which you will probably abandon at the first opportunity!

The syllabus and its topics

One of your first tasks when you began your course was to ensure that you thoroughly understood your **syllabus**. Check now to see if you can write down the **topics** it comprises from memory. You will see that the chapters of this WorkBook are each devoted to a topic. This will help you decide which are the key chapters relative to your revision programme. Though you should allow some time for glancing through the other chapters.

The topic and its key points

Again working from memory, analyse what you consider to be the key points of any topic that you have selected for particular revision. Seeing what you can recall, unaided, will help you to understand and firmly memorise the concepts involved.

Using the WorkBook

Relevant questions are provided for each topic in this book. Naturally, as typical examples of examination questions, they do not normally relate to one topic only. But the questions in each chapter *will* relate to the subject matter of the chapter to a degree. You can choose your method of consulting the questions and solutions, but here are some suggestions (strategies 1–3). Each of them pre-supposes that you have read through the author's notes on key points and question analysis, and any other preliminary matter, at the beginning of the chapter. Once again, you now need to practise working from *memory*, for that is the challenge you are preparing yourself for. As a rule of procedure constantly test yourself once revision starts, both orally and in writing.

Strategy 1

Strategy 1 is planned for the purpose of *quick revision*. First read your chosen question carefully and then jot down in abbreviated notes what you consider to be the main points at issue. Similarly, note the cases and statutes that occur to you as being

REVISION AND EXAMINATION TECHNIQUE

relevant for citation purposes. Allow yourself sufficient time to cover what you feel to be relevant. Then study the author's *skeleton solution* and skim-read the *suggested solution* to see how they compare with your notes. When comparing consider carefully what the author has included (and concluded) and see whether that agrees with what you have written. Consider the points of variation also. Have you recognised the key issues? How relevant have you been? It is possible, of course, that you have referred to a recent case that *is* relevant, but which had not been reported when the WorkBook was prepared.

Strategy 2

Strategy 2 requires a nucleus of *three hours* in which to practise writing a set of examination answers in a limited time-span.

Select a number of questions (as many as are normally set in your subject in the examination you are studying for), each from a different chapter in the WorkBook, without consulting the solutions. Find a place to write where you will not be disturbed and try to arrange not to be interrupted for three hours. Write your solutions in the time allowed, noting any time needed to make up if you *are* interrupted.

After a rest, compare your answers with the *suggested solutions* in the WorkBook. There will be considerable variation in style, of course, but the bare facts should not be too dissimilar. Evaluate your answer critically. Be 'searching', but develop a positive approach to deciding how you would tackle each question on another occasion.

Strategy 3

You are unlikely to be able to do more than one three hour examination, but occasionally set yourself a single question. Vary the 'time allowed' by imagining it to be one of the questions that you must answer in three hours and allow yourself a limited preparation and writing time. Try one question that you feel to be difficult and an easier question on another occasion, for example.

Mis-use of suggested solutions

Don't try to learn by rote. In particular, don't try to reproduce the *suggested solutions* by heart. Learn to express the basic concepts in your own words.

Keeping up-to-date

Keep up-to-date. While examiners do not require familiarity with changes in the law during the three months prior to the examination, it obviously creates a good impression if you can show you are acquainted with any recent changes. Make a habit of looking through one of the leading journals – *Modern Law Review*, *Law Quarterly Review* or the *New Law Journal*, for example – and cumulative indices to law reports, such as the *All England Law Reports* or *Weekly Law Reports*, or indeed the daily law reports in *The Times*. Specialist journal(s) for the subject eg *Public Law* are also helpful sources.

(B) EXAMINATION SKILLS

Examiners are human too!

The process of answering an examination question involves a *communication* between you and the person who set it. If you were speaking face to face with the person, you would choose your verbal points and arguments carefully in your reply. When writing, it is all too easy to forget *the human being who is awaiting the reply* and simply write out what one knows in the area of the subject! Bear in mind it is a person whose question you are responding to, throughout your essay. This will help you to avoid being irrelevant or long-winded.

The essay question

Candidates are sometimes tempted to choose to answer essay questions because they 'seem' easier. But the examiner is looking for thoughtful work and will not give good marks for superficial answers.

The essay-type of question may be either purely factual, in asking you to *explain the meaning* of a certain doctrine or principle, or it may ask you to *discuss* a certain proposition, usually derived from a quotation. In either case, the approach to the answer is the same. A clear programme must be devised to give the examiner the meaning or significance of the doctrine, principle or proposition and its origin in common law, equity or statute, and cases which illustrate its application to the branch of law concerned.

The problem question

The problem-type question requires a different approach. You may well be asked to advise a client or merely discuss the problems raised in the question. In either case, the most important factor is to take great care in reading the question. By its nature, the question will be longer than the essay-type question and you will have a number of facts to digest. Time spent in analysing the question may well save time later, when you are endeavouring to impress on the examiner the considerable extent of your basic legal knowledge. The quantity of knowledge is itself a trap and you must always keep within the boundaries of the question in hand. It is very tempting to show the examiner the extent of your knowledge of your subject, but if this is outside the question, it is time lost and no marks earned. It it inevitable that some areas which you have studied and revised will not be the subject of questions, but under no circumstances attempt to adapt a question to a stronger area of knowledge at the expense of relevance.

When you are satisfied that you have grasped the full significance of the problem-type question, set out the fundamental principles involved. You may well be asked to advise one party, but there is no reason why you should not introduce your answer by:

'I would advise A on the following matters ...'

and then continue the answer in a normal impersonal form. This is a much better technique than answering the question as an imaginary conversation.

You will then go on to identify the fundamental problem, or problems posed by the question. This should be followed by a consideration of the law which is relevant to

REVISION AND EXAMINATION TECHNIQUE

the problem. The source of the law, together with the cases which will be of assistance in solving the problem, must then be considered in detail.

Very good problem questions are quite likely to have alternative answers, and in advising A you should be aware that alternative arguments may be available. Each stage of your answer, in this case, will be based on the argument or arguments considered in the previous stage, forming a conditional sequence.

If, however, you only identify one fundamental problem, do not waste time worrying that you cannot think of an alternative – there may very well be only that one answer.

The examiner will then wish to see how you use your legal knowledge to formulate a case and how you apply that formula to the problem which is the subject of the question. It is this positive approach which can make answering a problem question a high mark earner for the student who has fully understood the question and clearly argued his case on the established law.

Examination checklist

1   Read the instructions at the head of the examination carefully. While last-minute changes are unlikely – such as the introduction of a *compulsory question* or *an increase in the number of questions asked* – it has been known to happen.
2   Read the questions carefully. Analyse problem questions – work out what the examiner wants.
3   Plan your answer *before* you start to write. You can divide your time as follows:
    a) working out the question (5 per cent of time);
    b) working out how to answer the question (5 to 10 per cent of time);
    c) writing your answer.
    Do not overlook (a) and (b).
4   Check that you understand the rubric *before* you start to write. Do not 'discuss', for example, if you are specifically asked to 'compare and contrast'.
5   Answer the correct number of questions. If you fail to answer one out of four questions set you lose 25 per cent of your marks!

Style and structure

Try to be clear and concise. Basically this amounts to using paragraphs to denote the sections of your essay, and writing simple, straightforward sentences as much as possible. The sentence you have just read has 22 words – when a sentence reaches 50 words it becomes difficult for a reader to follow.

Do not be inhibited by the word 'structure' (traditionally defined as giving an essay a beginning, a middle and an end). A good structure will be the natural consequence of setting out your arguments and the supporting evidence in a logical order. Set the scene briefly in your opening paragraph. Provide a clear conclusion in your final paragraph.

TABLE OF CASES

Allighan (Gary) MP, Case of (1947) HC 138   *87, 96*
Amendment of the Constitution of Canada, Re (1982) 125 DLR (3d) 1   *6, 13, 15*
Amministrazione delle Finanze dello Stato v Simmenthal SpA Case 106/177 [1978] ECR 629   *38, 40, 45, 182*
Argyll v Argyll [1967] Ch 302   *156, 160*
Arrowsmith v Jenkins [1963] 2 QB 561   *141*
Associated Provincial Picture Houses Ltd v Wednesbury Corporation [1948] 1 KB 223   *7, 195*
Attorney-General v BBC (1987) The Times 18 December   *160*
Attorney-General v De Keyser's Royal Hotel [1920] AC 508   *191, 192*
Attorney-General v English [1983] 1 AC 116; [1982] 2 WLR 278   *158, 161*
Attorney-General v Guardian Newspapers (No 1) [1987] 1 WLR 1248; [1987] 3 All ER 316   *8, 123, 158, 163, 197*
Attorney-General v Guardian Newspapers (No 2) [1988] 3 WLR 776; [1988] 3 All ER 545   *8, 155, 156, 160, 161, 163*
Attorney-General v Jonathan Cape [1976] QB 752   *6, 14, 17, 156*
Attorney-General v News Group Newspapers Ltd [1987] QB 1   *161*
Attorney-General v Newspaper Publishing plc [1987] 3 All ER 276   *158*
Attorney-General v Observer Newspapers Ltd [1988] 1 All ER 385   *160*
Attorney-General v Times Newspapers Ltd [1974] AC 273; [1973] 3 All ER 54   *122, 157*
Attorney-General for Ceylon v De Livera [1963] AC 103   *86, 92, 93, 95*
Attorney-General for New South Wales v Trethowan [1932] AC 526   *25*
Attorney-General's Reference (No 3 of 1977) [1978] 3 All ER 1166   *157*

BBC v Johns [1965] Ch 32   *191, 192*
Beach v Freeson [1972] 1 QB 14   *86, 92*
Beatty v Gillbanks (1862) 9 QBD 308   *149*
Bonham's (Dr) Case (1610) 8 Co Rep 118a   *196, 197*
Bradlaugh v Gossett (1884) 12 QBD 271   *87, 97, 101*
British Coal Corporation v R [1935] AC 500   *40*
Brown (WJ) MP, Case of (1947)   *88, 92, 93*
Brutus v Cozens [1973] AC 854   *142*
Bulmer (HP) v J Bollinger SA [1974] Ch 401; [1974] 2 All ER 1226   *4, 34, 40*
Burgoin v Ministry of Agriculture [1986] QB 716   *46*
Burmah Oil Co v Lord Advocate [1965] AC 75   *24, 40, 169*

Calder, John (Publishers) Ltd v Powell [1965] 1 QB 509   *157*
Campbell v United Kingdom (1992) The Times 1 April   *123*
Campbell and Cosans v United Kingdom [1982] 4 EHRR 293   *122*
Carltona Ltd v Commissioners of Works [1943] 2 All ER 560   *107*
CCSU v Minister for the Civil Service – see Council for Civil Service Unions v Minister for the Civil Service
Chandler v DPP [1964] AC 763   *155, 162, 165*
Christie v Leachinsky (1947) CLC 6152   *133, 136*

TABLE OF CASES

Church of Scientology of California v Johnson-Smith [1972] 1 QB 522   *86, 92, 93, 95, 99*
Commission v UK (Re Bathing Water Directive) [1994] 1 CMLR 760   *36*
Conegate v HM Customs and Excise [1987] 2 WLR 39   *36*
Cook v Alexander [1974] QB 279   *87, 92, 93*
Costa v ENEL [1964] CMLR 425; [1964] ECR 585   *27, 31, 35, 38, 40, 43, 45, 182*
Council for Civil Service Unions v Minister for the Civil Service [1985] AC 374; [1985] ICR 14; [1984] 3 All ER 935   *4, 136, 165, 192, 195*

Derbyshire County Council v Times Newspapers Ltd [1993] 1 All ER 1011   *121, 123, 134, 138*
DPP v A and BC Chewing Gum Ltd [1968] 1 QB 159   *157*
DPP v Hawkins [1988] 1 WLR 1166   *173*
DPP v Luft [1977] AC 962; [1976] 2 All ER 569   *48, 50, 51, 186, 187*
D'Souza v DPP [1992] 1 WLR 1073   *173, 176*
Dudgeon v UK (1981) 4 EHRR 149   *136*
Duke v GEC Reliance [1988] 1 All ER 626   *45*
Duncan v Jones [1936] 1 KB 218   *141, 149*
Duport Steels v Sirs [1980] 1 All ER 529   *183, 184*

Egan v Macready (1921) 1 IR 265   *168*
Ellen Street Estates Ltd v Minister of Health [1934] 1 KB 590   *25, 27, 29, 31, 38, 40, 122, 128, 131, 181, 182*
Entick v Carrington (1765) 19 St Tr 1030   *4, 7, 13, 133, 136*

Faccini Dori v Recreb Srl Case C–91/92 [1995] 1 All ER (EC) 1   *35*
Finnegan v Clowney YTP [1990] 2 AC 407   *34*
Fox v Stirk [1970] 2 QB 463   *47*
Francovich v Italy [1992] IRLR 84   *35, 36, 41, 46*

Garland v British Rail Engineering Ltd [1983] 2 AC 751   *32, 36, 39, 182*
GCHQ case – see Council for Civil Service Unions v Minister for the Civil Service
Goldsmith v Pressdram Ltd [1976] 3 WLR 191   *155*
Grieve v Douglas-Home 1965 SC 315   *48, 50, 51, 186, 188*

Harman v Secretary of State for the Home Department [1982] 2 WLR 338   *121, 157*
Harper v Home Secretary [1955] Ch 238   *48*
Harris v DPP, Fehmi v DPP [1993] 1 All ER 562   *172*
Henderson (DFS) MP, Case of (1945)   *92, 93*
Hipperson v Electoral Registration Officer for Newbury [1985] QB 1060   *4, 13, 47*
Hirst and Agu v Chief Constable for West Yorkshire [1987] Crim LR 330   *141*
Hubbard v Pitt [1976] QB 142   *140*

Inquiry under the Company Securities (Insider Dealing) Act 1985, Re an [1988] AC 660   *158*

Jordan v Burgoyne [1963] 2 QB 744; [1963] 2 All ER 225   *142, 143, 151, 155*

Kent v Metropolitan Police Commissioner (1981) The Times 15 May   *143*
Knuller v DPP [1973] AC 435   *157*

Lamb v DPP [1990] Crim LR 58   *173*
Lewis v Chief Constable of South Wales Constabulary [1991] 1 All ER 206   *173*
Lion Laboratories Ltd v Evans [1985] QB 526; [1984] 3 WLR 539   *160*
Litster v Forth Dry Dock and Engineering Co [1990] 1 AC 546   *181, 182*
Liversidge v Anderson [1942] AC 206   *13*
Lord Advocate v Scotsman Publications [1990] 1 AC 812   *156*

M v Home Office [1993] 3 All ER 537; [1992] 1 QB 270   *17, 21, 22, 179, 183*
Macarthys Ltd v Smith [1979] 3 All ER 325; [1981] QB 180   *28, 32, 36, 37, 38, 41, 131, 181, 182*
Madzimbamuto v Lardner-Burke [1969] 1 AC 645   *6, 13*
Malone v Metropolitan Police Commissioner [1979] Ch 344   *125, 134, 196, 197*
Malone v United Kingdom [1985] 7 EHRR 14   *5, 121, 131, 134, 156, 196, 197*
Mandla v Dowell Lee [1983] 2 AC 548   *143, 155*
Manuel v Attorney-General [1983] Ch 87   *25*
Marleasing SA v La Comercial Internacionale de Alimentacion SA Case C–106/89 [1992] 1 CMLR 305; [1990] ECR 1   *36, 41, 45*
Marshall v BBC [1979] 3 All ER 80   *48*
Marshall v Southampton and South West Hampshire Area Health Authority [1986] QB 401   *35*
Marshall v Southamptom and South West Area Health Authority (No 2) [1993] 4 All ER 586   *35*
Meek v Lothian Regional Council 1983 SLT 494   *186, 188*
Mortensen v Peters 1906 14 SLT 227   *24, 40*
Moss v McLachlan (1984) 149 JP 167   *141*

Observer, The and The Guardian v United Kingdom [1992] 14 EHRR 153   *156*
O'Moran v DPP [1975] QB 364   *143*

Page v Hull University Visitor [1993] 1 All ER 97   *194, 195*
Pepper v Hart [1993] 1 All ER 42   *18, 19, 20, 86, 89*
Pickin v British Railways Board [1974] AC 765   *7, 25, 97, 121, 128, 196, 197*
Pickstone v Freemans plc [1988] 2 All ER 803   *36*
Piddington v Bates [1960] 3 All ER 660   *141*
Prebble v Television New Zealand Ltd [1994] 3 WLR 970   *89*

R v Aitken [1974] Crim LR 639   *160*
R v Arrowsmith [1975] QB 678   *154*
R v Boundary Commission for England, ex parte Foot [1983] QB 600; [1983] 1 All ER 1099   *48, 50, 51, 55, 58*
R v Caunt (1948) unreported   *154*
R v Chief Constable of Devon and Cornwall, ex parte CEGB [1982] QB 458; [1981] 3 WLR 967   *141*
R v Chief Metropolitan Stipendiary Magistrate, ex parte Choudhury [1991] 1 QB 429   *158*

TABLE OF CASES

R v Clarke (No 2) [1964] 2 QB 315   *153*
R v Davison [1992] Crim LR 31   *142*
R v Fulling [1987] 2 All ER 65   *177, 178*
R v Graham-Campbell, ex parte Herbert [1935] 1 KB 594   *87, 94*
R v Griffiths [1957] 2 QB 52   *163*
R v Hailwood [1928] 2 KB 277   *48*
R v Hebron [1989] Crim LR 839   *142, 150*
R v HM Treasury, ex parte Smedley [1985] 1 All ER 589   *20*
R v Home Secretary, ex parte Northumbria Police Authority [1989] QB 26   *191, 192*
R v Home Secretary, ex parte McWhirter [1969] CLY 2636   *48, 51*
R v Horseferry Road Magistrates' Court, ex parte Siadatan [1990] Crim LR 598   *142*
R v Howell [1982] QB 416   *141*
R v Inland Revenue Commissioners, ex parte Rossminster Ltd [1980] 1 All ER 80   *7*
R v Jockey Club, ex parte Aga Khan [1993] 1 WLR 909   *194*
R v Lemon [1979] AC 617   *155*
R v Manchester University, ex parte Nolan (unreported)   *194, 195*
R v Mason [1988] 1 WLR 139   *174, 178*
R v Metropolitan Police Commissioner, ex parte Blackburn [1973] QB 241   *157*
R v Morpeth Ward Justices, ex parte Ward and Others [1992] Crim LR 497   *145*
R v Panel on Takeovers and Mergers, ex parte Datafin plc [1987] QB 815; [1987] 1 All ER 564   *194*
R v Penguin Books [1961] Crim LR 176   *157*
R v Ponting [1985] Crim LR 318   *160*
R v Rowe, ex parte Mainwaring and Others [1992] 1 WLR 1059   *49*
R v Rule [1937] 2 KB 375   *86, 92, 95*
R v Samuel [1988] 2 All ER 135   *177, 178*
R v Secretary of State for Foreign and Commonwealth Affairs, ex parte Everett [1989] QB 811; [1989] 1 All ER 655   *191, 193*
R v Secretary of State for the Home Department, ex parte Bentley [1993] 4 All ER 442   *191, 193*
R v Secretary of State for the Home Department, ex parte Binbasi [1989] Imm AR 595   *191, 193*
R v Secretary of State for the Home Department, ex parte Brind [1991] 2 WLR 588; [1991] 1 All ER 720   *121, 123, 134, 139, 158, 194, 195*
R v Secretary of State for the Home Department, ex parte Hosenball [1977] 1 WLR 766   *14, 165*
R v Secretary of State for Transport, ex parte Factortame (No 1) [1990] 2 AC 85; [1989] 2 WLR 997; [1989] 2 All ER 692 (HL)   *42, 182, 183*
R v Secretary of State for Transport, ex parte Factortame [1990] 3 CMLR 807 (Eur Ct)   *41, 43*
R v Secretary of State for Transport, ex parte Factortame (No 2) [1991] 1 AC 603; [1990] 3 WLR 818; [1991] 1 All ER 70 (HL)   *11, 28, 32, 36, 37, 39, 41, 42, 45, 181, 183*
R v Self [1992] 1 WLR 476   *176*
R v Tronoh Mines [1952] 1 All ER 697   *48, 50, 51, 186, 187, 188*

TABLE OF CASES

Republic of Ireland v United Kingdom [1978] 2 EHRR 25 *136*
Rivlin v Bilainkin [1953] 1 QB 485 *86, 92, 93, 95*
Rost v Edwards (1990) The Times 16 February *99, 102*

Schering Chemicals v Falkman Ltd [1982] QB 1; [1981] 2 All ER 321 *160*
Secretary of State for Defence v Guardian Newspapers Ltd [1984] 2 WLR 268; [1984] 1 All ER 453 *155, 158, 161, 164, 167*
Shaw v DPP [1962] AC 220 *7, 157, 185*
Sheriffs of Middlesex, The, Case of (1840) 11 Ad & E 273 *88, 101*
Sim v Stretch (1936) 52 TLR 669 *158*
Simmenthal SpA v Amministrazione delle Finanze dello Stato [1977] 2 CMLR 1; [1978] 3 CMLR 263 *35*
Stockdale v Hansard (1839) 9 Ad & E 1 *88, 90*
Stourton v Stourton [1963] P 302 *87*
Strauss (GWR) MP, Case of (1957–58) HC 227 *86, 92, 93, 96, 98, 102*
Sunday Times, The v United Kingdom [1979] 2 EHRR 245 *136*
Sunday Times, The v United Kingdom [1992] 14 EHRR 229 *156*

Thomas v Sawkins [1935] 2 KB 249 *141, 173*
Thomas v University of Bradford [1987] AC 795 *194*
Torfaen Borough Council v B & Q plc [1990] 1 All ER 129 *36*
Tyrer v United Kingdom [1978] 2 EHRR 1 *122, 134*

Van Duyn v Home Office [1974] ECR 1337; [1974] 3 All ER 178 *34, 41*
Van Gend en Loos v Netherlands [1963] ECR 1 *35, 45*
Vauxhall Estates v Liverpool Corporation [1932] 1 KB 733 *25, 31, 38, 40, 122, 128, 131, 136, 181, 182*

Wason v Walter (1869) LR 4 QB 73 *87*

X (a minor), Re [1975] 2 WLR 335 *161*
X v Morgan Grampian (Publishers) Ltd [1991] 1 AC 1 *158, 161*

Yorkshire Area Council of National Union of Mineworkers, Case of (1975) *88, 96*

Zamora, The [1916] 2 AC 77 *155*

TABLE OF STATUTES

Act of Settlement 1700   *4, 24, 183, 184*
Act of Union with Scotland Act 1706   *122*
Acquisition of Land (Assessment of Compensation) Act 1919   *31*
    s7(1)   *31*
Appellate Jurisdiction Act 1876   *184*

Bill of Rights 1688   *4, 13, 129, 132, 133, 191, 192*
    Article 9   *86, 96, 99, 101, 102*
Broadcasting Act 1981   *164*
Broadcasting Act 1990   *49, 164, 186*
    s6   *48*
    s6(1)(b)   *188*
    s6(1)(c)   *188*

Canada Act 1982   *25*
Caravan Sites Act 1968   *145*
Children and Young Persons (Harmful Publications) Act 1955   *157*
Cinemas Act 1985   *157*
Colonial Laws Validity Act 1865   *128*
Commonwealth of Australia Act 1901   *122*
Companies Act 1985   *186, 188*
Contempt of Court Act 1981   *157, 161, 163*
    s1   *158*
    s2   *161*
    s3   *158, 163*
    s5   *161*
    s10   *158, 161, 164, 167*
Criminal Justice Act 1988
    s159   *162, 163*
Criminal Justice and Public Order Act 1994   *8, 125, 127, 140, 144, 145, 146, 148, 151, 153, 175, 198*
    s34   *175*
    s35   *175*
    s36   *175*
    s37   *175*
    s38   *175*
    s39   *175*
    s61   *144*
    s63   *145*
    s64   *145*
    s65   *145*
    s66   *145*
    s67   *145*
    s68   *144*
    s70   *144*

TABLE OF STATUTES

Criminal Justice and Public Order Act 1994 (continued)
    s71   *144*
    s75   *144*
    s76   *144*
    s77   *144*
    s80(1)   *145*
    s154   *145*
    s155   *145*
Customs Consolidation Act 1876   *157*

Defamation Act 1954   *93*
    s7   *92*
Defence of the Realm Acts 1914–15   *169*

Education Act 1994   *195*
Education Reform Act 1988   *64, 200*
Emergency Powers Act 1920   *168, 169, 171*
Emergency Powers Act 1964   *169*
Emergency Powers (Defence) Acts 1939–40   *100, 169*
Equal Pay Act 1970   *41*
European Communities Act 1972   *4, 7, 11, 25, 28, 30, 32, 33, 35, 36, 37, 39, 40, 41, 42, 43, 44, 45, 122, 131, 135, 136, 181, 182, 183*
    s2   *44*
    s2(1)   *31, 35, 37, 38, 39, 40, 45, 182*
    s2(2)   *35*
    s2(4)   *26, 27, 31, 35, 37, 38, 39, 40, 43, 45, 182, 183, 198*
    s3   *40, 44, 45, 182*
    s3(1)   *34, 39*
    Schedule 2   *35*
European Communities (Amendment) Act 1993   *25, 44*

Highways Act 1980   *141*
    s137(1)   *152*
His Majesty's Declaration of Abdication Act 1936   *24*
House of Commons Disqualification Act 1975   *7, 68, 103, 183, 184*
    s1   *184*
    s2   *184*
House of Commons Redistribution of Seats Acts 1949, 1958, 1979   *48, 50*
Housing Act 1925   *31*
Housing Act 1988   *200*

Incitement to Disaffection Act 1934   *154*
Intelligence Services Act 1994   *22*
Interception of Communications Act 1985   *156, 167*
Ireland Act 1949
    s1(2)   *24, 29*

Justices of the Peace Act 1361   *199*

TABLE OF STATUTES

Life Peerages Act 1958   *74, 75, 77, 190*
Local Government Act 1888   *199*
Local Government Act 1894   *199*
Local Government 1972   *199, 200*
    s79   *199*
Local Government Act 1992   *200*
    s13   *200*
Local Government Finance Act 1982   *200*
Local Government Finance Act 1988   *64, 68*
Local Government Finance Act 1992   *200*

Merchant Shipping Act 1988   *36, 39, 41, 42, 45, 182*
Metropolitan Police Act 1839
    s52   *152*
Ministerial and Other Salaries Act 1975   *103*
Municipal Corporations Act 1835   *199*

National Audit Act 1983   *62, 65, 67*
Northern Ireland Act 1973
    s1   *25, 28, 29*

Obscene Publications Act 1959   *156*
    s1   *156*
    s3   *157*
    s4   *157*
Obscene Publications Act 1964   *157*
Official Secrets Act 1911   *162*
    s1   *155, 162*
    s2   *155, 160, 162*
Official Secrets Act 1920   *162*
Official Secrets Act 1989   *155, 159, 160, 161, 162, 167*
    s1   *167*
    s5   *160*

Parliament Act 1911   *13, 17, 24, 25, 47, 64, 75, 78, 82, 128, 189, 190, 197*
Parliament Act 1949   *13, 24, 25, 64, 75, 78, 82, 128, 189*
Parliamentary and Municipal Elections Act 1872   *187*
Parliamentary Commissioner Act 1967
    s10(5)   *86*
Parliamentary Constituencies Act 1986   *57*
Parliamentary Elections (Corrupt and Illegal Practices) Act 1883   *187*
Parliamentary Papers Act 1840   *87*
Parliamentary Proceedings Act 1987   *102*
Peerage Act 1963   *75*
Police Act 1964   *141*
    s51(1)   *153*
    s51(3)   *149, 153*
    s53   *154*

TABLE OF STATUTES

Police and Criminal Evidence Act 1984   *133, 136, 140, 143, 149, 170, 172, 177*
    s1   *172, 177*
    s2   *172, 177*
    s3   *172, 177*
    s4   *173*
    s11   *173*
    s14   *173*
    s17   *173, 174, 177*
    s17(5)   *140*
    s17(6)   *140, 173*
    s18   *173, 177*
    s19   *173*
    s24   *173*
    s28   *173*
    s32   *173*
    s56   *174*
    s58   *174, 177, 178*
    s76   *174, 177, 178*
    s78   *174, 175, 177, 178*
    s82   *174*
Police and Magistrates' Courts Act 1994   *200*
Post Office Act 1953   *157*
Prevention of Terrorism (Temporary Provisions) Act 1989   *143, 168*
Protection of Children Act 1978   *157*
Public Meeting Act 1908   *153*
Public Order Act 1936   *141, 143, 146, 147*
    s1   *143*
    s3   *147*
    s5   *142, 147, 151, 153*
    s5A   *147*
Public Order Act 1986   *140, 141, 143, 145, 146, 147, 148, 149, 150, 151, 152, 153, 168, 170*
    s1   *141, 149, 150, 153*
    s2   *142, 149, 150, 151, 153*
    s3   *142, 149, 150, 151, 153*
    s4   *142, 143, 147, 149, 150, 153, 154*
    s4A   *145*
    s5   *142, 148, 149, 150, 151, 153, 170*
    s8   *142*
    s11   *143, 149, 152*
    s12   *143, 146, 147, 149, 152*
    s13   *143, 146, 147, 149, 152*
    s14   *144, 146, 147, 152*
    s16   *143, 147, 152*
    s17   *142, 143, 147, 155, 170*
    s18   *142, 155, 170*
    s19   *142, 145, 155, 170*
    s20   *142, 155, 170*

TABLE OF STATUTES

Public Order Act 1986 (continued)
    s21   *142, 155, 170*
    s22   *142, 155, 170*
    s23   *142, 155, 170*
    s30   *148*
    s38   *148, 153*
    s39   *144, 148*
    s40   *140*

Race Relations Act 1976   *133, 135*
Representation of the People Act 1983   *13, 47, 58, 186, 188*
    s75   *48, 50, 51, 186, 187*
    s75(1)(b)   *187*
    s76   *48, 51, 187*
    s93   *48*
    s97   *153*
    s120   *186*
    s121   *186*

Security Service Act 1989   *22*
Sex Discrimination Act 1975   *41, 133, 136*
Statute of Westminster 1931   *28, 128, 136*
    s4   *25*
Supreme Court Act 1981   *184*
    s31(3)   *194, 195*
    s31(6)   *194*

Theatres Act 1968   *157*
Trade Union and Labour Relations Act 1974
    s15   *143*
Trade Union and Labour Relations (Consolidation) Act 1992   *188*

Unlawful Drilling Act 1819   *153*

Video Recordings Act 1984   *157*

War Crimes Act 1991   *76, 83, 191*
War Damage Act 1965   *24, 169*

From the European Union

European Convention on Human Rights 1953   *5, 8, 121, 122, 123, 124, 125, 126, 127, 128, 131, 133, 134, 135, 136, 137, 138, 139, 156*
    Article 5   *121*
    Article 6   *100, 145*
    Article 10   *123, 156, 159*
    Article 11   *121*
    Article 15   *121*

TABLE OF STATUTES

Single European Act 1986   *33*

Treaty of Accession 1972   *33, 37*
Treaty of Rome 1957   *4, 31, 32, 42, 43*
　　Article 2   *40*
　　Article 3(b)   *200*
　　Article 52   *45*
　　Article 119   *39, 41*
　　Article 177   *42*
　　Article 189   *27*
Treaty on European Union 1992   *33, 36, 44*

1 THE NATURE OF CONSTITUTIONAL LAW

1.1 Introduction
1.2 Key points

1.1 Introduction

Constitutions define political authority and the basis for the exercise of political authority. They regulate the relationships of the principal organs of government – legislature, executive and judiciary – to each other and define their function. A Constitution is essentially a framework of rules which make up the system whereby a state is governed.

In most modern states these rules are contained in a single document and usually include a Bill of Rights which guarantees to citizens of that state certain liberties. Such Constitutions are subject to judicial interpretation. The United Kingdom has no written Constitution and the sources are contained in statute, the common law and custom, usages and convention. Conventions play an important part in the United Kingdom but cannot be enforced in the courts.

1.2 Key points

a) *Written and unwritten Constitutions*

   The term 'written Constitution' is used in relation to those countries with a single document (or a group of documents) that contains the basic rules and to which reference can be made. By contrast with an 'unwritten Constitution' no such document exists and the rules have to be established from the ordinary laws of the land.

b) *Flexible and rigid Constitutions*

   Most countries with a written Constitution require some special procedure before constitutional changes can be effected – for example a referendum or a two-thirds majority of the elected chamber. Flexible Constitutions are so described because constitutional change can be achieved by the same procedure as changes in laws generally. This is the position in the United Kingdom.

c) *Other classifications*

   i) A system of government which is accountable to the people is described as democratic government. Constitutions define the way in which a government is to be responsible and the way in which it is elected.

   ii) Federal states are those states in which regions enjoy autonomous law making power. Unitary states are those in which power is focused on central government. The United Kingdom has a unitary system of government in that

Parliament is the supreme law making body, while the United States is a federal state.

iii) The head of state can vary in form. It may be a monarch, a president or a chairman. The extent of their powers is defined by the Constitution so that, for example, while the President of the USA enjoys significant powers, the President of the Republic of Ireland enjoys a position analogous to our own Monarch – that is to say most of their executive powers are exercised by ministers.

d) A Constitution is in a sense a higher form of law. It is the basis upon which all other laws derive their validity and force. However, it remains valid only for as long as those subject to it accept its rules as binding. It can be argued that acceptance can be imposed as in a dictatorship.

Students need to appreciate the basic features of Constitutions to provide a reference point from which to analyse the British Constitution.

2 THE CHARACTERISTICS OF THE BRITISH CONSTITUTION

2.1 Introduction
2.2 Key points
2.3 Recent cases and statutes
2.4 Analysis of questions
2.5 Questions

2.1 Introduction

The British Constitution has evolved over centuries and the 'rules' of constitutional behaviour are not contained in any single document. A point of comparison can be made with the USA where, following the American War of Independence, a written document was prepared which established fundamental constitutional principles and safeguarded the rights of citizens. Our constitution has evolved over a period of time and through the actual process of government 'rules' have emerged which relate to our constitutional order. It is these rules and their application that must be understood.

2.2 Key points

a) *The main features*

The constitution of the United Kingdom applies throughout England, Wales, Scotland and Northern Ireland.

   i) The Parliament at Westminster is the only body with ultimate legislative authority. The United Kingdom constitution is unitary as opposed, for example, to the USA which is federal, the states having certain original law-making powers.

   ii) The United Kingdom Parliament is sovereign. There is no limit on the competence of Parliament to enact legislation (but see here the constitutional implications of our membership of the European Union). Furthermore, constitutional changes can be achieved by ordinary legislation, ie a simple majority in each house of Parliament and the Royal Assent.

   iii) The legislature of the United Kingdom comprises the House of Lords and the House of Commons – a bi-cameral system. The House of Lords is an unelected chamber, a politically controversial feature of the legislature.

   iv) The Head of State is the Queen but the role of the monarch is largely ceremonial and circumscribed by convention. Residual powers of the crown are in fact excercised by the government.

   v) Government is democratic, ie membership of the House of Commons is dependent on elections and the government is ultimately accountable to the electorate. The electoral system in the UK – 'first past the post' as opposed to any form of proportional representation – arouses occasional political controversy.

vi) The Constitution is described as unwritten – there is no single document to which reference can be made and individual liberties are not safeguarded by a Bill of Rights but by remedies available in the ordinary law. Conventions (see below) play a significant part in defining the constitutional order.

vii) In the absence of a written constitution there is a greater dependence on the government's respect for the rule of law as there is no clear line on what is constitutionally legitimate.

viii) It is argued that British society is in need of a written Constitution which would better protect the individual rights of citizens, include a reformed House of Lords, a 'fairer' electoral system based on proportional representation, better ensure the accountability of Government to Parliament and attempt to achieve more open government – see the proposals of Charter 88.

b) *Sources of the Constitution*

Because we have an unwritten Constitution the sources are to be found in the general law, ie statute and precedent, and in practices that have become firmly established over time, ie conventions. In addition our membership of the European Union has important consitutional implications.

i) Statute

There are many statutes which relate either to the system of government or to the rights of the citizens. Identifying statutes of constitutional significance can be difficult. Major examples are the Bill of Rights 1688 which laid down the foundations of the modern constitution, the Act of Settlement 1700 which provided for the succession to the throne and the European Communities Act 1972 by which the United Kingdom acceded to the Treaty of Rome.

ii) Case law

Decisions of the courts can contain important rules of constitutional behaviour see: *Entick* v *Carrington* (1765) 19 St Tr 1030; *Council for Civil Service Unions* v *Minister for the Civil Service* [1984] 3 All ER 935.

On statutory interpretation see: *Hipperson* v *Electoral Registration Officer for Newbury* [1985] QB 1060.

iii) European law

The United Kingdom became a member of the European Communities from 1 January 1973 – see European Communities Act 1972. The impact on the United Kingdom constitution can be seen in *Bulmer (HP)* v *J Bollinger SA* [1974] 2 All ER 1226 at 1231.

- Treaty of Rome.
- Regulations. Main source of European Union law and directly applicable in United Kingdom courts.

2 THE CHARACTERISTICS OF THE BRITISH CONSTITUTION

- Directives. Community objectives which must be complied with.
- Decisions of the European Court of Justice on European law. Binding in the United Kingdom.

iv) The Royal Prerogative – the residual powers, privileges and immunities belonging to the Crown. Such powers are exercised in accordance with convention.

v) The European Convention on Human Rights

The United Kingdom has not incorporated the treaty into domestic law. Nevertheless, decisions of the European Court of Human Rights have an impact on human rights in the United Kingdom: *Malone* v *United Kingdom* [1985] 7 EHRR 14.

vi) Conventions

Definition: Conventions are 'rules of constitutional behaviour which are considered to be binding by and upon those who operate the constitution but which are not enforced by the law courts ... nor by the presiding officers of the Houses of Parliament.' (Dicey)

Some examples of conventions:

- The Monarchy
  - The Sovereign should act on the advice of her ministers.
  - The Sovereign should ask the leader who commands a majority in the House of Commons to form a government.
  - The Sovereign should dissolve Parliament at the request of the prime minister.
  - The Sovereign should not refuse the Royal Assent.
- The Executive
  - Ministers are collectively and individually responsible to Parliament.
  - Ministers must be members of the House of Commons or House of Lords.
  - The Government must resign if it loses the confidence of the Commons.
- Parliament
  - Public expenditure measures must originate in the House of Commons.
  - The House of Lords ought ultimately to defer to the will of the House of Commons.
- The Judiciary
  - A judge's professional conduct should not be questioned in either House except on a motion for dismissal.
  - A judge should not be active in party politics.

c) *The importance of conventions*

i) The aim of conventional rules is the smooth working of government. See Sir Ivor Jennings on the test for recognising a valid convention:

- Is there a precedent?
- Do those who operate the constitution accept that the convention is binding?
- Is there a good political reason for the convention?

ii) To ensure the accountability of the executive. It is debatable however whether the conventions of Cabinet responsibility do ensure accountability – see chapter 9.

iii) Dicey argued that breach of convention could give rise to a breach of the law.

iv) There can be significant political repercussions on breach, ie the refusal of a government to resign on losing the confidence of the House of Commons. Such repercussions are dependent on the perceived importance of the conventional rule. Rules of political practice do change and conventions can change accordingly. This gives the constitution flexibility.

d) *Conventions and the courts*

Conventions are not enforceable in the courts because they are not rules of law – see *Madzimbamuto* v *Lardner-Burke* [1969] 1 AC 645.

However, the courts do recognise the existence of conventions: see *Attorney-General* v *Jonathan Cape* [1976] QB 752 and *Re Amendment of the Constitution of Canada* (1982) 125 DLR (3d) 1.

e) *The limitations on the exercise of power*

In constitutional democracies the powers of government are limited in a number of ways:

i) Bill of Rights. The constitution itself often confines the activities of government and allows for judicial interpretation of Acts of Parliament on the basis of constitutionality – see USA.

ii) The separation of powers

The three basic and essential organs of state are legislative, executive and judicial. With a view to avoiding the potential for an autocratic and tyrannical form of government it has been considered theoretically desirable for the functions to be kept separate. In 1748 the French jurist Montesquieu developed the doctrine of the separation of powers which argues the need for checks and balances to exist between the three. It is a useful concept for analysing the nature of our parliamentary democracy.

- Legislature and executive

There is a significant overlap. Ministers head departments of state. The government initiates legislation and has the controlling voice in Parliament. Ministers and local authorities have a limited law making function through delegated legislation.

- Executive and judiciary

The Lord Chancellor heads the judiciary, presides in the House of Lords and has a seat in Cabinet. Judges are appointed by the Lord Chancellor or by the Queen on the advice of the Lord Chancellor.

2 THE CHARACTERISTICS OF THE BRITISH CONSTITUTION

The judiciary control the executive authorities from exceeding their powers: see *Associated Provincial Picture Houses Ltd v Wednesbury Corporation* [1948] 1 KB 223.

- Judiciary and legislature

  A degree of separation exists: House of Commons Disqualification Act 1975. Judges do, however, to a certain extent make law: see *Shaw v DPP* [1962] AC 220.

  Within our Constitution Parliament is supreme and the courts cannot challenge an Act of Parliament. In many countries with written Constitutions the courts can challenge an act of the legislature as unconstitutional: see *Pickin v British Railways Board* [1974] AC 765.

  Our membership of the European Union obliges the United Kingdom to legislate in a way that is consistent with European law. In theory, however, Parliament could repeal the European Communities Act 1972, so any loss of sovereignty is 'limited and partial'.

iii) Rule of law

'An abstract concept based on the principle that government must be seen to be legitimate' in the sense that it is impartial, fair and obeyed even when disagreed with.

Dicey's propositions

1) No man is punishable except for a distinct breach of the law and then only in the ordinary courts and in the manner prescribed by law.

   This is contrasted with arbitrary and discretionary power. Governments in the twentieth century do enjoy wide discretionary powers – welfare benefits, public health, sentencing policy, etc.

   Wide arbitrary powers are avoided and attempts made to ensure accountability.

2) No-one is above the law and everyone should be subject to the jurisdiction of the ordinary courts: *Entick v Carrington* (1765) 19 St Tr 1030. Disputes between government and citizen are settled in the ordinary courts. But note the part played by administrative tribunals.

   Whilst the courts cannot challenge an Act of Parliament, they will review administrative action.

   Note also the fact of parliamentary supremacy and the wide powers of governmental officials. See *R v Inland Revenue Commissioners, ex parte Rossminster Ltd* [1980] 1 All ER 80.

3) Principles of constitutional law are contained in judicial decisions which serve to ensure that individual liberties are protected.

   This is contrasted with the position in countries with a written constitution where a single document seeks to establish citizens' rights and places reliance on the judiciary to develop laws which protect liberties. The extent to which our liberties are protected in the absence of a Bill of Rights is currently a matter of debate.

CONSTITUTIONAL LAW

4) The International Rule of Law

Increasingly, political attempts are made to establish internationally binding codes of basic human rights. See: The Declaration of Delhi 1959; European Convention of Human Rights 1953.

2.3 Recent cases and statutes

An up-to-date knowledge of recent political debate and legislative changes is important.

The Criminal Justice and Public Order Act 1994 has been criticised as further undermining civil liberties in the United Kingdom.

The Nolan Report (see chapter 8) on Standards in Public Life has again raised the question as to whether certain 'rules' relating to government ministers should be codified.

The 'Spycatcher' case (*Attorney-General* v *Guardian Newspapers (No 1)* [1987] 1 WLR 1248; *(No 2)* [1988] 3 WLR 776 focused on the issue of whether there should be a right to free expression, in which case any restriction on publication would have to be justified.

Recent developments in the style of Cabinet government can be seen as undermining the conventions that apply to that forum. This also has implications for the separation of powers.

2.4 Analysis of questions

Questions on conventions are popular with examiners. Care must be taken to answer the question asked and not simply provide the examiner with a 'list'. The separation of powers and the rule of law may be examined in their own right but remember that both are concepts which can be used as a yardstick to evaluate other topics ie prime ministerial power or a Bill of Rights, both of which come later in the syllabus.

2.5 Questions

QUESTION ONE

To what extent, if any, do you agree with the statement that 'conventions constitute probably the most discussed and least definable source of the Constitution' (Norton).

University of London LLB Examination
(for External Students) Constitutional Law June 1987 Q1

General Comment

A relatively difficult question. Unless you can deal with the specific point raised concerning the definition of conventions you should not attempt this question. The danger with such a question is that your answer becomes too general and there is the temptation to fill it out by simply producing a list of conventions.

2 THE CHARACTERISTICS OF THE BRITISH CONSTITUTION

Skeleton Solution

- Introduction – what are conventions of the constitution?
- The difficulty of defining conventions. The lack of written form; their political nature; lack of legal form; effect of disagreement; absence of pre-existing usage; flexibility.
- Why conventions are discussed. Distinction between law and convention; why conventions are obeyed; the advantage of conventions over legal rules.

Suggested Solution

A great many of the rules of the British Constitution, which are observed by the Sovereign, the Prime Minister, Ministers, Members of Parliament, the judiciary and civil servants, are not contained in Acts of Parliament or judicial decisions, but are to be found in those rules of conduct called constitutional conventions. These have been described as 'rules of constitutional behaviour which are considered to be binding by and upon those who operate the Constitution but which are not enforced by the law courts ... nor by the presiding officers in the Houses of Parliament': Marshall & Moodie, *Some Problems of the Constitution*, 5th ed 1971 pp22–23. These conventions of the Constitution are obeyed by those to whom they apply not because of the threat of any legal sanction in case of breach, but because of the political difficulties which may follow if they are not obeyed.

Some conventional rules are very well known and have great authority but many others have been developed on a very informal basis so as to avoid the sort of strictness one usually associates with changes in the law. This informality associated with conventions of the Constitution often means that, while some may be publicly recorded, others are not formulated in writing, having simply evolved as practice over a period of time. It is for this reason that at a given moment in time it may be impossible to ascertain whether practice on a certain matter has crystallised into a conventional rule. This, together with the fact that they operate in a political context, often means that disputes may arise about the existence and content of conventional rules. Whereas disputes about the existence and content of legal rules are settled by judicial decisions, no formal judicial mechanism exists to settle disputes concerning conventional rules.

Problems may arise therefore when attempting to identify conventional rules. By their definition conventions of the Constitution are forms of political behaviour based upon usage and regarded as obligatory, but at the same time lacking legal sanction. But when or how does such a non-binding usage become binding? One answer is of course that usage becomes binding because those to whom the usage applies consider that there is an obligation on their part to continue to behave in that way. But the dominant motive is not always apparent. Is the usage obeyed out of a sense of obligation or for some other reason? Also, what if there is substantial disagreement as to the existence or content of a convention. Political expediency or personal prejudice may result in divided interpretations of the obligation, if any, to be assumed. Certainly the opinions of politicians may differ as to the scope of the conventions they should observe. The fact that conventions may be created without any evidence of pre-existing usage also results in problems of identification.

CONSTITUTIONAL LAW

Their non-legal nature also means that conventions are very flexible in the sense that they may lose their binding force or undergo a change in content without the need for any formal mechanism being followed. Conventions established by express agreement may be superseded or changed by agreement. Decisions taken by the Prime Minister or the Cabinet about the way Cabinet is to operate, for example, may be superseded by new decisions. Changes in circumstance may result in a convention losing its force, or indeed, the fact that a convention has been disregarded with impunity. Other conventions disappear with general acquiescence.

It is therefore probably true to say that conventions constitute the least definable source of the Constitution. They are also probably the most discussed source especially as regards their interrelationship with the legal rules of the Constitution. The differences between law and convention, the reasons why conventions are obeyed, whether or not conventions should be codified as law and the attitudes of the courts towards conventions are all matters which have occupied constitutional writers for many years and no doubt will continue to do so into the future.

QUESTION TWO

'A written Constitution for the United Kingdom would preserve the best of the existing constitutional practices and would remove the major defects.'

Discuss.

University of London LLB Examination
(for External Students) Constitutional Law June 1986 Q2

General Comment

A difficult question which should only be attempted as a last resort. It is, however, currently a very topical issue.

Skeleton Solution

- Introduction: What is a Constitution?: The unwritten nature of the United Kingdom Constitution.
- The defects of our constitutional system: the absence of a higher form of law; the sovereignty of Parliament.
- The benefits of our constitutional system: the flexible nature of the Constitution; the process of evolution.
- Conclusion: adoption of a written Constitution need not result in rigidity, but even if desirable is change necessary?

Suggested Solution

The Constitution of a state may be defined as the body of rules relating to the structure, functions and powers of the organs of state, their relationship to one another, and to the private citizen. The word 'constitution' is also used to refer to a document having a special legal sanctity which sets out the framework and the principal functions of the organs of government within the state, and declares the principles by which those organs must operate. This document has usually been enacted by the legislature or adopted by some other constituent body, for example a Constituent Assembly. In this sense of the word, as de Tocqueville observed, the United Kingdom has no Constitution. There is no single document from which is derived the authority of the main organs of government, such as the Crown, the Cabinet, Parliament and the courts of law. No single document lays down the relationship of the primary organs of government one with another, or with the people.

Within the United Kingdom therefore there is no written Constitution which can serve as fundamental law. This can create certain difficulties. In most states the Constitution is a higher form of law in the sense that other laws must conform with it. The Constitution imposes limits on what may be done by ordinary legislation and the courts may declare certain legislative acts void. But in the United Kingdom, in the absence of a written Constitution to serve as the foundation of the legal system, the vacuum is filled by the legal doctrine of the legislative supremacy of Parliament. The result is that formal restraints upon the exercise of power which exist in other states do not exist in the United Kingdom. Parliament may make or unmake any law. There is no limit to its competence to legislate. No Parliament may bind its successors or be bound by its predecessors and the courts cannot question the validity of an Act of Parliament. Note, however, that since our membership of the European Union and the developing jurisprudence of the European Court of Justice, it has been established that our courts can grant an injunction suspending part of a statute which is inconsistent with European law: see *R* v *Secretary of State for Transport, ex parte Factortame (No 2)* (1991).

A major defect therefore of the United Kingdom Constitution is that the absence of any higher form of law makes it virtually impossible to ensure that the rights of minorities and individual citizens are protected against legislative infringement by Parliament. Moreover, the absence of a written Constitution means that there is no special procedure prescribed for legislation of constitutional importance. For example, before the Republic of Ireland could join the EC, a constitutional amendment to the Irish Constitution had to be approved by a referendum of the people. In the United Kingdom, however, while the European Communities Act 1972 was debated at length in Parliament, the Act was passed by essentially the same procedure as would apply to any legislation of purely domestic concern. The absence of a written Constitution means that in practice the British Constitution depends far less on legal rules and safeguards and relies much more upon political and democratic principles. But can the politicians be trusted to observe these informal restraints on their power?

These problems could, it is argued, be overcome if the United Kingdom adopted a formal written Constitution which defined the scope, and set out the legal limitations on, the functions and powers of the organs of government. But it must be remembered that no written document alone can ensure the smooth working of a system of government. A written document has no greater force than that which persons in authority are willing to attribute to it. Also our present unwritten Constitution founded as it is partly on Acts of Parliament and judicial decisions, partly upon political practice, and partly upon detailed procedures established by the various organs of government for carrying their own tasks, provides a complex and comprehensive system of government which has served the United Kingdom well. In particular, as all law in the United Kingdom, including laws relating to the

CONSTITUTIONAL LAW

Constitution, may be enacted, repealed or amended by the Queen in Parliament using the same legislative procedure, our Constitution is highly flexible and can adapt to meet changes in social, moral and political circumstances. Indeed this facility for gradual evolution has been one of the major contributions to the political and social stability of the United Kingdom.

But the adoption of a written Constitution need not necessarily destroy this flexibility altogether. A written Constitution cannot contain all the detailed rules upon which government depends and accordingly a written Constitution usually evolves a wide variety of customary rules and practices which attune the operation of the Constitution to changing conditions. These customary rules and practices will usually be more easily changed than the Constitution itself and their constant evolution will reduce the need for formal amendment of the written Constitution. For example the rules for electing the legislature are usually found not in the written Constitution but in ordinary statutes enacted by the legislature within the limits laid down by the Constitution. Such statutes can when necessary be amended by the ordinary process of legislation whereas amendments to the Constitution may require a more elaborate process, such as a special majority in the legislature or approval by a referendum.

Therefore it may well be the case that a written Constitution for the United Kingdom would preserve the best of the existing constitutional practices and would remove the major defects. But, in spite of the defects, so long as our present constitutional system works so well, why change?

QUESTION THREE

'Conventions are unlike legal rules because they are not the true product of a legislative or judicial process' (Geoffrey Marshall *Constitutional Conventions*).

The University of Wolverhampton
Constitutional Law June 1990 Q10

General Comment

A question that requires students to explain the part played by conventions in the British Constitution, distinguish law and convention and examine both the consequences of breach and the court's approach to conventions.

Skeleton Solution

An outline of the sources of the British Constitution emphasising its unwritten character. Definition of conventions followed by examples of the part they play. Distinguish law and examine the court's approach to conventions.

Suggested Solution

The Constitution of the United Kingdom is described as unwritten – that is to say there is no single document to which reference can be made to establish constitutional principles of government or the safeguards that exist to ensure government is accountable and that individual liberties are safeguarded. To describe the United Kingdom constitution as unwritten is a little misleading, however, because of course much of the source material is written in the form of statutes and case law or common

2 THE CHARACTERISTICS OF THE BRITISH CONSTITUTION

law. For example many statutes contain important constitutional rules, eg the Bill of Rights 1688, the Parliament Acts 1911 and 1949, the Representation of the People Act 1983 and so on. Many decisions of the courts contain important constitutional 'statements' which form the basis of judicial reasoning, for example, *Entick* v *Carrington* (1765), *Hipperson* v *Electoral Registration Officer for Newbury* (1985). The point of course about both written constitutions and in the case of the United Kingdom statute and case law sources is that the courts can adjudicate directly on the source.

The United Kingdom constitution has been described as the product of evolution rather than revolution. The consequence is that many non-legal rules supplement the legal sources. Described as conventions, these non-legal rules play a significant part in the constitution. Conventions have been defined as '... rule of constitutional behaviour which are considered to be binding by and upon those who operate the constitution but which are not enforced by the law courts ... nor by the presiding officers in the Houses of Parliament'.

Conventions can be seen to operate in all areas of the constitution. The sovereign's relationship with the executive is significantly defined by convention, ie the sovereign must act on the advice of her ministers, must not exercise her own initiative in refusing to assent to Bills which have passed through both Houses of Parliament, and must appoint as Prime Minister the person who can command a majority of seats in the Commons.

Conventions relating to the legislature include: the House of Lords ought ultimately to defer to the will of the House of Commons; Parliament must be summoned to meet at least once a year. Conventions relating to the Judiciary include: judges shall not be active in party politics; Lords of Appeal who sit in the House of Lords must not participate in the political affairs of the House. In addition the whole basis of cabinet government is convention – ministers are collectively and individually responsible to Parliament.

Dicey drew a clear distinction between law and convention. Laws are enforceable in the courts, conventions are not. To this extent conventions are unlike legal rules. However, the general values inherent in the constitution, expressed in the rule of law, are interrelated with conventions and sanctions exist for the breach of a convention. Dicey argued that the breach of a convention 'will almost immediately bring the offender into conflict with the courts and the law of the land'. This is palpably not the case and Sir Ivor Jennings suggests that conventions are obeyed because of the political difficulties which follow if they are not. The failure of a minister to abide by the doctrine of collective responsibility will result in dismissal/resignation. The failure of a government to resign on losing the support of the House of Commons would precipitate a political uproar supported by public opinion. Sometimes the failure to follow a convention can result in a change in the law so for example the refusal of the House of Lords to support Liberal reforms in 1909–1910 led to the Parliament Act 1911.

The courts do not recognise conventions as legal rules – see *Madzimbamuto* v *Lardner-Burke* (1969) and *Re Amendment of the Constitution of Canada* (1982) where the Canadian Supreme Court recognised but refused to apply a convention. However, conventions can indirectly influence a decision; in *Liversidge* v *Anderson* (1942) and

CONSTITUTIONAL LAW

R v *Secretary of State for the Home Department, ex parte Hosenball* (1977) reference was made to the responsibility and accountability of the Home Secretary to Parliament. In *Attorney-General* v *Jonathan Cape* (1976) the government based its case on the convention of cabinet secrecy. Lord Widgery stated that the convention was relevant to establishing a balance between the public interest and confidentiality.

Conventions are, then, unlike legal rules in that the courts cannot give direct effect to them. However, other sanctions can result in adherence to convention in much the same way as adherence to a legal rule, more particularly in respect of those where breach would be fundamentally unconstitutional.

QUESTION FOUR

'When an Englishman speaks of the conduct of a public man being constitutional or unconstitutional, he means something wholly different from what he means by conduct being legal or illegal.'

Discuss.

University of London LLB Examination
(for External Students) Constitutional Law June 1989 Q1

General Comment

A relatively difficult question which requires students to analyse the term 'constitution' as a higher form of law in the context of the United Kingdom.

Skeleton Solution

- Explain the meaning of the quotation setting it in context by showing what would be meant by the words in a system with a written constitution.
- Look at role of convention and statute in British constitution.

Suggested Solution

Today most countries of the world possess a 'Constitution' ie a document or series of documents laying down the fundamental rules relating to the organisation of the state. In such countries if a person decries a law or an action as being unconstitutional or illegal what he means is that it offends against the higher law laid down in the Constitution, which is normally protected from later legislative changes by the need to follow a more difficult prescribed legislative process ie the Constitution is entrenched. To a degree the two adjectives are in these countries interchangeable. Even in such countries convention plays a part but a role which cannot be compared to the position of conventions in the British constitution. To discover the fundamental rules governing the Constitution in Britain one has to look to various sources – statute, judicial decisions and conventions of the constitution. Conventions of the constitution are rules of political practice regarded as biding by those to whom they apply but which are not enforced by the Courts or by Parliament. The important point to grasp is that although statute is the most important source of our Constitution and a statute can always override a convention, nevertheless one would not understand how the British Constitution operated without an understanding of conventions. For instance the existence of the Prime Minister, Cabinet and other ministers is dependent on convention and their relationships to each other and to Parliament are regulated by conventions of ministerial responsibility. Furthermore if one looks strictly at the legal powers of the Monarch those are immense until one appreciates the convention that for the most part the Monarch follows the advice of her Government. Conventions are also important in the functioning of the legislature and even of the judiciary.

The quotation in the question is therefore alluding to the difference between statute and convention as a source of the British constitution. If an Englishman spoke of something as 'illegal' he would normally be referring to a breach of a statute or common law rules. If he is talking of something being 'unconstitutional' he would be taken to be referring to a breach of a convention. This is however somewhat of an oversimplification for sometimes in speaking of a breach of a statute or case law rule of constitutional importance the Englishman might at once describe the behaviour as 'unconstitutional' and 'illegal', but what is unconstitutional is not necessarily illegal, although it may be.

Mallory said 'for the Americans anything unconstitutional is illegal, however right or necessary it may seem; for the British, anything unconstitutional is wrong, no matter how legal it may be'.

Some conventions are well known and possess great authority whilst others have developed on an informal basis. This means that some conventions are not even recorded in writing in public documents having evolved informally over a period of time. Indeed this is one of the reasons why disputes arise as to the existence and content of conventional rules. There is no judicial procedure or mechanism to settle disputes concerning such rules. One of the results of these uncertainties is that the phrase 'unconstitutional' is often used by politicians in circumstances where it may not strictly be appropriate, thus devaluing the term.

For example in 1932 the National Government's agreement to differ and the 1975 Labour Government waiver of collective responsibility, over the EC referendum were both described by some commentators as 'unconstitutional' but these occasions were both without precedent and should, some would argue, merely be seen as developments and glosses on a convention. The twin conventions of collective and individual responsibility (see in particular the 1954 Crichel Down affair on individual responsibility) do give rise to uncertainty as to whether a minister's behaviour merits resignation and whether breach of the convention amounts to action which is unconstitutional. Recent controversy over MPs' personal interests and the tabling of questions for cash in the House of Commons highlight this dilemma.

The courts will not enforce conventions but conventions are taken into account. The Crossman diaries are a good example illustrating the 'grey area' between legal and non-legal rules. In that case the Attorney-General tried to prevent the breach of a conventional rule and to establish the existence of a legal obligation. It was held that former cabinet ministers could be restrained by injunction from publishing confidential information – there is a legal obligation to respect confidentiality. The court, however, must not be thought to have enforced a convention in this case. Collective responsibility (the convention in question) was no more than one factor taken into account by the judge in establishing the limits of the legal doctrine of confidence. In *Re Amendment of the Constitution of Canada* (1982) the Canadian

Supreme Court recognised, but refused to apply, a convention. It could well be argued that what the government was proposing was legal but unconstitutional.

Some jurists take the view that all constitutional rules ought to be enacted as law. To a large degree this is what would happen if the United Kingdom were to entrench a written constitution. If that were done a Supreme Court (or Law Lords in the House of Lords) would interpret constitutional articles. It is true that some areas would be quite difficult. For example, to anticipate every possible eventuality in which the Sovereign might be required to invite a new Prime Minister to form a government. Also it could be argued that even if all present non-legal rules were susceptible to a written code, new conventions could be born at any time. (Note Wade and Bradley say that 'provisions contained in a written constitution' are not *all* suitable for judicial enforcement. This, however, may not be valid as some constitutional lawyers will maintain that *all* provisions/articles of a written constitution have equal standing; it is either an article or not.) This argument, however, is not entirely satisfactory – the main point about codification is that all non-legal rules (conventions) are brought under a legal footing, namely, a constitution. Were conventions fully codified then the use in Britain of the phrases 'unconstitutional' and 'illegal' would alter to resemble that in other countries.

QUESTION FIVE

Should all or any of the conventions of the constitution be given statutory force?

University of London LLB Examination
(for External Students) Constitutional and Administrative Law June 1992 Q5

General Comment

This is a standard question on conventions. It is not an opportunity to list every known convention, but obviously examples are needed. This suggested solution adopts the view that conventions need not be given statutory force – but that is not the 'right' answer!

Skeleton Solution

- Definition.
- An example of a convention.
- Problem of scope.
- Difficulty of definition.
- Enactment in case of breach.
- Flexibility.
- Illegality and recognition by the courts.
- Certainty if enacted.
- Conclusion.

Suggested Solution

Conventions have been described as 'rules of constitutional behaviour' (Marshall & Moodie, *Some Problems of the Constitution*). They are unwritten and they are not

2 THE CHARACTERISTICS OF THE BRITISH CONSTITUTION

enforced by the courts. Nevertheless they are considered binding upon those whom they cover. If that is the case, what is to be gained by giving some or all of them statutory force?

A good example of a convention is that the Prime Minister and the Chancellor of the Exchequer should both belong to the House of Commons. The last member of the House of Lords to hold office as Prime Minister was Lord Salisbury in 1902, making this a comparatively recent convention. Yet, in 1963, the 14th Earl of Home felt constrained to renounce his title so that he could enter the House of Commons as Harold Macmillan's successor (although it took four days from his appointment as Prime Minister to the disclaimer!). Thus, an unwritten rule both enforced and reflected the political impossibility of a Prime Minister governing from the House of Lords.

In theory, all conventions could be given statutory force and this has been the practice in several Commonwealth countries. However, there are various reasons why this is unnecessary. Firstly, conventions cover a very wide area, involving executive, judiciary and legislature. No single code could embrace them all.

Secondly, there is the difficulty of definition. For example, ministers are responsible both collectively and individually, and resignation is the appropriate response. It is impossible to define the limits of that responsibility – as much as anything, it is a question of political judgment. In 1954, Sir Thomas Dugdale resigned over the Crichel Down affair. In 1982, Lord Carrington resigned over the Falkland Islands' occupation. Yet, Kenneth Baker as Home Secretary did not resign over the escape from Brixton Prison of IRA suspects nor after he was held to be in contempt of court in *M* v *Home Office* (1993) following the deportation of an asylum seeker. Putting merits aside, no draftsman could cover such diverse situations.

Thirdly, a breach of convention can always be corrected by statute if necessary. In 1909, the House of Lords rejected the Liberal Government's Finance Bill. Until then, the Commons had asserted their authority when it came to the passage of money bills and the Lords had generally acknowledged this convention. The crisis that followed in 1909 led to the Parliament Act 1911 which – in terms – enacted the convention.

Fourthly, while it may seem questionable to wait for a breach before enactment, conventions are largely followed because they describe how the constitution works. They are also, in their unwritten form, sufficiently flexible to reflect change. By convention, the Queen appoints as Prime Minister the person who can command a majority in the Commons. Until 1965, the death or retirement of a Conservative Prime Minister required the Queen – to some extent – to make a choice, but since then there has been a system within the party for electing a new leader. The convention remains, but it has become a formality.

However, what would happen if the Queen decided to ignore it? That may be a fanciful idea, but at present, while breach of a convention may cause political difficulty – which may also be its strongest restraint – it does not result in illegality. (Dicey argued that if Parliament did not follow the convention of meeting each year it would have to raise taxes illegally, but that is an exception). Similarly, although recognised by courts (as in *Attorney-General* v *Jonathan Cape* (1976)) they are not legally enforceable. Enactment would alter that, although one might consider whether

CONSTITUTIONAL LAW

the present court structure would be adequate for 'trying' resultant breaches of the law.

Another argument in favour of enactment is that of certainty. For example, the Sovereign's conventional power with regard to the dissolution of Parliament and the appointment of Ministers is – on paper – considerable but ill-defined. Is it enough to say that in practice it is not a problem?

In conclusion, it is submitted that – despite these arguments – there is no need to give all conventions statutory force. If they are breached then that is the time for enactment. However, they are obeyed because they reflect constitutional practice and, unlike laws, when they are no longer relevant, they simply fade away.

QUESTION SIX

'It must be conceded that the constitution of the United Kingdom deviates from a pure concept of separation of powers. Nevertheless the concept is respected and adequate safeguards exist to prevent abuse of power.'

Discuss.

University of London LLB Examination
(for External Students) Constitutional Law June 1993 Q1

General Comment

A straightforward question that calls for a clear narrative of the workings of the British Constitution and the ways in which the democratic principle is upheld in a system without a rigid constitutional separation of powers. The challenge is to present the material in an original and lively way, because many average students will simply regurgitate large sections of traditional textbooks on this topic. Hence the suggested solution concentrates on a particular theme (the separation between law and politics) and very specialised illustrations, with no attempt to cover the entire (very wide) field of the distribution of power in modern British society. It is one approach; there are many others. It is a useful reminder that, for law exams, there are no 'model' answers, merely suggested approaches to solutions.

Skeleton Solution

- Definition of Montesquieu's 'pure' concept of separation of powers.
- The British Constitution and the overlapping of organs and functions.
- Safeguards, illustrated by detailed discussion of one area: the separation of law and politics through constitutional conventions.
- Application to the office of Lord Chancellor.
- Do the particular conventions work?
- The decision in *Pepper* v *Hart* and Lord Mackay's significant dissent.
- The courts and Parliament: Speaker Boothroyd's views and those of Lord Donaldson MR.
- Alternatives to the conventional approach.
- Difficulties in the American system of government.

2 THE CHARACTERISTICS OF THE BRITISH CONSTITUTION

Suggested Solution

The 'pure' concept of the separation of powers is that propounded by Montesquieu:

'The three main powers of government, namely, the legislative, executive and judicial, should be organically and functionally separated in order to avoid the risk of too much power being accumulated in one person or institution, ie the risk of tyranny': from *L'Esprit des Lois* (1748).

The theory proved of great influence in the drafting of the American Constitution in 1787, but is clearly not strictly followed by the British Constitution, which has developed in an unwritten, pragmatic fashion since the Norman Conquest of 1066. Today the three main organs of government can be found in one institution: Parliament. The functions of government are also shared, to take the most famous and obvious example: the Lord Chancellor, who combines the functions of judge, Cabinet minister and legislator in the House of Lords (where he also acts as Speaker).

Yet, as the assertion in question points out, respect is paid to the spirit of Montesquieu's theory, if not the letter of it. Safeguards have developed to minimise the risks of abuse of power from institutions such as Parliament and the Lord Chancellor. Whether they are adequate, however, is another matter, and one which has generated controversy among lawyers and politicians for generations.

Conventions of the constitution have assumed great importance in checking the exercise of power. Conventions are 'unwritten' guidelines designed to persuade decision-makers to act fairly, responsibly, democratically and morally. For example, the holder of the office of Lord Chancellor will be expected, by convention, to separate his party political views from the views he must take when acting in the capacity as head of the judiciary, whether he is appointing judges or himself sitting as a judge to hear an appeal taken to the House of Lords.

It has been argued that conventions such as these are followed either because of the integrity and sense of honour of the office holder (an 'internal' limit) or because of the fear of the adverse political consequences of a breach of a fundamental convention (loss of reputation, removal from office, etc: an 'external' limit). A person who is appointed as Lord Chancellor is expected to command the confidence of the judiciary, the legal profession and the public generally when exercising judicial functions and hence the internal limit is more likely to operate in his case than with any other politician. Even the most passionate kinds of politician, eg Lord Hailsham, have been able to exercise dispassionate judgment when exercising those functions of the office of Lord Chancellor that require impartiality and independence from the executive.

Nevertheless the fear remains that, as a member of the Cabinet, the Lord Chancellor may be unable to separate his functions in the sophisticated and subtle manner which may be required. To take a recent example (and one is not questioning the integrity of Lord Mackay on this point) in the case of *Pepper* v *Hart* (1993) six of the seven Law Lords (Lord Mackay LC dissenting) were prepared to allow access to Hansard for lawyers and judges when considering issues of statutory construction. Lord Mackay dissented solely on the ground that to permit such access would add greatly to the costs of litigation. One must be tempted to wonder whether his responsibility

CONSTITUTIONAL LAW

for public spending on the legal aid scheme (an executive, political responsibility) may have proved decisive in reaching this particular judgment, since none of the other Law Lords considered costs to be a major problem. If the Lord Chancellor were not permitted to sit as an appeal judge would the decision in this case be unanimous if an 'ordinary' Law Lord had taken his place?

The curious point that emerges from the decision is that, in practical terms, Lord Mackay may be proved right, since use of Hansard has increased dramatically since that landmark decision and the impact on the costs of litigation is likely to be significant. This shows how a merger of powers and functions can be useful in (perhaps) influencing a decision and making it better informed than it otherwise would have been. Lord Mackay's judgment in *Pepper* v *Hart* reveals experience of empirical research which is lacking in the other judgments, which tend to rely heavily on abstract issues of principle.

The separation between law and politics is certainly regarded as a desirable objective in the British Constitution, even if the two areas are not organically and functionally separated by rigid written rules. In the recent controversy over the legality of ratification of the Maastricht Treaty, the Commons Speaker, Betty Boothroyd, took the unusual step of reminding the courts not to get involved in politics when they came to exercise judicial review on the issue. In return, she said, Parliament and politicians respect the independence of the judiciary. This echoes part of a judgment given by Lord Donaldson MR in *R* v *HM Treasury, ex parte Smedley* (1985):

'Although the UK has no written constitution, it is a constitutional convention of the highest importance that the legislature and judiciary are separate and independent of one another ... It therefore behoves the courts to be ever sensitive to the paramount need to refrain from trespassing upon the province of Parliament ... I would hope and expect that Parliament would be similarly sensitive to the need to refrain from trespassing upon the province of the courts.'

What if the British pragmatic approach, based on convention, fails to work? The answer is probably a written constitution, with a Bill of Rights, providing for a compartmentalisation of organs and functions and a system of American-style checks and balances. But the price may be high: less well informed decision-making and less efficient and effective government. The American experience of 'gridlock' between President and Congress in recent years is testimony to that risk.

QUESTION SEVEN

'The Rule of Law is too vague a concept to be of practical relevance to an evaluation of the actions of Government.'

Discuss.

University of London LLB Examination
(for External Students) Constitutional Law June 1993 Q3

General Comment

This is a straightforward question largely requiring descriptive analysis. The challenge must be to make it as original and as critical as possible, with as many useful illustrations as possible, especially any of topical interest. It is important to give equal emphasis to each of Dicey's components of the Rule of Law; it is a common mistake, for example, to concentrate overmuch on equality under the law.

Skeleton Solution

- Modern versions of the Rule of Law.
- The Declaration of Delhi 1959.
- Contrast with Dicey's 19th century formula.
- The three elements and objectives of Dicey's Rule of Law.
- Their influence in establishing safeguards against abuse of power.
- Delegated legislation and tribunals.
- Trades unions and security services.
- Ministers of the Crown and *M v Home Office*.
- Judicial review.
- Conclusion.

Suggested Solution

Modern versions of the Rule of Law tend to be formulated in broad political language embracing concepts such as 'justice', 'the rights of man', 'fundamental freedoms' etc. They tend to be too vague to serve as quality tests for the democratic behaviour of governments. An example is the Declaration of Delhi 1959:

'The Rule of Law means the principles, institutions and procedures, not always identical, but broadly similar, which the experience and tradition of lawyers in different countries of the world, often having themselves varying political structures and economic backgrounds, have shown to be important to protect the individual from arbitrary government and to enable him to enjoy the dignity of man.'

The absence of precise legalistic analysis from this Declaration probably allows various dictatorships around the world to claim that the Declaration has been transplanted, with 'modifications', into the soil of their constitution and legal system. The Rule of Law becomes a political concept made of clay to be moulded into the shape desired by the potter.

However, if one reverts to the classic, albeit largely discredited, theory of the Rule of Law as propounded by the Victorian Oxford Professor A V Dicey one finds a formal legal analysis which is at least capable of being used to measure the actions of government, and which even today is invoked from time to time to criticise abuses of power. It might well still be a political concept dressed up as law, but it is not as vague as the Declaration of Delhi or other modern variants.

Dicey contended that the Rule of Law has three essential elements:

a) that no one should be punished or lawfully made to suffer in body or goods except for a distinct breach of the law established in the ordinary legal manner before the ordinary courts of the land;

b) that no one should be above the law: that every person, whatever his rank or condition, should be subject to the ordinary law and answerable to the ordinary courts; and

c) that the general principles of the constitution, such as the right to personal liberty and the right of public meeting, are the result of judicial decisions and that so we have a judge-made constitution.

Dicey summed up the objective of those three elements as being 'the absolute supremacy or predominance of regular law as opposed to the influence of arbitrary power, and the exclusion of arbitrariness, of prerogative or even of wide discretionary authority on the part of government': from *Introduction to the Study of the Law of the Constitution* (1885).

Dicey's views proved immensely influential on thinking throughout the twentieth century in the British Constitution. Element (a) lay behind Parliament's caution in setting up tribunals and in granting delegated law-making powers to ministers and others. Committees such as Donoughmore (1932) and Franks (1957) recommended safeguards against the risks of abuse of power by ministers, tribunals and inquiries, which, of necessity, had to operate in a fashion far removed from the 'due process of law' administered by the 'ordinary' courts of the land. Supervisory bodies such as Parliament's Committees on Statutory Instruments and the independent Council on Tribunals, as well as the relatively modern British phenomenon of Ombudsmen (imported from Sweden), show how the British Constitution has adapted to the social welfare needs of the twentieth century without losing sight of Diceyan concepts.

Element (b) of Dicey's theory, concerning equality under the law, was said to have been gravely weakened by certain 'power groups' in society which were able to operate at times seemingly with utter contempt for the law, eg the mineworkers' union in the period of 1972–4 which flouted statutory income restraint legislation; trades unions generally in the period 1974–9; and the state security services where control and accountability seemed so minimal as to be virtually non-existent until very recently. However the 'Thatcher Years' of 1979–90 witnessed a reassertion of the rule of law over trades unions (it took a year-long miners' strike to end in failure to achieve it, in 1984) and steps were even taken to establish a statutory framework and system of parliamentary control for the security services, first with the home service, MI5, under the Security Service Act 1989 and then, during John Major's government, with the foreign service, MI6, under the Intelligence Services Act 1994. Even the long established common law immunities of the Crown, which sometimes seemed to put Ministers above the law, suffered a blow with the recent historic decision that Ministers, in their public capacity as Crown servants, could be made subject to the law of contempt of court, a decision which Sir William Wade QC hailed as a tremendous victory for the Rule of Law: *M v Home Office* (1993).

Dicey's third element, which some have regarded as descriptive rather than normative in character, has also proven a useful weapon in the armoury of those who believe in vigorous judicial review of administrative action and perhaps the creation eventually of a domestic human rights court to enforce a Bill of Rights against an over-mighty executive (ironically Dicey was against a Bill of Rights because he thought it would undermine Parliamentary sovereignty; but in his day Parliament was not the executive-dominated institution which it is today; if he had lived to see the power of the Whips and executive patronage Dicey may well have changed his view). The rapid growth of principles of judicial review in the last 30 years is regarded by many senior judges as their most significant contribution to establishing constitutional restraints

2 THE CHARACTERISTICS OF THE BRITISH CONSTITUTION

against abuse of power and, indeed, Wade & Bradley call judicial review a modern constitutional fundamental.

So Dicey's formula, far from being vague and transitory, has proven of solid and lasting value in influencing the development of controls over decision-makers and in bringing Government back within the law.

3 SOVEREIGNTY OF PARLIAMENT

3.1 Introduction
3.2 Key points
3.3 Analysis of questions
3.4 Questions

3.1 Introduction

It is important to understand in outline the means by which Parliament's legislative supremacy came to be established, and to understand the ways in which the British Constitution differs markedly from countries with a written Constitution. The British Constitution has evolved out of the long struggle between the Crown and Parliament, which culminated in Parliament exercising the powers previously enjoyed by the Crown.

Countries with a written Constitution place limits on the legislature and the courts can rule whether an act of the legislature is 'unconstitutional'. This is the case for example with the American Constitution.

The major issue on sovereignty is the question whether any Parliament can entrench legislation – that is to say limit in some way its future repeal – which could of course be of importance in the enactment of a Bill of Rights for the UK.

3.2 Key points

The phrase 'sovereignty of Parliament' is generally used to mean the absence of any legal restraint on the legislative powers of the United Kingdom Parliament. This absence of legal restraint has three aspects – see (a) to (c) following.

a) *Parliament is legally competent to legislate on any subject matter*

   i) The Act of Settlement 1700 and His Majesty's Declaration of Abdication Act 1936.

   ii) *Burmah Oil Co v Lord Advocate* [1965] AC 75 and the War Damage Act 1965.

   iii) *Mortensen v Peters* 1906 14 SLT 227.

   iv) Parliament Acts 1911 and 1949.

   v) Ireland Act 1949 s1(2).

b) *No Parliament can bind its successors or be bound by its predecessors*

   'There is one and only one limit to Parliament's legal power: it cannot detract from its own continuing sovereignty.' (Dicey, *Law of the Constitution*.)

   i) A later Parliament can expressly repeal an earlier statute.

ii) A later Parliament can impliedly repeal an earlier statute: *Vauxhall Estates* v *Liverpool Corporation* [1932] 1 KB 733; *El'en Street Estates Ltd* v *Minister of Health* [1934] 1 KB 590.

c) *Once Parliament has legislated no court or other person can pass judgment upon the validity of the legislation*

All the courts may do when faced with an Act of Parliament is apply it, subject to their limited powers of statutory interpretation. At common law a Bill becomes an Act of Parliament when it has been approved by the House of Commons and the House of Lords (unless passed under the provisions of the Parliament Acts), and has received the Royal Assent. The enforcement of these procedural rules is entirely a matter for the House concerned and the courts refuse to consider the question as to whether there have been any procedural defects in the passage of a Bill through Parliament: *Pickin* v *British Railways Board* [1974] AC 765.

d) *Limitations upon the exercise of parliamentary sovereignty*

Only Parliament can limit its own sovereignty and such limitations must have been enacted in the form of a statute. However, no Parliament can bind its successors. Therefore, whatever limitations are imposed upon the sovereignty of Parliament by one statute may be repealed by a subsequent Act. However, in practice there are limitations upon the sovereignty of Parliament.

i) Limitation as to the scope and subject matter of Parliamentary legislation: Statute of Westminster 1931, s4.

ii) Limitation as to the manner and form which legislation must take: *Attorney-General for New South Wales* v *Trethowan* [1932] AC 526 – but note that this applied to a colonial legislature.

iii) Other practical limitations on the exercise of sovereignty

- The doctrine of the mandate
- Public opinion
- Political and economic constraints

  – The impact of the European Communities Act 1972 and the European Communities (Amendment) Act 1993 and the effect on parliamentary sovereignty is significant and continues to arouse political controversy. Whilst the UK remains a member of the European Union, European law must be given effect and is seen as an ever increasing area of regulation.
  – Northern Ireland Act 1973, s1.

iv) Convention: Canada Act 1982; *Manuel* v *Attorney-General* [1983] Ch 87.

3.3 Analysis of questions

Questions can be either essay or problem. Problem questions tend to focus on the issue as to whether or not Acts of Parliament can be entrenched against future repeal. Essay questions are more wide ranging and may examine the student's knowledge of the relationship between parliamentary sovereignty and conventions of the Constitution.

CONSTITUTIONAL LAW

An example of each follows. Note that the problem question also demands a knowledge of the EU. (See chapter 4: *Sovereignty of Parliament and the EU.*)

3.4 Questions

QUESTION ONE

In July 1993 Parliament based the Puffins Act: s1 provides that it shall be a criminal offence to kill a puffin; s2 provides that no Bill to repeal the Puffins Act shall be laid before Parliament unless the consent of the Birds Council has previously been obtained.

In 1994 a Bill repealing the Puffins Act is laid before Parliament, without the consent of the Birds Council having been previously obtained, and this is subsequently enacted as the Puffins Repeal Act 1994.

Advise the Birds Council whether they can challenge the 1994 Act and still bring a prosecution against Mr Toad who killed a puffin in 1995.

How, if at all, would your advice differ if the European Commission had made a Regulation in October 1993 providing that puffins were vermin and that a cash premium would be paid in respect of each puffin killed?

Adapted from University of London LLB Examination
(for External Students) Constitutional Law June 1986 Q3

General Comment

A relatively simple question on the sovereignty of Parliament and the effects of membership of the European Union. As regards the first part of the question, after stating the content of the doctrine of parliamentary supremacy, students should argue as best they can the likely effect of the Puffins Repeal Act. There is no answer; just state the likely alternatives. The second part of the question is more straightforward as the supremacy of Community law over national rules is now firmly established in situations such as the one in the problem.

Skeleton Solution

- Introduction: the content of the doctrine of parliamentary sovereignty.
- The Puffins Repeal Act 1994: the application of the doctrine of parliamentary sovereignty to the Act; the effects of s2 of the Act on the traditional doctrine.
- The European Communities Act 1972 s2(4); the supremacy of Community law over national laws.

Suggested Solution

Under the doctrine of the sovereignty of Parliament there exists no legal limitation upon the legislative competence of the United Kingdom Parliament. This absence of legal restraint has three aspects: Parliament is legally competent to legislate upon any subject matter, no Parliament can bind its successors or be bound by its predecessors, and, once Parliament has legislated, no court or other person can pass judgment upon the validity of the legislation.

3 SOVEREIGNTY OF PARLIAMENT

This rule that Parliament may not bind its successors (and that no Parliament is bound by Acts of its predecessors) is often cited both as a limitation upon legislative supremacy and as an example of it. As Dicey says, 'The logical reason why Parliament has failed in its endeavours to enact unchangeable enactments is that a sovereign power cannot, while retaining its sovereign character, restrict its own powers by any parliamentary enactment' (*The Law of the Constitution*, 10th edition, 1959, p68). It is inherent in the nature of a legislature that it should continue to be free to make new laws and, within the United Kingdom legal system therefore, all statutes that have been enacted by the Queen in Parliament remain in force until they are repealed or amended. An Act can be repealed either expressly or impliedly (see *Ellen Street Estates Ltd* v *Minister of Health* (1934)). In the latter case if Parliament passes an Act which is contrary to a previous statute (or certain provisions of the earlier statute) the earlier statute (or those particular provisions) are held to have been repealed.

The doctrine therefore consists, in essence, of a rule which governs the legal relationship between the courts and the legislature, namely that the courts are under a duty to apply the legislation made by Parliament and may not hold an Act of Parliament to be invalid or unconstitutional.

In order for the Birds Council to challenge the Puffins Repeal Act 1994 and prosecute Mr Toad, the Council will have to satisfy the courts that the Act is invalid due to the failure to comply with the consultation provisions of the 1993 Act. Normally of course, under the doctrine of parliamentary supremacy, there will be no problem. The courts will consider the 1994 Act to have expressly repealed the 1993 Act. But in the present case, what is the effect of s2? The principle that the Parliament which passed the 1993 Act cannot bind the Parliament which purports to enact the 1994 Repeal Act may mean simply that, notwithstanding s2, the repeal is valid and the courts will be bound to give effect to the express wishes of the legislature. However it can also be argued that s2 creates a provision as to the manner by which repeal of the 1993 Act must be achieved and that this will be binding upon future Parliaments until s2 itself is expressly repealed. Therefore any attempt to repeal the whole Act without first removing s2 will be invalid. Of course it may also be argued that by expressly repealing the whole of the 1993 Act Parliament is in any case impliedly repealing the consultation provisions of s2.

The situation concerning the effect of the purported repeal is therefore somewhat uncertain. No uncertainty would exist, however, had the European Commission made a Regulation in October 1993 providing that puffins were vermin and that a cash premium would be paid in respect of each puffin killed. Section 2(4) of the European Communities Act 1972 provides in effect that United Kingdom Acts of Parliament shall be construed and have effect subject to directly applicable Community law. Under Article 189 of the Treaty of Rome, Regulations have direct applicability and are binding in all member states without requiring implementation or adoption by national law. Therefore any Regulation made by the European Commission in October 1993 would have supremacy over national laws and take effect notwithstanding the conflict with the then already existing Puffins Act 1993. In this respect it is both clear from the Treaty and from statements made by the European Court of Justice (see *Costa* v *ENEL* (1964)) that Community law should prevail over national law in all circumstances and therefore any United Kingdom constitutional law doctrine of the legislative supremacy of Parliament is irrelevant.

CONSTITUTIONAL LAW

Of course, the approach taken by the European Court of Justice indicated above runs completely contrary to the traditional doctrine of the sovereignty of Parliament. This has resulted in controversy, with some arguing that, while the doctrine of implied repeal has been abandoned so far as Community law is concerned, the doctrine of express repeal of earlier law, including Community law, is nevertheless retained. However it is yet to be seen how the United Kingdom courts would act if faced by a United Kingdom Act of Parliament expressing an intention of Parliament to legislature contrary to Community law. It is worth noting, however, that in *R* v *Secretary of State, ex parte Factortame (No 2)* (1990) the House of Lords did, following a reference to the European Court, grant an injunction effectively suspending the operation of a UK statute to the extent that it was inconsistent with European law. Such a situation is, perhaps, unlikely to arise since it would amount to a blatant repudiation by the United Kingdom of its international obligations under the European Community Treaties. But, in the absence of such express repeal of Community law by our Parliament, it is clear that as in *Macarthys Ltd* v *Smith* (1979), where a conflict does exist between United Kingdom legislation and Community law, the latter will prevail and accordingly, not withstanding the Puffins Act 1993 and its provisions, the Community Regulation of October 1993 will bind our courts.

QUESTION TWO

Section 1 of the Northern Ireland Act 1973 reads:

' ... it is hereby affirmed that in no event will Northern Ireland ... cease to be part of ... the United Kingdom without the consent of the majority of the people of Northern Ireland voting in a poll held for the purposes of this section ...'

Is this a law or a convention or both? Is it a restriction on parliamentary sovereignty?

University of London LLB Examination
(for External Students) Constitutional Law June 1983 Q2

General Comment

Be careful only to answer the question and not to digress into any sort of political discussion − it might be interesting but it is irrelevant for examination purposes. The question requires definitions and discussions of basic constitutional ideas − conventions and parliamentary sovereignty. It can be answered either under two separate headings or by amalgamating your answer into a continuous essay − but keeping both parts distinct.

Skeleton Solution

- Relationship between law and convention.
- The courts and conventions.
- Sovereignty of Parliament − doctrine of implied repeal.
- Political consequences. Statute of Westminster, European Communities Act 1972.

Suggested Solution

In a number of constitutional contexts the distinction between law and convention is blurred. Dicey was quite clear that conventions were not 'laws' in the strict sense for if any were broken no court would 'enforce' them. Laws, he felt, were simply rules enforced or recognised by the courts. But this is really over simplifying the nature of a convention for courts do take notice of conventions and use them as aids to interpretation. Constitutional conventions do influence judicial decisions. They may be compared to a preamble in an Act of Parliament.

Section 1 of the Northern Ireland Act is a curious case. It reads like the affirmation of a constitutional convention. It replaces s1(2) of the Ireland Act 1949 which stated the same thing but with a reference to the Parliament of Northern Ireland. As a constitutional convention it is not legally binding on the United Kingdom Parliament but by placing it within the statute it might suggest it was a law. Generally matters within a statute are law and enforced and recognised by courts. Because it is within the statute it cannot be challenged in the courts as being void or unconstitutional. Statutes are the prime source of law and it would be a bold argument to suggest that s1 was not a law. If the government decided to ignore s1, without passing a statute, then a declaration could be sought to state that the government was acting unlawfully.

Section 1 is a good example of the close relationship between law and convention. It is a law and might also be a convention. While it remains on the statute book it will be obeyed predominantly for political reasons and not through fear of litigation.

Is it a restriction on parliamentary sovereignty?

Parliamentary sovereignty is shorthand for the principle that Parliament is competent to make or unmake any law whatsoever on any matter whatsoever and that no court can question the validity of an Act of Parliament. Section 1 purports to bind future Parliaments and thus would seem to run contrary to the principle.

There is no method in law by which sections of statutes can be entrenched, and in strict legal terms Parliament could now pass an Act to grant independence to Northern Ireland or to cede it to Eire and thereby impliedly repeal s1. In his judgment in *Ellen Street Estates Ltd* v *Minister of Health* (1934) Maugham LJ stated 'The Legislature cannot, according to our Constitution, bind itself as to the form of subsequent legislation'. In reality it is unlikely that Northern Ireland would cease to be part of the United Kingdom without a referendum – the politics of the situation would demand it and it might be seen as political suicide to determine otherwise. Strictly s1 cannot be seen as a restriction on sovereignty.

Historically the formal giving away of parliamentary sovereignty by granting independence to a nation has followed the de facto independence of the country in question. This actual state of independence has not been reached and may never be reached in Northern Ireland.

QUESTION THREE

'Attempts to entrench legislation by legal means will inevitably be futile unless the basic rule of the United Kingdom's Constitution is abandoned.'

Discuss.

University of London LLB Examination
(for External Students) Constitutional Law June 1991 Q1

CONSTITUTIONAL LAW

General Comment

A question requiring an explanation of the terms used, particularly 'entrenchment', and 'the basic rule of the constitution'. It is important to explain how parliamentary sovereignty manifests itself thus indicating the difficulties with entrenchment. Obviously the impact of European Union membership upon parliamentary sovereignty also needs to be considered.

Skeleton Solution

- Explain nature of sovereignty.
- Express and implied repeal – examples.
- Nature of European Communities Act – decisions thereunder.
- *Factortame* cases – conclusion.

Suggested Solution

Entrenchment of legislation involves the enactment of clauses that prevent the Act concerned from being repealed by simple majority vote by the legislative body. A typical example is provided by Article V of the United States constitution under which two thirds of the members of Congress have to approve an amendment to the constitution, which in turn has to receive the support of three quarters of the state legislatures. The purpose of entrenchment is clearly to protect those constitutional measures which are seen as being particularly fundamental. A constitution that could not be altered at all would soon become obsolete and disregarded in practice. One that could be changed by a simple majority vote would be at the mercy of passing political trends, especially where a small party held power because an election had produced a 'hung' parliament. The question under consideration refers to attempts at entrenchment within the British constitution being futile because of the constitution's basic rule. By this it is assumed that the question is referring to the doctrine of parliamentary sovereignty, under which Parliament has the ultimate power to pass or repeal any legislation it sees fit. In short it is being suggested that it will not avail Parliament to include entrenchment provisions in a piece of legislation in an effort to protect it, as a natural consequence of parliamentary sovereignty is that no parliament can bind its successor parliaments. To what extent does the operation of the British constitution support this view?

Traditionally constitutional lawyers have pointed to the operation of two doctrines as evidence of the inability of any parliament to bind its successors; express repeal and implied repeal. Under the former, any parliament could enact legislation expressly repealing existing legislation. The effect of the doctrine was that the courts would always apply the most recent legislation. Where two pieces of legislation appeared irreconcilable, but the later Act did not expressly state that its effect was to repeal the terms of the earlier Act, the latter doctrine of implied repeal would be brought into play by means of which the courts would assume that it was implicit in the passage of the later legislation that Parliament had intended to repeal the earlier legislation since they could not stand together. Attempts by Parliament to circumvent the doctrine of implied repeal in the earlier part of the 20th century met with little success.

3 SOVEREIGNTY OF PARLIAMENT

This is illustrated by the cases of *Vauxhall Estates* v *Liverpool Corporation* (1932), and *Ellen Street Estates Ltd* v *Minister of Health* (1934).

In the first of these cases, the Corporation of Liverpool proposed a scheme for the improvement of a certain area of the city. The Minister of Health confirmed the scheme in an order which incorporated the provisions of the Acquisition of Land (Assessment of Compensation) Act 1919 and the Housing Act 1925. These two Acts each provided a different scheme of compensation for compulsorily acquired land. The 1919 Act provided in s7(1):

'The provisions of the ... order by which the land is authorised to be acquired, or of any Act incorporated therewith, shall in relation to the matters dealt with in this Act, have effect subject to this Act, and so far as inconsistent with this Act those provisions shall ... not have effect.'

The question arose as to whether the compensation due to the appellants should be calculated in accordance with the 1919 Act or in accordance with the 1925 Act. The appellants argued that, because of s7(1) of the 1919 Act, it must be calculated in accordance with that Act.

It was held that the compensation should be assessed in accordance with the later Act. Parliament had exercised its power of overriding the provisions of s7(1) of the 1919 Act by enacting in the later Act of 1925 a set of provisions totally inconsistent with those of the 1919 Act. Similarly in the *Ellen Street* case it was held that the provisions of an earlier Act could always be repealed, by implication, by provisions in a later Act which were inconsistent with those in the earlier Act. Maugham LJ stated the effect of the doctrine as follows:

'... The Legislature cannot, according to our constitution, bind itself as to the form of subsequent legislation, and it is impossible for Parliament to enact that in a subsequent statute dealing with the same subject-matter there can be no implied repeal.'

It should be clear from the above that the doctrine of parliamentary sovereignty depends in large measure on the adherence by the judiciary to the practice of applying the later Act in preference to an earlier one.

Since the entry into the European Community (EC) by the United Kingdom, however, the assumptions implicit in the question need to be re-assessed, however. Section 2(1) of the European Communities Act 1972 provides that all EC law became part of United Kingdom law with effect from 1 January 1973. Section 2(4) further provides that '... any such provision (of any such extent) as might be made by Act of Parliament, and any enactment passed or to be passed, other than one contained in this Part of this Act, shall be construed and have effect subject to the foregoing provisions of this section ...'. In other words any subsequent Act passed by the United Kingdom Parliament was to take effect only to the extent that it did not conflict with the provisions of EC law. This was clearly another attempt to bypass the doctrine of implied repeal, but it was one that was necessary if the United Kingdom was going to be able to abide by its obligations under the terms of the Treaty of Rome, which requires each member state to give primacy to EC law, see *Costa* v *ENEL* (1964). The result has been that the domestic courts have modified the doctrine of implied repeal as regards domestic law and EC legislation, by holding that domestic law should always be interpreted in a manner that produces a result consistent with the United Kingdom's obligations under the Treaty; see *Macarthys Ltd* v *Smith* (1981), and *Garland* v *British Rail Engineering Ltd* (1983), wherein Lord Diplock stated that, in a case of clear conflict, domestic courts would still have to produce an interpretation of domestic law that ensured conformity with EC law, '... no matter how wide a departure from the prima facie meaning may be need to achieve consistency.'

Following *R* v *Secretary of State for Transport, ex parte Factortame (No 2)* (1990), it is now clear that the domestic courts have to be prepared to go as far as suspending the operation of an Act of Parliament if it is impugned on the ground that it conflicts with EC law whilst that issue is being considered by the European Court of Justice. It is submitted that short of the United Kingdom reneging upon its obligations under the Treaty of Rome, unilaterally withdrawing from the EU, and expressly repealing the European Communities Act 1972, the Act effectively entrenches EU law, by making it impossible for any later Act to be applied in preference to EU law by means of implied repeal.

Note that this result is achieved because of the existence of bodies outside the United Kingdom (such as the European Commission and Court of Justice) given jurisdiction by the United Kingdom Parliament over matters formerly within its control, and further given power to invoke sanctions against the United Kingdom if it attempts to re-assert that sovereignty by indirect means.

4 SOVEREIGNTY OF PARLIAMENT AND THE EUROPEAN UNION

4.1 Introduction

4.2 Key points

4.3 Recent cases and developments

4.4 Analysis of questions

4.5 Questions

4.1 Introduction

a) The political integration of European countries has been a post-war objective within Europe. In 1957 Belgium, France, West Germany, Italy, Luxembourg and the Netherlands signed the Treaty of Rome establishing the European Economic Community. In 1973 Denmark, Ireland and the United Kingdom became members.

b) The United Kingdom became a member by virtue of the Treaty of Accession 1972. It was necessary for Parliament to pass legislation incorporating the provisions into domestic law. This was achieved by the European Communities Act 1972.

c) Political and legal integration has proceeded since then. The political and legal issues are:

   i) The extent to which our Parliament is obliged to pass legislation which is consistent with Community provisions – a negation of sovereignty?

   ii) The position of our courts where Community law and UK law conflict.

d) Following the Single European Act 1986 the process of integration has continued apace, and the creation of a single market is well under way. These factors together with decisions of the European Court of Justice re-affirming the supremacy of Community law over national legislation are causing political controversy.

e) Following the Treaty on European Union signed at Maastricht in February 1992, the basic structure is now:

CONSTITUTIONAL LAW

4.2 Key points

a) *The Community organs*

The Community has law making, executive and judicial powers.

i) The Council of Ministers – The final policy and law making body of the Community. It has representatives from each member state with a president holding office for six months. Note the decision-making process of the council.

ii) The European Commission – Members are chosen by national governments. The commission can propose law, make law itself and enforce Community law against member states.

iii) The European Parliament – Members of the European Parliament are directly elected by member states. They are independent of national party policies. The parliament has no law making powers but is consulted by the council. Both the council and the commission are accountable to the parliament. There are proposals to give the Parliament greater powers.

iv) The European Court of Justice – The ECJ consists of 15 judges appointed by member states. Its function is to enforce Community law and treaty provisions. The role of the court is crucial to Community law being applied uniformly through all member states (see below).

b) *The sources of Community law*

i) The Treaties

Proceedings can be brought in the European Court if a member state fails to fulfil its obligations.

ii) Acts of the Community Institutions

- Regulations – Made by Council of Ministers or the Commission, these are directly applicable in member states.
- Directives – These establish Community objectives but leave the responsibility of implementation to member states: see *Van Duyn* v *Home Office* [1974] 3 All ER 178.

iii) Decisions of the Court of Justice

- Actions against member states
- Rulings on the interpretation of Community law referred by national courts: Article 177; see *Bulmer (HP)* v *J Bollinger SA* [1974] Ch 401 and *Finnegan* v *Clowney YTP* [1990] 2 AC 407.

Note s3(1) European Communities Act 1972 – 'for the purpose of all legal proceedings any question as to the meaning or effect of any of the treaties or as to the validity meaning or effect of a community instrument ... shall be for determination as such in accordance with the principles laid down by ... the European Court.'

4 SOVEREIGNTY OF PARLIAMENT AND THE EUROPEAN UNION

c) *Direct applicability*

Section 2(1) of the European Communities Act 1972 provides:

'All such rights, powers, liabilities, obligations and restrictions from time to time created or arising by or under the Treaties, and all such remedies and procedures from time to time provided for by or under the Treaties, as in accordance with the Treaties are without further enactment to be given legal effect or used in the United Kingdom shall be recognised and available in law, and be enforced, allowed and followed accordingly; and the expression "enforceable Community right" and similar expressions shall be read as referring to one to which this subsection applies.'

The effect of this subsection is that all the provisions of Community law which are, in accordance with Community law, intended to take direct effect in the United Kingdom are given the force of law. This applies to Community law made both before and after the coming into force of the Act.

d) *Direct effect*

Community law now creates rights and obligations which can be enforced in national courts. The sources of Community law are: (i) Treaty provisions; (ii) directives; and (iii) regulations. Community law which has vertical direct effect refers to those obligations which are imposed upon the state. Horizontal direct effect applies to rights which individuals can enforce against one another. Regulations give rise to law which has horizontal direct effect. Treaty provisions and directives create obligations on the state. Note, however, that the developing jurisprudence of the ECJ has resulted in some Treaty provisions and directives having horizontal direct effect: see *Van Gend en Loos* v *Netherlands* [1963] ECR 1; *Van Duyn* v *Home Office* [1974] ECR 1337; *Marshall* v *Southampton and South West Hampshire Area Health Authority* [1986] QB 401; *Francovich* v *Italy* [1992] IRLR 84. But see now decisions which deny horizontal direct effect to directives: *Marshall* v *Southampton and South West Area Health Authority (No 2)* [1993] 4 All ER 586 and *Faccini Dori* v *Recreb Srl* Case C–91/92 [1995] 1 All ER (EC) 1.

e) *The supremacy of Community law over national rules*

Section 2(4) of the European Communities Act provides:

'The provision that may be made under subsection (2) above includes, subject to Schedule 2 of this Act, any such provision (of any such extent) as may be made by Act of Parliament, and any enactment passed or to be passed, other than one contained in this part of this Act, shall be construed and have effect subject to the foregoing provisions of this section.'

The 'foregoing provisions' include s2(1) which states that directly applicable Community law shall have effect in the United Kingdom. Therefore s2(4) seems to amount to a statement that United Kingdom Acts of Parliament 'shall be construed and have effect subject to' directly applicable Community law.

The primacy of Community law over national law can be seen in decisions of the European Court of Justice: *Costa* v *ENEL* [1964] ECR 585; *Simmenthal SpA* v *Amministrazione delle Finanze dello Stato* [1977] 2 CMLR 1.

CONSTITUTIONAL LAW

f) *Community law and the UK*

European law will be followed in preference to inconsistent pre-1972 statutes: *Conegate* v *HM Customs and Excise* [1987] 2 WLR 39.

It is suggested that there is a new canon of statutory interpretation so that relevant provisions of UK law can bear a meaning that is consistent with Community law: *Garland* v *British Rail Engineering Ltd* [1983] 2 AC 751; *McCarthys Ltd* v *Smith* [1979] 3 All ER 325; *Pickstone* v *Freemans plc* [1988] 2 All ER 803.

More radical approaches are being adopted which suggest that the duty of the national court is to give effect to Community law and frustrate the provisions of an Act of Parliament where there is a conflict. In *R* v *Secretary of State for Transport, ex parte Factortame Ltd and Others (No 2)* [1990] 3 WLR 818 the court granted interim relief suspending those parts of the Merchant Shipping Act 1988 which conflicted with Community law.

g) *Conclusion*

The doctrine of direct applicability and the supremacy of Community law over national rules has led to a surrender of sovereignty on the part of the Westminster Parliament. But while there can be no implied repeal of Community law by national legislation, the position regarding the express repeal of Community law by Act of Parliament is a matter of controversy. While the European Court of Justice maintains that a national court should give effect to Community law even when subsequent national legislation is inconsistent with it, some lawyers argue that the express wish of Parliament must prevail. Two points are however clear:

i) It is only a partial surrender of sovereignty in that it only affects those matters within the competence of the European Community Treaties.

ii) It is only a temporary surrender of sovereignty in that it only applies so long as the European Communities Act 1972 is in force.

4.3 Recent cases and developments

Francovich v *Italy* [1992] IRLR 84.

R v *Secretary of State for Transport, ex parte Factortame (No 2)* [1990] 3 WLR 818.

Marleasing SA v *La Comercial Internacionale de Alimentacion SA* Case C–106/89 [1990] ECR 1.

Torfaen Borough Council v *B & Q plc* [1990] 1 All ER 129.

Commission v *UK (Re Bathing Water Directive)* [1994] 1 CMLR 760 – a good example of the policing role of the European Commission.

Treaty on European Union 1992 ('Maastricht Treaty') – implemented by the European Communities (Amendment) Act 1993.

4.4 Analysis of questions

The extent to which the UK Parliament remains sovereign becomes an ever more important political question. The legal issue raised in exam questions focuses on the

4 SOVEREIGNTY OF PARLIAMENT AND THE EUROPEAN UNION

relationship between EU law and UK law where there is a conflict and the approach of the judiciary to such a conflict.

4.5 Questions

QUESTION ONE

Parliament wishes to promote affirmative action and decides to allow women to be paid more than men for the same work. It passes the Turning the Tables Act 1995, s1 of which states:

'This Act is to be given effect notwithstanding any decision of the European Court of Justice or any provisions of Community law or any provisions of the European Communities Act 1972.'

Would a British judge still give primacy to Community law if this new Act came into conflict with it?

Adapted from University of London LLB Examination
(for External Students) Constitutional Law June 1987 Q3

General Comment

A relatively simple question concerning the effect of membership of the European Communities on the sovereignty of the Westminster Parliament.

Skeleton Solution

- Introduction. The European Communities Act 1972.
- The principles of direct applicability and the supremacy of Community law over national rules. Section 2(1) and s2(4) of the European Communities Act 1972.
- The sovereignty of Parliament. Express repeal and the doctrine of implied repeal. Effect of Community law.
- Effect of parliamentary legislation expressly contrary to Community law: *Macarthys Ltd* v *Smith* (1979); *R* v *Secretary of State for Transport, ex parte Factortame (No 2)* (1990).
- The position with regard to the Turning the Tables Act 1995.

Suggested Solution

The United Kingdom became a member of the European Communities with effect from 1 January 1973, by virtue of the Treaty of Accession 1972. For the Treaty of Accession and the Community treaties and law to have legal effect in the United Kingdom it was necessary for Parliament to pass legislation incorporating them into domestic law. This was achieved by the European Communities Act 1972.

The legal regime of the European Community is founded upon the principle of direct applicability. Certain rules of Community law contained both in the treaties and in regulations made by the Council or the Commission are directly applicable in that, of their own force, they create legal rights and duties enforceable in municipal courts. Community law also forms part of the national law of every member state. The European Court of Justice has held that Community law prevails over national

37

law to the extent that they are inconsistent with one another. These two principles are given effect in the law of the United Kingdom by virtue of s2(1) and s2(4) of the European Communities Act 1972.

By virtue of s2(4) of the European Communities Act 1972 therefore all United Kingdom legislation shall only take effect to the extent that it is consistent with Community law however clearly it may appear from the United Kingdom legislation that it is intended to have effect notwithstanding any Community law to the contrary: *Costa* v *ENEL* (1964); *Amministrazione delle Finanze dello Stato* v *Simmenthal SpA* (1978). It is clear both from the treaty and from statements made by the European Court of Justice that community law should prevail over national law in all circumstances. Any United Kingdom constitutional law doctrine of the legislative sovereignty of Parliament is irrelevant. This approach taken by the European Court of Justice runs completely contrary to the traditional doctrine of the sovereignty of Parliament as enunciated in *Vauxhall Estates* v *Liverpool Corporation* (1932) and *Ellen Street Estates Ltd* v *Minister of Health* (1934). Certainly the doctrine of implied repeal as set out in *Ellen Street Estates* v *Minister of Health*, that later United Kingdom legislation always, by implication, repeals earlier legislative provisions with which it is inconsistent, would not survive.

But what about the situation such as that under the Turning the Tables Act 1995, where Parliament legislates expressly contrary to Community law. In such a case it may be possible to treat s2(4) as amounting to a rule of interpretation that there shall be a presumption that the United Kingdom Parliament, in passing legislation, intends to legislate consistently with Community law. This approach allows that if the United Kingdom Parliament were to make it clear in a piece of legislation that it intended to legislate contrary to Community law or that it intended the legislation to take effect notwithstanding any provision of Community law to the contrary, then the United Kingdom legislation would prevail over the inconsistent Community law. This is the approach that was favoured by the Court of Appeal in *Macarthys Ltd* v *Smith* (1979). A man had been employed as a stockroom keeper at £60 per week. Subsequently a woman was employed in this position at £50 per week. She took the matter to an industrial tribunal on the grounds that this was contrary to law. Two questions arose. Firstly, was this contrary to article 119 of the Treaty of Rome which provides that each member state shall ensure and maintain the application of the principle that men and women should receive equal pay for equal work? Secondly, in the event of a conflict between the United Kingdom legislation and article 119 of the Treaty, which should prevail in English courts?

In the Court of Appeal Lord Denning MR felt that if there were a conflict between the United Kingdom legislation and article 119 of the Treaty, article 119 should prevail since this is required by s2(1) and s2(4) of the European Communities Act 1972. Lord Denning here assumed that Parliament, when it passes legislation, intends to fulfil its obligations under the Treaty. But he felt that if the time should come when Parliament deliberately passes an Act with the intention of repudiating the Treaty or any provision in it or intentionally of acting inconsistently with it and says so in express terms, then it would be the duty of the United Kingdom courts to follow the Act of Parliament. But unless there is such an intentional and express repudiation of the Treaty, it is the duty of the United Kingdom courts to give priority to the Treaty.

4 SOVEREIGNTY OF PARLIAMENT AND THE EUROPEAN UNION

Thus Lord Denning put forward the view that if Parliament in an Act stated an express intention to legislate contrary to Community law or notwithstanding Community law, then in that one situation the United Kingdom court would give preference to the United Kingdom legislation over the Community law. This interpretation was also favoured by Lord Diplock in *Garland* v *British Rail Engineering Ltd* (1983) when he too stated that statutes must be construed in a way consistent with Treaty obligations if they are capable of bearing such a meaning.

This amounts to a retention of the doctrine of express repeal of earlier law by later legislation, but involves the abandonment of the doctrine of implied repeal as far as Community law is concerned. In the case of *R* v *Secretary of State for Transport, ex parte Factortame (No 2)* (1990) the court granted temporary injunctive relief suspending those parts of the Merchant Shipping Act 1988 which were in conflict with Community law. A reference to the European Court of Justice ruled that domestic courts were required to give effect to directly enforceable provisions of Community law. The approach is not consistent with the traditional United Kingdom doctrine of the sovereignty of Parliament. However, it is yet to be seen how the United Kingdom courts would act if faced with a United Kingdom Act of Parliament expressing a clear intention of Parliament to legislate contrary to Community law. Regarding the Turning the Tables Act 1995 therefore the position is far from clear. The court may be inclined to uphold the express wish of Parliament and give effect to the Act notwithstanding article 119 of the Treaty of Rome. However the European Court of Justice would almost certainly declare this to be invalid and hold that s1 of the 1995 Act amounts to a blatant repudiation by the United Kingdom of its international obligations under the European Community Treaties.

QUESTION TWO

The United Kingdom Parliament is said to have forfeited its sovereignty by the European Communities Act 1972. However this forfeiture of sovereignty is better described as a limited and partial surrender of sovereignty.

Discuss.

The University of Wolverhampton
Constitutional Law September 1991 Q1

General Comment

A topical question which continues to arouse political controversy. Our membership of the European Union has far reaching political and constitutional implications.

Skeleton Solution

- An outline of the idea of parliamentary sovereignty.
- The European Communities Act 1972 ss2(1), (4) and 3(1).
- Sources of Community law and its integration into the UK.
- The response of the UK courts.
- Conclusion.

CONSTITUTIONAL LAW

Suggested Solution

The doctrine of parliamentary sovereignty according to Dicey means that Parliament has the right to make or unmake any law whatever, that no person or body is recognised by the law of England as having a right to override or challenge the legislation of Parliament and that Parliament cannot bind its successors. Thus Parliament has passed legislation which has retrospective effect, see *Burmah Oil Co* v *Lord Advocate* (1965), legislation which conflicts with international treaties – see *Mortesen* v *Peters* (1906) – and the cases of *Vauxhall Estates* v *Liverpool Corporation* (1932) and *Ellen Street Estates Ltd* v *Minister of Health* (1934) illustrate the principle that Parliament cannot detract from its own continuing sovereignty – that is to say it cannot bind a future Parliament.

There are of course certain ultimate limitations on what Parliament can do which derive from the influence of public opinion and the political realities any government faces – see Lord Sankey in *British Coal Corporation* v *R* (1935). By and large such issues tend to be academic. However, the United Kingdom's membership of the European Union has posed a constitutional dilemma in that the United Kingdom is obliged to legislate in a way that is consistent with treaty obligations and European law has direct effect in the United Kingdom.

The United Kingdom became a member of the European Communities with effect from 1 January 1973. The Community Treaties and Community law were given legal effect by the European Communities Act 1972. The objective of the Community is to create a 'partnership' of member states. To achieve this a degree of harmonisation of individual states' laws is necessary. The objectives of the Community are contained in Article 2 of the Treaty of Rome and whilst specifically aimed at commercial and agricultural activity they permeate many other areas of United Kingdom law, for example sex discrimination and environmental control.

Community law originates from the Community Treaties, Acts of the Community institutions and decisions of the European Court of Justice. Whilst the United Kingdom is not bound by international treaties the particular feature of the Community is that laws made by the Community organs are transferred into United Kingdom law by virtue of the European Communities Act and furthermore the United Kingdom must legislate in a way consistent with Community law and Community Treaties, see *Bulmer* v *Bollinger* (1974). Community law has become a source of law in the United Kingdom. Where then does this leave the doctrine of Parliamentary supremacy as defined by Dicey?

Section 2(1) of the European Communities Act 1972 provides that 'rights, powers, liabilities, obligations and restrictions ... and all such remedies and procedures from time to time provided for under the Treaties ... are without further enactment to be given legal effect ... in the United Kingdom ...' Section 2(4) provides that United Kingdom Acts of Parliament 'shall be construed and have effect subject to directly applicable Community Law'.

The approach of the European Court of Justice, which under s3 of the Act is the ultimate authority on the interpretation of Community law, is to assert the primacy of that law: see *Costa* v *ENEL* (1964) and the *Simmenthal* case (1978). The approach of the United Kingdom courts has been to interpret both treaty provisions and directives (see *Van Duyn* v *Home Office* (1974)) in a way consistent with treaty obligations. This was the case in *MacCarthys Ltd* v *Smith* (1979), which concerned the equal pay provisions under article 119 of the Treaty of Rome. In that particular case there was a degree of interpretative latitude under the Equal Pay Act 1970 as amended by the Sex Discrimination Act 1975, and Denning MR argued that the court could look to the treaty provisions as an aid to construction, the assumption being that the United Kingdom Parliament would not intend to legislate in a way inconsistent with European law.

The case of *R* v *Secretary of State for Transport, ex parte Factortame (No 2)* (1990) further underlines the conflict. The Merchant Shipping Act 1988 contained provisions at variance with Community law. On a reference to the European Court of Justice the court predictably ruled that measures of EC law rendered any conflicting national law inapplicable. The House of Lords granted an injunction effectively suspending the provisions of the Act that were in conflict thus frustrating, albeit temporarily, the objectives of the statute. The developing jurisprudence of the European Court can be seen in two cases: *Marleasing SA* v *La Comercial Internacionale de Alimentacion SA* (1990) and *Francovich* v *Italy* (1992). In *Marleasing* the court held that national courts should interpret their existing national law taking account of a clearly worded directive, notwithstanding it had not been implemented. In *Francovich* an individual was given the right to sue the state for damages for the non-implementation of a directive which would, if implemented, have conferred a remedy.

It can therefore be seen that, in the context of our membership of the European Union, the purist view of parliamentary sovereignty is no longer tenable. Forfeiture of sovereignty is limited and partial in the sense that in the United Kingdom constitution it is not possible to entrench legislation and the European Communities Act could be repealed. However, a 'European constitutional order' is emerging despite some political resistance and the present integration of the United Kingdom into the Community does mean a limited sovereignty in practical terms.

QUESTION THREE

'The *Factortame* decision of the Court of Justice of the European Communities is little more than a reaffirmation of the supremacy of Community Law.'

Critically assess this statement.

University of London LLB Examination
(for External Students) Constitutional Law June 1991 Q7

General Comment

A question that clearly requires a very good knowledge of recent case law. Note that it was set before the European Court of Justice handed down its decision as to the validity of the Merchant Shipping Act 1988, and thus refers to the decision on the availability of remedies in domestic law.

Skeleton Solution

- Facts of case. Legal proceedings.

CONSTITUTIONAL LAW

- Reference to legal framework of the 1972 Act.
- Discussion of the decision's impact.
- Conclusion.

Suggested Solution

a) *The background to the decision*

Under the Common Fishing Policy established by the European Economic Community, limits were set upon the amount of fish that could be caught by fishing fleets registered with each member state, the purpose being to ensure that each state could have a fair access to the community's total allowable catch. Many Spanish owners set up British registered companies running fishing fleets which counted against the British quota, even though the companies had little connection with Britain. The UK government objected to this 'quota hopping', arguing that the UK's quota was being plundered by ships flying the British flag but which had little if any connection with the United Kingdom. In 1988 the Merchant Shipping Act came into force, and regulations enacted thereunder introduced new requirements that would have to be met by any shipowner wishing to register his ship as British. Inter alia, the company owning the 'British' vessels would have to have its principal place of business in the UK, and 75 per cent of its shareholders would have to be British nationals. The effect of these new provisions was to effectively de-register the Spanish owned ships, as their owners could not satisfy the new requirements, and could therefore no longer fish against the British quota. Ninety-five companies were affected by this change. The Spanish trawler owners sought judicial review of the minister's decision that they should be de-registered; his determination that theirs were no longer 'British' ships; and the relevant parts of the Act and regulations which sought to prevent them from fishing. As to remedies, the applicants sought a declaration that the minister's decision should not take effect because of its inconsistency with European Community law; an order of prohibition to prevent the minister from regarding the ships as de-registered; and an interim injunction suspending the operation of the legislation pending the ruling of the European Court of Justice.

b) *The legal rulings*

The question of whether or not interim injunctive relief was available to suspend the operation of an Act of Parliament was considered by the House of Lords, who in turn referred the question to the European Court of Justice under article 177: *R v Secretary of State for Transport, ex parte Factortame (No 1)* (1989). On the question referred to it by the House of Lords, the European Court of Justice ruled that the Treaty of Rome required the courts of member states to give effect to the directly enforceable provisions of European Community law. Such measures of European Economic Community law rendered any conflicting national law inapplicable. A court which would grant interim relief to protect community rights, but for a rule of domestic law, should set aside that rule of domestic law in favour of observing community obligations. This ruling was considered by the House of Lords in *R v Secretary of State for Transport, ex parte Factortame (No 2)* (1991). Noting that the ruling recognised their lordships' jurisdiction to grant interim relief, but that it did not provide any indication as to how that power should be exercised in the instant case, Lord Bridge explained that, in determining whether an injunction should be granted, the determining factor should not be the availability of damages as a remedy, but the balance of convenience, taking into account the importance of upholding duly enacted laws.

c) *The significance of the decision*

The United Kingdom Parliament, in enacting the European Communities Act 1972, which provided for the direct applicability of Community law in the United Kingdom, and the enforceability of Community rights before United Kingdom courts, laid the foundations for the judgment of the European Court of Justice in the *Factortame* case. Section 2(4) of the Act provides (inter alia) that ' ... any such provision (of any such extent) as might be made by Act of Parliament, and any enactment passed or to be passed, other than one contained in this Part of this Act, shall be construed and have effect subject to the foregoing provisions of this section ...' This is a tolerably clear statement that EC law is to prevail over all existing and future domestic legislation.

It is also clear both from the Treaty of Rome and from statements made by the European Court of Justice that the Community view is that Community law should prevail over national law in all circumstances. Thus, the European Court of Justice, in *Costa* v *ENEL* (1964), stated that accession to the European Communities 'has as a corollary the impossibility, for the Member State, to give preference to an unilateral and subsequent measure against a legal order accepted by them on a basis of reciprocity'.

The significance of the decision would seem to be that the courts can now, at least temporarily, disapply the provisions of an Act of Parliament where there appears to be a violation of Community law. There was predictable outrage in the House of Commons when the decision of the European Court of Justice was published, (the Speaker refused a motion for an emergency debate on the issue) but many commentators regarded the outcome as an inevitability that had been slow in materialising. The need for some mechanism by which the existence of rights, purported to have been created by community law, could be protected whilst the matter was litigated, should be obvious.

There is clearly a need to develop some jurisprudence as to how this newly found power to is to be exercised. The availability of damages as an appropriate remedy may persuade a court not to suspend the operation of an Act. The decision at least serves as a reminder to the legislature to be more mindful of Community obligations when enacting legislation.

d) *Conclusion*

The conclusion must be that the *Factortame* decision is a predictable consequence of European Community membership, and does amount to a reaffirmation of the supremacy of European Community law, in areas where the Member States have agreed that the European Community should have sovereignty.

CONSTITUTIONAL LAW

QUESTION FOUR

'The traditional doctrine of Parliamentary sovereignty requires revision in light of the United Kingdom's membership of the European Communities.'

Do you agree?

University of London LLB Examination
(for External Students) Constitutional Law June 1993 Q2

General Comment

Despite its mild, almost understated appearance, this is probably the most difficult of all questions which a constitutional student is likely to face. The effect of EU membership on national sovereignty involves very sophisticated and intricate analysis; there will be no time to give elementary explanation of concepts at any length, and so the examiner will be prepared to assume a large degree of knowledge, eg on the character of EU Articles, Regulations and Directives, the differences between horizontal and direct effect, etc. It is essential to concentrate on rulings of the European Court of Justice in recent cases which have spelled out the enormity of the constitutional changes. It is unlikely that the examiner expected detailed discussion of the Treaty of Maastricht, which had not been ratified by member states or incorporated into English law at the time of the examination. But, following subsequent ratification and incorporation, it is likely that future questions of this sort will invite more detailed appraisal of the effect of those decisions.

Skeleton Solution

- Brief definition of concept of sovereignty.
- Brief outline of changes made by European Communities Acts 1972 and 1993.
- Detailed consideration of 1972 Act, ss2 and 3.
- Rulings of ECJ on harmonisation of national laws and supremacy of EU law.
- Ruling of ECJ on methods of interpreting national laws so as to comply with EU Directives.
- Ruling of ECJ on remedies for failure to implement Directives.
- Brief reference to likely effect of ratification of Treaty of Maastricht.
- Conclusion.

Suggested Solution

The traditional doctrine of parliamentary sovereignty contends that Parliament can make or unmake any law whatsoever; that no Parliament can bind future Parliaments as to the manner or form of legislating or as to the policy of legislation; and that no court is competent to question the validity of an authentic Act of Parliament. The doctrine evolved in the context of the UK's unwritten constitution as a result of Parliament's struggle for power against the monarchy and judges in the seventeenth century. However, the enactment of the European Communities Act (ECA) 1972 and the recent incorporation of the Maastricht Treaty on European Union by the European Communities (Amendment) Act 1993 changed all that. It would, indeed, be something of an understatement to say that the traditional doctrine requires mere revision; it must be questionable whether it even exists any more, since the ECA 1972 gave the UK an external written constitution superior (in cases of conflict) to the internal unwritten one. EU Law today affects so much of English law that, so far as fundamentals are concerned, it would be fantasy to assert that UK judges could continue to recognise a claim to sovereignty which had effectively been surrendered to (or 'pooled with') a different kind of sovereignty, that of the EU.

The combined effect of the 1972 Act, s2(1) and s2(4) is that conflicts between English law and EU law must be resolved in favour of EU law, whether the English law existed before or after the coming into force of the 1972 Act. The effect of the 1972 Act s3 is to make the European Court of Justice at Luxembourg the supreme judicial authority for deciding issues of EU law, including conflicts of law. Long before the UK joined the EC, the ECJ had made rulings for other member states emphasising the primacy of EC law in order to facilitate harmonisation of laws, regarded as essential to lay the foundations for a Single Market and eventual economic and political union: *Van Gend en Loos* (1963) and *Costa* v *ENEL* (1964). National courts were instructed by the ECJ to suspend conflicting national law by granting injunctions to applicants without waiting for their national legislatures to bring in amending legislation: the *Simmenthal* case (1978). It was only a matter of time before the ECJ was given an opportunity to rule that the same obligation applied to UK judges and that any national doctrine (such as parliamentary sovereignty) which appeared to stand in the way was 'irrelevant' and could and should be ignored: the *Factortame (No 2)* case (1991).

The acceptance of that ruling by the House of Lords and the consequent disapplication of the Merchant Shipping Act 1988 (found to have been in conflict with article 52 of the Treaty of Rome) illustrated what Bingham LJ (as he then was, in the Court of Appeal) described as the 'constitutional enormity' of the change to the British Constitution made by the UK's membership of the EC. One academic commented in the following terms:

'The House of Lords has given the clearest indication yet that the British courts accept the full implication of the constitutional foundations of the Community legal order; and that the British constitutional doctrine of parliamentary sovereignty can no longer be relied on in the British courts to frustrate the application of Community Law': Gravells ([1991] PL 180 at 181).

There appears to be no escape from the logical consequences of belonging to a system in which the objective is the harmonisation of laws. Thus, even attempts by UK judges to preserve a degree of national sovereignty by giving a literal interpretation to laws passed prior to EU membership have been rejected by the ECJ's adoption of a 'broad' approach under which national judges are obliged to construe such law so as to comply as far as possible with EU law (especially Directives), even if this means considerable judicial rewriting of the statutory text and ignoring the intentions of the parliament which passed the pre-ECA 1972 law in question: see *Duke* v *GEC Reliance* (1988), which cannot now stand with the ruling of the ECJ in the *Marleasing* case (1992).

The impact of *Marleasing* will be considerable because although Directives strictly have only vertical effect (imposing duties on national state authorities only), the broad approach to construction will permit Directives to be 'interposed' in purely private disputes between Community citizens and therefore give them a kind of horizontal effect, thereby immensely extending the scope of existing Directives. This is precisely what the ECJ hoped to achieve, because the ECJ had been faced with the problem that the efficacy of EU law was being undermined by the difficulty of enforcing EU harmonisation rules contained in non-implemented Directives because of the absence of horizontal effect.

The extent of State liability for failure to implement Directives was considered by the ECJ in the *Francovich* case (1992) in which it was held that any national rules on remedies which prevented effective protection of the rights of EC citizens must be set aside and that damages could be awarded against the state for ultra vires non-implementation (or misimplementation) of Directives. This will change English law, which has traditionally denied the general remedy of damages in respect of ultra vires acts: *Bourgoin* v *Ministry of Agriculture* (1986), now a doubtful authority in view of the *Francovich* ruling.

Time does not permit detailed discussion of the effect of the UK's ratification of the Maastricht Treaty; suffice to say that the passionate debates it has generated and its turbulent passage through Parliament indicate the far-reaching changes involved in the creation of a European Union based (eventually) on full economic and political union. National sovereignty will be replaced by the concept of subsidiarity, under which decisions are to be taken at the most appropriate level of government depending on their subject matter and effect. But the concept is vague and who decides the level is still open to doubt; probably, ultimately, the ECJ. Sovereignty seems no longer to have a place in the dictionary of the British constitutional lawyer.

5 THE ELECTORAL SYSTEM

5.1 Introduction
5.2 Key points
5.3 Recent cases and statutes
5.4 Analysis of questions
5.5 Questions

5.1 Introduction

The membership of the House of Commons is elected on the basis of adult suffrage. A general election must be held at least every five years: Parliament Act 1911.

5.2 Key points

a) *The franchise*

In order to vote in a parliamentary election a person must be included on the electoral register for a parliamentary constituency: Representation of the People Act 1983. To qualify for inclusion a person must:

i) be 18 years of age (or be due to attain his eighteenth birthday within twelve months of the publication of the register);

ii) be a British subject or a citizen of the Republic of Ireland;

iii) not be subject to any legal incapacity;

iv) be resident in the constituency on the qualifying date for compiling the register: *Fox* v *Stirk* [1970] 2 QB 463; *Hipperson* v *Electoral Registration Officer for Newbury* [1985] QB 1060.

b) *Disqualification*

The following persons are not entitled to vote, even if their names appear on the register.

i) Aliens (excluding citizens of the Republic of Ireland).

ii) Minors (persons under 18 years of age).

iii) Peers and peeresses in their own right (Irish peers may vote).

iv) Convicted persons serving sentences of imprisonment.

v) Persons convicted of corrupt practices at elections are disqualified from voting for five years. Persons convicted of illegal practices at elections are disqualified from voting for five years in the constituency in question.

vi) Those who for reasons such as mental illness, subnormality or other infirmity lack the capacity at the moment of voting of understanding what they are about to do.

CONSTITUTIONAL LAW

c) *Parliamentary constituencies*

The United Kingdom is divided into constituencies each of which is represented by a Member in the House of Commons.

i) Constituency boundaries are delimited by the Boundary Commissioners.

ii) The basic principle that each constituency should have the same number of electors is to ensure that all votes have equal value.

Quota = no. of electors divided by no. of constituencies

iii) Boundary Commissioners have discretion to depart from strict application of the rules if there are special geographical or other considerations that render departure desirable: House of Commons Redistribution of Seats Acts 1949–79; see, too, Schedule II.

iv) The re-drawing of the constituency map can result in challenges: *R v Boundary Commission for England, ex parte Foot* [1983] 1 All ER 1099; *Harper v Home Secretary* [1955] Ch 238; *R v Home Secretary, ex parte McWhirter* [1969] CLY 2636.

d) *Electoral campaign*

i) It is an offence to incur expenditure 'with a view to promoting or procuring the election of a candidate at an election' without authorisation of the candidate or his agent for public meetings and displays and advertisements or 'otherwise presenting to the electorate the candidate or his views or the extent or nature of his backing or disparaging another candidate': s75 Representation of the People Act 1983.

ii) There are limits placed on the amount a candidate can spend: s76 Representation of the People Act 1983; *R v Hailwood* [1928] 2 KB 277; *R v Tronoh Mines* [1952] 1 All ER 697; *Grieve v Douglas-Home* 1965 SC 315; *DPP v Luft* [1976] 2 All ER 569.

e) *Broadcasts*

i) Other broadcasts: *Marshall v BBC* [1979] 3 All ER 80. See s93 Representation of the People Act 1983.

ii) Broadcasting Act 1990: see s6 requiring impartiality in relation to 'major matters'.

f) *The election of Members of Parliament*

At present Members of Parliament are elected under the simple majority voting system. Each parliamentary constituency returns a single member. Each elector can vote for one candidate only and the candidate who polls the most votes within a given constituency wins the seat.

i) Disadvantages of the simple majority voting systems

- There are many wasted votes.
- It is a very crude system.

5 THE ELECTORAL SYSTEM

- There is no relationship between the number of votes cast nationally for a particular party and the number of seats allocated to that party in the House of Commons.
- The system produces exaggerated majorities for the two major parties and discriminates against the minority parties.

ii) Advantages of the simple majority voting system
- The voting procedure is simple and the results may be quickly calculated.
- There is a link between the member and his constituency.
- One party usually obtains an absolute majority of seats in the House of Commons thus leading to strong government.

g) *Electoral reform*

The three main alternatives to our present system are:

i) The Alternative Vote. Voters list the candidates in order of preference. If no candidate gains an absolute majority of first preference votes then the lowest candidate is eliminated and his second preference votes are distributed among the other candidates. The process may be repeated until a candidate emerges who has an absolute majority.

ii) The Party List System. One constituency comprising the whole country. The parties present lists of candidates and electors vote not for individual candidates but for the whole party list. Seats are then allocated to the parties in proportion to the votes received by each party list.

iii) The Single Transferable Vote. Requires multi-member constituencies of between five and seven members. Voters list the candidates in order of preference. The candidate needs a quota of votes to be elected. Any votes he receives beyond this figure are surplus and so they are redistributed among the other candidates according to second preference. The quota is usually established by the following formula:

$$\frac{\text{number of votes cast} + 1}{\text{number of seats} + 1}$$

5.3 Recent cases and statutes

R v *Rowe, ex parte Mainwaring and Others* [1992] 1 WLR 1059.

The Boundary Commission Report 1995.

Broadcasting Act 1990.

Note that the matter of electoral reform is again being debated in the context of a written constitution for the UK.

5.4 Analysis of questions

Questions on this area seem to be set when the subject is topical ie just before or just after an election. Examiners favour essay type questions on the voting system in

CONSTITUTIONAL LAW

the UK – its advantages and disadvantages – a question that requires students to have some knowledge of alternative systems.

Students need to be aware of the role of the Boundary Commissioners and the problems that can arise when they report.

Problem questions could be set on the rules governing elections.

5.5 Questions

QUESTION ONE

a) What is the function of the Boundary Commission and what problems can occur when it reports?

b) Rupert is a newspaper proprietor. He stood as candidate for the Freedom Party at a general election. His newspapers carried advertisements extolling the virtues of the Freedom Party and urging people to vote for it. Rupert was elected.

Blake, a constituent, seeks to challenge Rupert's election as MP on the grounds that he incurred unauthorised expenditure.

Discuss.

Written by the Editors

General Comment

An easy question if students know the cases and statutes below.

Skeleton Solution

a) • The function of the Boundary Commission – House of Commons Redistribution of Seats Acts 1949–79.
   • An explanation of the effect on political parties when constituencies are redefined.
   • *R* v *Boundary Commission for England, ex parte Foot* (1983).

b) • The provisions of s75 Representation of the People Act 1983.
   • An analysis of cases on unauthorised expenditure: *R* v *Tronoh Mines* (1952); *Grieve* v *Douglas-Home* (1965); *DPP* v *Luft* (1976).

Suggested Solution

a) The function of the Boundary Commission as laid down by the House of Commons Redistribution of Seats Acts 1949–1979 is to regulate the size of parliamentary constituencies in the United Kingdom. The purpose is to achieve, as far as is practicable, constituencies which are approximately equal in terms of voters. A figure is arrived at by dividing the number of voters by the number of constituencies which produces a current figure of approximately 65,000.

The commissioners do have, however, discretionary powers to vary the size of constituencies taking into account county boundaries and special geographical considerations including the size, shape and accessibility of a constituency. In the exercise of their discretion the commissioners should observe a balance between the countries of the UK, ie Great Britain should not have substantially more or less seats than 613, Scotland should not have less than 71, Wales 35 and Northern Ireland between 16 and 18.

Under their powers the commissioners present their recommendations to the Home Secretary whose duty it is to lay these before Parliament for approval. The objective is to remove the decision from the political process because changes are perceived by one party or another as disadvantaging them and political agreement is therefore unlikely. The only circumstances in which a review of their decision is likely is if 100 or more affected voters petition or if a County Council petitions. The only other way is to challenge through judicial review the exercise of the commissioners' discretion.

The Labour party has traditionally been disadvantaged by changes largely because of migration from urban areas, traditionally labour strongholds, to the country. In the late 1960s the Labour Party sought to delay the implementation of proposals: see *R v Home Secretary, ex parte McWhirter* (1969). More recently Foot, then leader of the Labour Party, sought to challenge the proposals on the grounds that the commissioners had exercised their powers wrongly and that the decision was ultra vires: *R v Boundary Commission for England, ex parte Foot* (1983). The court held that the discretion of the commissioners was very wide and that they had not acted unreasonably. The challenge failed.

b) Section 75 of the Representation of the People Act 1983 makes it an offence to incur expenditure with a view to promoting or procuring the election of a candidate at an election without the authority of the candidate or his agent and s76 goes on to place limits on the candidate's expenditure. The amount is varied from time to time by means of statutory instrument. The objective here is to ensure that one candidate does not gain advantage by virtue of the fact that he may have substantial personal wealth to wage a campaign and can be contrasted with other countries notably America where there are no limits.

There are however no limits in this country on the amount that a national party can spend on a campaign. It can be argued that this is a disadvantage to some political parties, more particularly the smaller parties whose ability to wage a national campaign is limited by a lack of money. It is a tradition in this country that political parties grow out of grass roots support. The issue in the question therefore would seem to be simply whether the newspaper advertisement can be seen as essentially part of a national campaign or whether the intention and effect is to ensure the election of the local candidate Rupert.

In support of the principle that expenditure incurred cannot exceed the permitted maximum it has been held that a local campaign urging the electorate not to vote for a particular candidate falls foul of s75 because by implication it is of advantage to the other: see *DPP v Luft* (1976). However on the question of national newspaper campaigns it has been held that an advertisement advocating the defeat of a Labour government was not an election expense within the meaning of s75: see *R v Tronoh Mines* (1952). Furthermore, in *Grieve v Douglas-Home* (1965), an unsuccessful Communist candidate who argued that Douglas Home the then Prime Minister gained an unfair advantage in respect of his local campaign when he appeared on national television did not convince the courts. Such a broadcast was not held to be expenditure with a view to procuring his election.

CONSTITUTIONAL LAW

By analogy then it would seem unlikely that Blake would be successful in his challenge unless the advertisement referred to in the problem specifically relates to Rupert's own campaign. Whilst he may gain some advantage from such an advertisement, on the facts the advertisement is aimed at furthering the interests of the party nationally.

QUESTION TWO

What difference, if any, would reforming the electoral system make to the British Constitution?

Written by the Editors

General Comment

This is a very straightforward question involving discussion of the present electoral system and the effect reform would have on the British Constitution.

Skeleton Solution

- Introduction. The operation of the relative majority system (the first-past-the-post system).
- The problems with the present system. Parliamentary seats not allocated on a proportional basis; discrimination against small parties; wastage of votes; problems with constituency size.
- The advantages of the present system. Simplicity; results in strong government; constituency link with MP.
- Effect of reform. Loss of the advantages of the present system; election of a Parliament but not a government.

Suggested Solution

Under the present parliamentary electoral system the United Kingdom is divided into 651 parliamentary constituencies, each of which returns a single member to the House of Commons. Each elector may vote for one candidate only and the successful candidate is the one who receives the highest number of valid votes in the constituency. This system of 'first past the post' is known as the relative majority system as wherever there are more than two candidates in a constituency, the successful candidate need not have received an absolute majority of votes, but simply a majority over the runner-up. This system has the advantage of being very simple, but as a means of providing representation of the electorate in Parliament it is very crude. It is a system which, according to its critics, is not truly democratic and one which has several inherent disadvantages which, it is argued, can only be overcome by reform.

Certainly any reform of the present electoral system will seek to remedy the major problem that at present the system does not ensure that the distribution of seats in the House of Commons is in any way proportionate to the national distribution of votes. There is no consistent relationship between the number of votes cast nationally for a political party and the seats which they obtain. This is well illustrated by the June 1983 election results. The Conservative Party polled 42.4 per cent of the votes cast

5 THE ELECTORAL SYSTEM

and won 397 seats. The Labour Party polled 27.6 per cent of the votes cast and won 209 seats. But the Liberal/SDP Alliance polled 25.4 per cent of the votes cast and won only 23 seats. The Alliance therefore was under-represented in relation to their national vote, while the Conservative Government achieved the largest parliamentary majority since the war, but received one of the smallest percentages of votes cast. Under this system a Conservative vote thus carried more weight than an Alliance vote.

This tendency of the system to exaggerate the representation of the large parties and reduce that of the smaller parties leads to the allegation that the present electoral system makes no provision for the representation of minority interests. It discriminates against the smaller parties whose support is evenly spread throughout the country rather than being concentrated in particular constituencies. Votes for the smaller parties are, in effect, wasted votes. It doesn't matter whether the person elected has one more or twenty thousand more votes than his nearest rival. So where there are more than two candidates a person may be elected by less than 50 per cent of the total votes cast in that constituency. The votes for the losing candidate have no parliamentary importance, they are in a sense wasted. This system, it is argued, perpetuates the two party system and helps destroy any possibility of consensus politics in the United Kingdom.

A further problem arises from the constituency basis of the present system. If votes are to carry equal weight throughout the country each constituency must be of equal size. The size of every constituency is determined by the Boundary Commissioners who keep the situation under constant review and try to ensure that each constituency has the same number of voters in it. However disparity does exist between constituency populations and as a result the weight of your vote may vary according to where you live.

Reforming the electoral system would therefore help remove these problems and help achieve fairer representation for all political parties in the House of Commons. But it must always be remembered that the present electoral system has considerable advantages and that these advantages may be lost as a result of any reform. For example the voting procedure itself is very simple and easy to understand, ensuring quick results. The outcome of the election is known within a matter of hours of the close of poll. The system also ensures a close link between the Member of Parliament and his constituency. The constituents know who their parliamentary representative is and can approach him with their problems. He in turn will serve their interests, in the knowledge that their continued support is necessary if he is to be re-elected.

But the major advantage claimed for the present system is its tendency to produce an absolute majority of seats in the House of Commons for one party. The function of a general election is to elect a government as well as a parliament and the present system does precisely that, producing strong government. The United Kingdom system avoids the problems, often found in European countries, which use different electoral systems, of coalition or minority governments which can find it difficult to govern effectively because of their unstable electoral position.

Despite these advantages there is a case for reforming the electoral system so as to secure better representation of minority parties and a distribution of seats which bears some relation to the votes cast. The most favoured alternative systems are the alternative vote system, the party list system and the single transferable vote system.

CONSTITUTIONAL LAW

The adoption of any one of these systems would bring about changes to the British Constitution which, while welcomed by some, would be abhorrent to others.

The major result of adopting these systems is that they will help achieve legislative representation which accords with the relative electoral strengths of the political parties. Minority parties and independent candidates will therefore stand a better chance of election and the number of wasted votes will be reduced. But while these systems may to an extent maintain a local basis for representation, they may weaken the link between Members of Parliament and constituents. These systems of election are also complex. Most important, however, is the likely result that the traditional two party system may be destroyed. To some of course this may be no bad thing but, if the European experience is repeated and one party is less likely to secure an absolute majority of seats in the House of Commons, this will lead to minority or coalition governments giving smaller parties political importance out of all proportion to their popular support. Such a system of government is totally alien to the British tradition.

QUESTION THREE

Comment on the following: 'The British electoral system is based on the slogan "one man, one vote" but in certain important ways each vote is not of equal value.'

University of London LLB Examination
(for External Students) Constitutional Law June 1983 Q3

General Comment

This question asks students to criticise the electoral system as it stands and not just to suggest different reforms that could be brought in. However, the word 'comment' allows students a degree of lee-way as to which direction the answer should go, so there is no right and wrong.

You should start with a description of the present system and state that there have been suggestions of reform throughout the century. Then give a fairly detailed analysis of why the system maybe undemocratic including percentage of vote, Boundary Commission etc, and then suggest alternatives – party list systems etc. In conclusion perhaps you would like to mention the views of the main parties on the topic and mention the advantages of the present system. Statistics are not needed in the answer but it would help if you remembered some – perhaps of the 1992 election.

Skeleton Solution

- Outline of voting system in UK.
- The constitutional problems: all votes do not carry the same weight as constituencies are unequal in numbers of electors; percentage of votes cast for each party does not equal the numbers of seats gained.
- Alternatives and consequences for the British political system.

Suggested Solution

At present Members of Parliament are elected on the simple basis that within a given constituency the person who polls the most votes wins. This is the 'one man one vote'

5 THE ELECTORAL SYSTEM

or 'first past the post' system or more properly election by relative majority. Throughout the last century there have been calls for reform of this system as it is felt not to be truly democratic. Recently there was a surge of public interest in electoral reform which partly arose from the temporary emergence of the Social Democratic Party as a political force. Electoral reform continues to be on the political agenda but not as a priority. The two major parties have again consolidated their position.

The first reason for suggesting that not all votes carry the same weight follows from the actual number of voters in each constituency. The size of each constituency is determined by one of the four Boundary Commissions. As a basic principle each constituency should have the same number of voters in it. However, a Boundary Commission is entitled to depart from the strict application of this principle if 'special geographical considerations' so require. The rearrangement of the constituencies can have important effects on the political 'colour' of a given area. There was such a rearrangement prior to the 1983 election which the Labour Party unsuccessfully challenged in the courts: *R v Boundary Commission for England, ex parte Foot* (1983). This has been given as one of the reasons for the increased Tory majority. In the case of *Baker v Carr* (1962) the US Supreme Court ruled that where the State of Tennessee had failed to provide constituencies of the equal average population that was a breach of the fourteenth amendment to the Constitution. Prior to the 1983 rearrangement the smallest constituency in the United Kingdom had about a quarter of the population of the largest. It can be said that the weight of your vote varies according to where you live.

The problems of varying size of constituency can to some extent be overcome. However the greatest failing of a relative majority system, and perhaps this is what makes it undemocratic, is that the percentage of votes cast throughout the country for a particular party do not reflect the number of seats it receives in the House of Commons. The situation was particularly highlighted in the 1983 election results. The Conservatives took 397 seats from 42.4 per cent, the Labour Party took 209 from 27.6 per cent of the votes and the Alliance took 23 from 25.4 per cent. This distortion created by the process of translating votes into seats has become a matter of some public concern. Under this system a vote for Conservative in 1983 had more weight than a vote for an Alliance candidate. In the 1983 election the Conservatives scored against the Alliance by reason of the favour the system bestows upon the largest party when confronted by nearly equally divided opposition. The Labour Party and the Ulster Unionists scored by reason of the favour bestowed on a party whose support is more concentrated than dispersed. The gross deformity in results in the 1983 election may be temporary during a transition in opposition or abortive challenge to the two party system. As it stands however the weight of a vote varies with the party for which it is cast.

The relative majority system means that no account is taken of the size of a majority. A Tory MP returned with a 30,000 majority is of equal status to a Labour MP returned with a majority of three. So all votes cast in the above example over the total necessary to defeat the other candidates are in a sense wasted and of no parliamentary importance.

There is obviously a case for reforming the electoral system with a view to reducing the discrepancy between votes cast for and seats won by a party campaigning on a national scale. The most favoured systems around the world are the alternative vote system, the party list system and the single transferable vote.

The introduction of an alternative vote system would require little change save for the voter placing the candidates in order of preference on the ballot paper. If no candidate obtains an absolute majority by counting first preferences, the candidate at the bottom of the poll is eliminated, and his second preference votes are distributed among the other candidates, and so on until one candidate has more than 50 per cent. The result may be that the candidate placed second on the first count wins the seats. This system is not a proportional system. Sir Winston Churchill dismissed it as being 'the worst of all possible plans in which the decision is to be determined by the most worthless votes given to the most worthless candidate', and one can see his point!

The only precise means of achieving direct proportionality is to have the country as one constituency with the parties presenting list of candidates and electors voting not for individual candidates but for the whole party list. Seats are then allocated to the parties in proportion to the votes received by each party. Under our present system although in theory people vote for the candidate they think will best represent them in Parliament in practice people vote for a party. The introduction of a party list system would merely confirm this practice. However it would pose difficulties in drawing up the list in particular the order of the candidates and it would destroy the territorial constituency system with its strong link between one MP and one constituency.

The Single Transferable Vote System (STV) is an alternative to the party list. It requires multi-member constituencies (five to seven members) and voters list the individual candidates in order of preference. In counting the votes the principle that applies is that a candidate only needs a certain number and any surplus votes are redistributed among the other candidates according to second preferences. The quota is usually the number of votes cast divided by the number of seats but there are several variations in procedure throughout the world. STV is used in Australia and Eire and many trade unions and professional organisations use it to elect their National Committees. The introduction of this system would produce a more representative House of Commons. This system of proportional representation was described as the 'linchpin of the entire programme of reform' outlined in the 1983 Alliance manifesto. It is argued that the first past the post system ensures the under-representation of all those who reject class as the basis of politics and that reform is necessary for democracy. The criticisms of STV are that it may not and usually does not produce a government with a working majority, it breaks up the local constituency and produces coalition governments with a consequent blurring of policy alternatives on major issues. Supporters of STV would say that this last was its strongest point and that polarisation and reversal politics of successions of Labour and Tory governments are not in the best interests of the country as a whole.

Whatever the arguments on either side the fact is that the suggestion that votes are of unequal value in the present system is obviously correct. But it begs the question – what makes a satisfactory electoral system? An electoral system reflects each country's politics of which it is both cause and effect. Majority voting is usually the norm in a two-party system, proportional representation in a multi-party system. The overriding requirement is that it is seen to be reasonable by the country to ensure

5 THE ELECTORAL SYSTEM

the best representation possible and may be in particular to safeguard the representation of minorities. One might think that a quarter of the population are at present under-represented in the House of Commons.

QUESTION FOUR

'In practice, the legal rules providing for the delineation of electoral constituencies and the rules regulating the conduct of election campaigns reveal many defects.'

Critically assess this statement.

University of London LLB Examination
(for External Students) Constitutional and Administrative Law June 1992 Q7

General Comment

This is a difficult question. It requires a detailed knowledge of a fairly restricted subject and many students would find it hard to provide sufficient information.

Skeleton Solution

- Introduction.
- The Parliamentary Constituencies Act 1986.
- Inconsistencies in size of constituency.
- Political objections.
- Finance in elections.
- Broadcasting.
- Conclusion.

Suggested Solution

There are very precise rules both for the delineation of constituencies and for the conduct of campaigns. However, no rules can cover all of the variables and the political impossibility of drawing lines in a way that pleases all parties or of regulating conduct during a contest to general approbation make it possible to find defects. However, what may seem a defect from one partisan view is seen as a strength from another.

Dealing firstly with the rules for the delineation of electoral constituencies: the Parliamentary Constituencies Act 1986 retains four permanent Boundary Commissions – for England, Wales, Scotland and Northern Ireland. Their purpose is continuously to review the distribution of seats and recommend, in a report to the Home Secretary at intervals of between ten and 15 years, such redistribution as they consider necessary.

The Home Secretary cannot ignore or reject these recommendations but he can, when he lays them before Parliament, add modifications. If they are approved by resolutions of each House the recommendations take effect as Orders in Council and operate from the next election.

What, if any, defects are there in the system? Firstly, the Act determines the minimum number of seats per Commission area. The electorate of a constituency is to be as near as practicable to the quota, which is found by dividing the total electorate of the area by the number of constituencies. Scotland and Wales have fewer electors per constituency than England and there is a wide variation nationally in size of constituency, both numerically and geographically. This is inevitable but it means that your vote can carry more weight depending upon where you live.

Secondly, each set of recommendations always proves controversial and might not be implemented. For example, the 1969 recommendations proposed major changes to 271 constituencies. The Labour Party feared losing some ten seats as a result, so the Labour Government decided to implement then only in part but could not get the Bill past the Lords. The Orders in Council containing the complete recommendations were not passed until after the next election, by a Conservative Government.

In 1983, the Labour Party again objected to the effects of recommendations and took the case to the Court of Appeal (*R* v *Boundary Commission for England, ex parte Foot* (1983)), which held that the Commission had acted reasonably. This ability to challenge the Commission through the courts is clearly a safeguard and a strength in the system.

Turning to the rules for regulating the conduct of election campaigns, these are contained in the Representation of the People Act 1983 (and to a lesser extent subsequent Representation of the People Acts).

Firstly, election expenditure is strictly controlled at a constituency level, but the national expenditure of the parties is not, which might seem anomalous in terms of advertising in the national press. The Conservative party in recent elections has had greater resources for this, therefore the attempt to avoid unfair advantage to the wealthier party at local level may be seen to have been avoided at national level.

Secondly, broadcasting at election times is also controlled and the major parties are allowed to make party political broadcasts on television. This does not favour small, minority parties. Thirdly, there is no limit on opinion polls, although after the 1987 election the Speaker's Conference on electoral law recommended they should be banned for the 72 hours before an election. The inefficiency of opinion polls in the 1992 election and their influence on news programmes with the consequent influence on voters would strengthen this recommendation.

However, if these are defects, there are many positive features of the rules on election campaigns. There are clear rules in the event of dispute, with an Election Court investigating any misconduct. Corrupt practices are vigorously opposed and it is significant how few complaints are made.

Overall, one might conclude that no single system will provide better solutions. On the one hand, there is a shifting population, unevenly distributed and locally diverse. On the other hand, there is a short period of intense campaigning involving massive expenditure, saturation coverage and mass participation. It is submitted that the system, in general terms, is a successful one.

6 LEGISLATURE I – THE HOUSE OF COMMONS

6.1 Introduction
6.2 Key points
6.3 Recent statutes and developments
6.4 Analysis of questions
6.5 Questions

6.1 Introduction

The monarch is one of the three constituent parts of the legislature but the role of the monarchy is now largely ceremonial and formal. The United Kingdom has a bicameral legislature – there are two Houses of Parliament – the House of Commons and the House of Lords. The House of Commons dominates.

One of the central issues relating to the legislature is the accountability of government to Parliament. The House of Commons is dominated by the government particularly if following a general election the government has a large majority. The House of Lords challenges the government at a political level on unpopular policies. However, ultimately the Commons can successfully achieve its political will in the unlikely event of a confrontation.

Textbook analysis of the topic describes the rules and procedures of the House of Commons. Students must be able to place this knowledge in the context of executive power and understand the nature of the relationship between government and the Commons – see chapter 9.

6.2 Key points

The main functions of Parliament include the passing of legislation and the scrutiny of the administration through debate, the committee system and the control of national finance.

a) *The legislative process*

   i) A distinction must be drawn between Public and Private Bills:

      - Public Bills seek to alter the general law and affect the whole community.
      - Private Bills affect only a section of the community and relate to matters of individual, corporate or local interest.
      - Hybrid Bills are Public Bills that are classified by the Speaker as having a particular effect on one section of the community.

   ii) Public Bill procedure

      Most Public Bills are Government Bills, but some may be Private Members

Bills introduced by backbench Members of Parliament. Bills may be introduced into either House, but legislation which is politically controversial, financial or electoral begins in the House of Commons.

- First reading: The Bill is presented to Parliament.
- Second reading: The House considers the principles and merits of the Bill.
- Committee stage: The Bill is normally referred to a standing committee for detailed clause by clause consideration.
- Report stage: The Bill as amended is reported to the whole House.
- Third reading: The Bill is debated in general terms with only oral amendments allowed.
- House of Lords stages and amendments: After its third reading, the Bill is sent to the House of Lords where it goes through stages similar to those in the Commons. But note the effects of the Parliament Acts 1911–1949.
- Royal assent: Now a formality. After the Royal Assent has been given the Bill becomes an Act.

iii) Private Member's Bill procedure

There are a number of procedures under which Private Members may initiate Bills.

- The Ballot: The Ballot establishes an order of priority enabling those Members successful in it to use the limited Private Members' time for debate of their Bills which, given the governments' control of the parliamentary timetable, might otherwise not make progress.
- The Ten Minute Rule: Not, in general, serious attempts at legislation. The Member may speak briefly in support of the Bill and an opponent may reply. The House may then decide on whether the Bill should be introduced.
- Standing Order No 39: Allows every Member the right to introduce a Bill of his choosing after due notice.

iv) Private Bill procedure

Private Bills are initiated by petition from persons or bodies outside Parliament. Full notice must be given to those whose legal rights may be affected by the proposed legislation so that they may oppose it. In the House of Commons the Bill is introduced by being presented at the Table by the Clerk of the Private Bill Office. It is then deemed to have been read for the first time. At the Second Reading Debate, the House determines whether the Bill is unobjectionable from the point of view of national policy. If read a second time, the Bill is committed to a committee of four Members in the Commons (or five Members in the Lords). The committee stage has some of the features of a quasi-judicial proceeding.

v) Hybrid Bill procedure

The Standing Orders for private business apply to a hybrid Bill so that if opposed after its second reading it goes before a Select Committee, where those whose legal rights are affected by the Bill may raise their objections and petition against it. After the petitioners have been heard by the Select Committee, the Bill then passes through its committee stage and later stages as if it were an ordinary Bill.

b) *Opportunities for debate in the House of Commons*

Apart from the opportunities for debate during the legislative process, there are various other opportunities for debate in the House of Commons.

i) Adjournment debates

At the end of every day's business, when the adjournment of the House is formally moved, half an hour is made available for a private Member to raise a topic in debate and for a ministerial reply to be given.

ii) Standing Order No 10 – Motion to Adjourn

This allows Members to suggest that a specific and important matter should have urgent consideration and that an emergency debate be held upon it.

iii) Other opportunities

The final day before each of the four parliamentary recesses is also devoted to a series of Private Members' debates and ten Fridays per session are also set aside for Private Members' Motions. Other opportunities for debate occur in the debate on the address in reply to the Queen's Speech, the debate on the Budget, debates on motions of censure, the twenty Opposition Days, the three Estimate Days and on the second reading of Consolidated Fund Bills.

iv) Devices for curtailing debate

Delay of Bills in the House of Commons is a threat to the government's legislative programme. To overcome this threat, various methods of curtailing debate have been adopted by the House.

- Standing Order 22: The Speaker or Chairman may require a Member to discontinue his speech if he persists in irrelevance or tedious repetition.
- The Closure: Any Member may move 'that the question now be put'. If not less than 100 members vote for the motion the debate ceases and the motion under discussion must be voted upon.
- The Kangaroo: This is the power of the Speaker at the Report Stage to select from amongst the various proposed amendments those which are to be discussed.
- The Guillotine Motion: Such a motion provides that one or more stages of a Bill be disposed of either by a fixed date, or by a fixed number of sittings.

c) *Parliamentary questions*

There are three categories of question:

i) Question for oral answer which is intended to be given an oral answer in the House during Question Time.

ii) Private notice question which can be asked if the Speaker judges its subject matter to be urgent and important. These are taken orally in the House at the end of Question Time.

CONSTITUTIONAL LAW

iii) Question for written answer, which is not taken orally in the House but is printed in the official report (Hansard).

d) *Parliamentary committees*

The committees of the House of Commons fall into two main categories:

i) Standing committees

These are responsible for the committee stage in the passing of a Bill.

ii) Select committees

- Ad-hoc select committees: These are set up for a specific purpose when the need arises.
- Sessional select committees: These are set up at the beginning of the session and remain throughout the session.
- Departmental select committees: These are appointed to examine the expenditure, administration and policy of the principal government departments and associated public bodies.

e) *Parliamentary control of national finance*

Parliamentary control of national finance has two aspects:

i) Parliamentary control of government expenditure

- Estimate Days: There are now three annual days devoted to consideration of the main and Supplementary Estimates.
- The Public Accounts Committee: This is a select committee concerned with public money already spent, to see that it has been spent economically, and not wastefully.
- National Audit Act 1983: This Act provides for the appointment of the Comptroller and Auditor General, establishing a Public Accounts Commission and a National Audit Office and making new provisions for promoting economy, efficiency and effectiveness in the use of public money by government departments and other authorities and bodies.

ii) Control over taxation

- Budget Resolutions and the Finance Bill: These provide an opportunity for Members to debate government proposals for taxation and duties etc.

6.3 Recent statutes and developments

Students need to follow the passage of contentious legislation and listen to, watch and/or read reports of debates during any parliamentary session to best understand the way in which the House of Commons operates in practice and to give immediacy to their studies. In May 1995 the first Report on Standards in Public Life, under the chairmanship of Lord Nolan, was published. The committee focused specifically on Members of Parliament, Ministers and civil servants and executive quangos. Seven principles of conduct are re-affirmed – selflessness, integrity, objectivity, accountability, openness, honesty and leadership. Public concern on standards initiated the commission of the Report, in particular concern regarding members' financial interests, paid outside employment, parliamentary consultancies, and the disclosure of interests. The committee's recommendations have not, to date, been adopted. The Nolan Report has relevance not only to a consideration of the legislature in general terms, but also to a study of the executive and to parliamentary privilege (see chapter 8).

Note also the Jopling Report on reforms of parliamentary procedures: [1995] PL 203.

6.4 Analysis of questions

Questions are essay type. They tend to examine the student's understanding of the relationship between government and the legislature and so require a broadly based knowledge which includes the separation of powers, conventions of the Constitution and Cabinet government.

6.5 Questions

QUESTION ONE

The parliamentary function of legislation has effectively passed to the Cabinet.

Discuss.

University of London LLB Examination
(for External Students) Constitutional Law June 1986 Q5

General Comment

This question revolves around the old argument as to whether Parliament legislates or merely legitimates Executive policy. As well as examining the role of the backbench MP and the House of Lords in the legislative process, students should also consider whether in fact today legislation is not so much decided by the Cabinet as the Prime Minister.

Skeleton Solution

- Introduction: the enactment of legislation by the Queen in Parliament.
- The House of Commons: does it legislate or merely legitimate; the control of the Commons by the Executive.
- The role of the House of Lords: the ability of the Lords to check the Executive.
- The role of the backbench MP: Private Members' Bills.
- Conclusion: Cabinet legislation or Prime Ministerial legislation.

Suggested Solution

For purposes of constitutional analysis, the functions of government have often been divided into three broad classes – legislative, executive and judicial. The legislative function involves the enactment of general rules determining the structure and powers of public authorities and regulating the conduct of citizens and private organisations. In the United Kingdom, legislative authority is vested in the Queen in Parliament: new law being enacted when it has been approved by Commons and Lords and has received the Royal Assent.

The passing of legislation therefore is one of the primary functions of Parliament. Bills, which may be either public or private, cannot become law until they have been passed by Parliament and received the Royal Assent. However many consider that Parliament no longer legislates but rather that it merely legitimates proposed legislation already decided upon by the Executive. Certainly, the great majority of Public Bills are prepared for Parliament by the government, which is also responsible for supervising their passage through each House. The Executive therefore participates actively in the process of legislation. Party domination of the House of Commons and the use of the whip system ensures that, generally speaking, when the government has a working majority in the Commons, no new legislation can be enacted by Parliament which is not approved also by the government and that those Bills which are approved are passed.

There are however occasions when in spite of the government's control of the Commons its Members may exert their independence and refuse to act as a mere rubber stamp for Executive policy. For example the Commons effectively blocked attempts by the Labour government to reform the House of Lords in 1968 and attempts by Mrs Thatcher to reform the law on Sunday trading were defeated following a backbench Conservative revolt in the Commons. One must also remember that Parliament also includes the House of Lords and that although the legislative powers of the Lords have been severely curtailed under the Parliament Acts 1911 and 1949 the chamber, retaining as it does a large degree of political independence, may still act as an effective check on Government Bills.

Although the House of Lords no longer has power over money matters, under the Parliament Acts their Lordships do retain the power to amend non-money Bills and although the House cannot impose its will on the Commons in legislation, it can effectively delay Government Bills for one year. In practice therefore where the government has a heavy legislative programme amendment or delay in the Lords can seriously threaten the legislative timetable for that particular session and the government will be forced to take notice and attempt a compromise with the Lords. If compromise fails and the government implements the procedure under the Parliament Acts, even a one year delay may prove fatal to the government's plans. Recent events have illustrated how the House of Lords can exert its independence and challenge government legislation. The Local Government Finance Act 1988 and the Education Reform Act 1988 both were amended by the House of Lords. It must however be conceded that a determined government will successfully achieve its purpose in the face of the House of Lords. Mrs Thatcher's first administration sustained 45 defeats in their Lordships' Chamber.

It must also be remembered that not all Public Bills are initiated by the Executive. Although the bulk of the legislative programme of Parliament is taken up by Government Bills, a small but significant part of the programme consists of Bills introduced by backbench MPs. Although the scope for legislative initiative by individual MPs is severely limited, both because of restricted parliamentary time and of the tight hold which the government maintains over departmental responsibilities, standing orders, while generally giving precedence to government business, nevertheless set aside ten Fridays in each session on which Private Members' Bills have priority. The fact that not many of these Bills reach the statute book does not detract from their value as expressions of the independent legislative function of Parliament.

However, in spite of the opportunities for Private Members to introduce their Bills, the independence of the House of Lords and the occasional rebellion amongst backbench members of the government party in the House of Commons, it is probably true to say that in the main the parliamentary function of legislation has effectively passed to the Cabinet, at least in the sense that the Cabinet is the core of collective responsibility.

Traditionally it is in the Cabinet where government policy is thrashed out before being put to Parliament for what has largely become the formality of approval. However this may not necessarily be the case today. In the 1980s, under Margaret Thatcher, we experienced a period of prime ministerial government where policy decisions were made by the Prime Minister and her small inner-Cabinet based largely upon the advice of Cabinet committees and the Prime Minister's own policy unit. The full Cabinet, if consulted at all, merely approved whatever was put before it. It did therefore mean that the parliamentary function of legislation had effectively passed to the Prime Minister. More recently, under John Major Cabinet Ministers have been more involved in the decision-making process. Much depends on the personality of the Prime Minister.

QUESTION TWO

Evaluate the following statement:

'A serious weakness of the House of Commons is the ineffectual role of so many backbenchers.' (de Smith)

University of London LLB Examination
(for External Students) Constitutional Law June 1984 Q3

General Comment

In this question de Smith is commenting upon the fact that backbench MPs have opportunities available to scrutinise Government policy but that because of the procedure of the Commons and the stranglehold of the Government over the legislative system, these opportunities are mostly ineffectual. However, following this quote in his *Constitutional and Administrative Law* de Smith goes on to describe the success of the select committees in increasing the effectiveness of backbench MPs. Students, in evaluating the statement, should therefore weigh against the traditional factors limiting the effectiveness of the backbench MP in the Chamber, the success and achievements of the specialist select committees. Mention should also be made of the benefits to the backbenchers' role following the passing of the National Audit Act 1983.

Skeleton Solution

- Introduction – an outline of the opportunities available to backbenchers to participate in the business of the House of Commons.
- Examination of the system of select committees including their function.
- Limitations of select committees and the role of backbenchers.
- Conclusion – evaluation of the backbenchers' role.

CONSTITUTIONAL LAW

Suggested Solution

The role of any backbenchers in the scrutiny of government policy and administration is largely ineffectual. Backbenchers have their opportunities to call the government to account on the occasions set aside for Private Members' Motions, on the motions for the adjournment each day and before a recess, at question time and, if any succeed in catching the Speaker's eye, in the course of general debate.

However, many Members of Parliament soon discover that their opportunities to contribute significantly to debate are few. All such debates are limited by the political framework in which they are held and individual members have no means of probing behind the statements of Ministers seeking to justify departmental decisions. The influence of the member on government policy from the backbenches or in opposition is also negligible, and it often seems that the conduct of public administration cannot be effectively scrutinised by the House of Commons. It has been said that any effective participation of backbench Members of Parliament in decision making will continue to present very great difficulties as long as governments maintain majorities in the House with the aid of an electoral system under which the winner can expect to take almost all, and as long as constitutional rules leave the spending power entirely in the hands of the Executive.

It is these limitations that have given rise to demands for other procedures by which the House may inform and concern itself more directly with the work of government. In this respect experience has shown that it is possible within the existing British parliamentary system for members to influence the conduct of administration and to modify aspects of policy by their scrutiny of administrative activity as members of select committees. Indeed many people have seen in the increased use of select committees the key to a more effective role for Parliament vis-à-vis government. Between 1967 and 1978 these committees did offer some detailed and imaginative suggestions for administrative reorganisation, and made themselves, the House in general and interested members of the public better informed about central administration and the views of the administration.

However, it was not until 1979 that a bold experiment to extend the opportunity for members to scrutinise the Executive through specialised select committees was started. Twelve select committees were established to monitor the activities of particular government departments or groups of departments. Their terms of reference were to examine the expenditure, administration and policy of the principal government departments, with the power to send for papers and witnesses and to appoint sub-committees. The committees also have the power to appoint technical advisors to supply information which is not readily available or to elucidate matters of complexity.

But while their investigation and reports show that they are effective in putting pressure on the government, there are limitations. No sanctions exist in respect of ministers who refuse to appear. There is still no guaranteed time for debating their reports. Also the Party Whips effectively choose the members of their party who are to serve on a particular committee. This enables the Party Frontbench to exclude from a committee any member who is likely to oppose frontbench policy. Thus the government will attempt to exclude from a committee members of its own party who are likely to join with the opposition to produce a report critical of the government.

Nevertheless, reports critical of the government are produced, but this 'packing' of committees by the Party Whips clearly reduces the potential effectiveness of select committees as a device for exercising control over the government. A further step towards increasing the effectiveness of members over government policy, this time in the field of national expenditure, has been the enactment of the National Audit Act 1983. The Act provides for the Comptroller and Auditor General to become an officer of Parliament and to head a National Audit Office. A Public Accounts Commission is also established consisting of the Chairman of the Public Accounts Committee, the Leader of the House and seven other MPs who are not Ministers of State. This has vastly increased parliamentary control over national expenditure.

Therefore the ineffectual role of so many backbenchers may be a serious weakness of the House of Commons. But while the role of the backbencher in the Chamber itself may be ineffectual, opportunities do exist through the select committee system for his full participation in serious and effective scrutiny of government policy and administration.

QUESTION THREE

Critically assess the statement that Parliament legitimates but does not legislate.

University of London LLB Examination
(for External Students) Constitutional Law June 1983 Q4

General Comment

This question requires discussion of the idea of a separation of powers in the British parliamentary system. You need to write an introduction explaining the basic principles of separation of power and then decide if, as between the Executive and Legislature, it exists in this country. Does the Executive control the Legislature or vice versa? Remember the statement does not mention the independence of the Judiciary – so you in answering should also not really discuss it. We are concerned only with Executive/Legislature relations.

Skeleton Solution

- The doctrine of the separation of powers with the example of the USA which is based on the theory.
- The evolution of Cabinet government in the UK with particular reference to government dominance in the Commons.
- The nature of the relationship between Parliament and the government with reference to parliamentary controls on government.

Suggested Solution

The doctrine of the separation of powers has taken several forms at different periods and in different contexts. Aristotle is probably its first exponent, followed much later by John Locke in his second treatise of Civil Government in 1690, and then given a more popular treatment by Montesquieu in the eighteenth century. John Locke simply reasoned that as power corrupts men 'The three organs of state must not get into one hand'. Montesquieu developed the theory basing his analysis on a idealised picture of the British Constitution in 1700s. He decided that there are three main classes of government function: the legislative, the executive and the judicial and that these should be exercised by three main organs of government – the Legislature, the Executive and the Judiciary. He felt that to concentrate more than one class of function in any one person or organ of government is a threat to individual liberty. For example the Executive should not be allowed to make laws, or adjudicate on alleged breaches of the law and it should be concerned only with the making and applying of policy and general administration.

The best modern model of the doctrine is in the United States. The President and his 'Cabinet', the Executive, cannot be members of Congress, the Legislature. The Judiciary can declare legislation void, however this has in reality produced judges who are political appointments. The doctrine is embodied in the Constitution. In contrast no one would claim that the separation of powers is a central feature of the modern British Constitution.

Since the evolution of the Cabinet system with the Ministers of the Crown exercising executive power, and also sitting in Parliament the legislative body, there has been a direct link between Executive and Legislature power. In a sense the statement in question is true, but to see how true it is, a closer examination of the system is needed.

By convention Ministers of the Crown who form the Cabinet should be members of one or other House of Parliament. However since the House of Commons Disqualification Act 1975 the maximum number of ministers in the Commons is 95. Except for these ministers, under the same statute, the vast majority of persons who hold positions within the Executive are disqualified from membership of the Commons, namely all members of the civil service, armed forces, police and holders of many other public offices. It is only really the Ministers who form part of the Legislature and the Executive.

The statement in essence is suggesting that the Executive controls the Legislature. Ultimately this is untrue as Parliament can oust a government it does not like by withdrawing support. However the system of electoral representation together with the use of Whips makes such a reversal highly unlikely. A government usually is returned with an overall majority in the House of Commons and has virtual control over Parliament. The government will have a majority on all House of Commons committees. The Whips ensure that the party line is not broken and also that a majority can be summoned at short notice to vote in the Commons. Devices such as the guillotine are used to curtail parliamentary debate of legislation. A government such as the one returned in 1987 under Mrs Margaret Thatcher with a large majority should have little trouble in pushing through legislation built to implement the Tory policies. In substance the Government does seem to make law.

It is possible to argue that the Legislature is not merely a 'rubber stamp' and that it controls the government through Ministers' Question Time, Adjournment Debates, select committees, Opposition Days and just general opposition to the Executive policy. It is true to say that probing questions can disturb the path of government policy. An example may be the Local Government Finance Act 1988. Matters of great public concern can usually be at the very least delayed by the Legislature.

6 LEGISLATURE I – THE HOUSE OF COMMONS

The Executive also produces a great number of statutory instruments which are a form of delegated legislation and not questioned in the Commons. This usually is to deal with details within the Minister's domain (eg Planning for the Secretary of State for the Environment) but it is in theory a powerful example of the Executive exercising the functions of the legislature. In conclusion it is true to say that on most occasions Parliament merely legitimates the actions of the Executive but this blending of Executive and Legislature is a fundamental characteristic of the British system of government. It existed to a lesser extent in Montesquieu's day and with the growth of Cabinet and Prime Ministerial government it has grown too – any attempt to change it would produce startling results for our unwritten Constitution.

QUESTION FOUR

'Parliamentary procedures provide adequate opportunities for back benchers to scrutinise government policy.'

Do you agree?

University of London LLB Examination
(for External Students) Constitutional Law June 1991 Q2

General Comment

A straightforward question requiring a brief account of procedural matters such as debates, question time and committee work, with a brief comment on their effectiveness.

Skeleton Solution

- Set out three main devices – debate – questions – committee work.
- Comment on the effectiveness of each.
- Conclusion.

Suggested Solution

There are three principal means by which backbenchers can scrutinise government policy: first, in general or specific debates in the House of Commons; secondly, through questions asked of Ministers at Question Time; thirdly, through cross examination of Ministers appearing before select committees.

a) *Debates*

   The main opportunities for debate in the House of Commons are provided by adjournment debates, debates on motions to adjourn, and debates that occur as part of the legislative process.

   The adjournment debate normally occurs at the end of the day's business, when the adjournment of the House is formally moved. Half an hour is made available for a Private Member to raise a topic in debate and for a ministerial reply to be given. Topics are selected by ballot. The topic under discussion is usually one of local interest, so the debates tend to be constituency orientated. Often, if a Member is dissatisfied with an answer he has received in correspondence with a

Minister and/or in answer to a parliamentary question he may raise the matter 'on the adjournment'. A serious drawback in terms of publicity generation is that these debates usually take place in an almost empty House and at an inconvenient time for press coverage.

Debates on motions to adjourn, held under Standing Order No 10, allow Members to suggest that a specific and important matter should have urgent consideration and that an emergency debate be held upon it. It is for the Speaker to decide whether the matter is sufficiently important and urgent to warrant giving it precedence; the Chair in general very seldom gives leave. If leave is granted, and if the motion is approved by the House or supported by 40 Members, the motion will be debated either that evening or the following day. Again, the length of time available for debate dictates that such devices can only be of limited use in bringing Ministers to account.

As part of the legislative process Members can question government policy during the debate on the Second Reading of a Bill. The general principles and policy behind the Bill are debated and a defeat at this stage will be fatal for the legislation in question.

The effectiveness of backbench scrutiny depends to a large extent on the role of the Speaker in ensuring that all members who wish to do so have the opportunity to speak. The Speaker acts as chairperson during debates and generally presides over the House, except when it is in Committee. It is the Speaker who calls Members to speak and decides how many supplementary questions shall be allowed at Question Time.

The effectiveness of backbench scrutiny can be limited by the Government's resorting to the various devices that exist for curtailing debate. Under the Closure motion (Standing Order 30), debate will cease where at least 100 members vote for the motion. Under the 'Guillotine Motion' (allocation of time motion), one or more stages of a Bill are disposed of either by a fixed date, or by a fixed number of sittings (either of the House, or a Committee, or both). The effect is clearly to leave some issues undiscussed in the House of Commons. On the whole, these devices are unpopular with parliamentarians because they can restrict valuable criticism and amendment of legislation. If used extensively (and they are being used increasingly), it can be argued that they deny the legislative role of Parliament.

b) *Parliamentary questions*

These can be questions for an oral answer in the House during Question Time; or Private Notice Questions, which can be asked if the Speaker judges their subject matter to be urgent and important (these are taken orally in the House at the end of Question Time); and questions for a written answer, the reply to which is printed in the Official Report (Hansard).

The effectiveness of Question Time as a means of scrutiny of Ministers by backbenchers is limited by a number of factors. Generally, the backbencher is no match for the Minister with his Civil Service brief. When a parliamentary Question is submitted it is passed immediately to the relevant government department, and the officials in that department will give priority to preparing a brief for the Minister enabling him to answer not only that question, but also any supplementary questions that the officials anticipate. The department knows by whom the question is asked and in preparing the brief will bear in mind the interest and concerns of the questioner and other MPs who are similarly interested and likely to put supplementary questions. Ministers rarely gain or lose in reputation at Question Time. Most of them can cope quite satisfactorily with it, having risen through the House themselves. Often a Minister will deal with a Question simply by a party gibe, stonewalling or evasion.

c) *Select committees*

The most powerful select committees are those shadowing the work of government departments. The present system of committees was instituted in 1979, with the aim of strengthening the accountability of Ministers to the House for the discharge of their responsibilities. The committees can send for persons, papers and records, and from time to time report to the House. The committees have proved to be a very effective way of allowing backbenchers to question Ministers, and their reports frequently engender publicity embarrassing to the Government of the day, but a number of limitations still exist.

There is still no effective sanction available against a Minister who refuses to appear, or refuses to allow civil servants to appear, before a Select Committee to give evidence. In the past, Ministers have sometimes refused to appear or to answer certain questions.

In the past, Select Committees, partly because of inadequate funding, have enlisted the assistance of too few support staff, viz secretarial staff, researchers and technical experts, and thus their inquiries and reports have not been as penetrating as they could have been. MPs themselves also have limited time available for committee work. There is still no guaranteed time set aside for debating Committee Reports (other than those of the Public Accounts Committee).

In conclusion it is submitted that whilst the formal methods of control, outlined above are important, Government backbenchers can have their greatest effect on government policy when they threaten to rebel and withdraw their support from Government sponsored legislation in the House of Commons. Such a threat is likely to result in 'horsetrading' between backbenchers and the Government whips, to produce the required modifications in policy.

QUESTION FIVE

In the British Parliament today, are a Government's back-benchers its most effective opposition?

University of London LLB Examination
(for External Students) Constitutional and Administrative Law June 1992 Q4

General Comment

This is not the usual question on the power of backbenchers, therefore it is not a general essay on the methods open to the backbencher to check the executive. It requires a discussion of the role of the Government's own backbenchers, who will often exercise their influence in less overt ways. As a result it is quite a difficult question to answer fully.

CONSTITUTIONAL LAW

Skeleton Solution
- Introduction.
- John Major's Government.
- The Whips.
- Backbench groups.
- Procedural opportunities.
- Debates.
- Restrictions on the backbencher.
- Conclusion.

Suggested Solution

A party which wins an election with an outright majority of seats in the House of Commons is virtually unassailable. Even if the Opposition gathers together all the minority parties, the Government cannot be defeated. In such a position, only a backbench revolt will threaten the Government. Where the majority is thinner, the need for party discipline increases. Whatever the case, it is true that the Government's backbenchers can be a most effective check on the Government.

John Major's Government in 1992 had an outright majority of 21 seats – 81 seats fewer than that of the previous Conservative Government. At the time of writing, his Government faces potential backbench revolt over the Maastricht Bill. While the Opposition is broadly pro-European but will find grounds for opposition, there is a significant number of diehard anti-Europeans within the Conservative Party. A failure to appease them will lead to defeat and probably resignation. Following the Government's climbdown over proposed pit closures, Mr Major is perhaps more aware than most Prime Ministers of how capable 'loyal' backbenchers are of turning against the Government.

What can the backbencher do? He is under the control of the party Whips, to the extent that they will try to ensure that MPs will turn up and vote when needed and will perform such Parliamentary duties as are required. Most of the time, most MPs obey the Whips. Ambitions of joining the front benches will soon be thwarted if an MP takes too independent a line, but, that apart, most of the time MPs willingly follow the party line.

The Whips also convey to the party leaders the feeling amongst the backbenchers. These feelings are more directly conveyed by backbench groups. For example, the Conservative 1922 Committee is quite capable of taking Ministers, even the Prime Minister, to task over their policies. The Chairman of the 1922 – currently Sir Marcus Fox, who is himself a former whip – is effectively spokesman for the Conservative backbenchers and any Conservative Prime Minister faced with contentious legislation must first ensure he has the 1922 on his side. Faced as he will be with unanimous opposition from the other parties, he needs to rely on his own members and these unofficial channels will tell him whether this support will be provided.

There are, of course, plenty of opportunities within House of Commons' proceedings, short of voting against the Government, by which a backbencher can make his voice

6 LEGISLATURE I – THE HOUSE OF COMMONS

heard. Parliamentary questions – both oral and written – are one such opportunity. Another would be through participation in Parliamentary committees. To some extent, the selection process will ensure that maverick MPs are kept away. However, the Select Committees have shown themselves quite capable of confronting Government policies and criticism may well come from the Government's backbench members as, for example, in the Select Committee on Defence during the 'Westland affair' (1986). In other words, their loyalty to the Government does not prevent them from taking a critical stance. The Government is not directly threatened by that stance and yet its source probably makes the criticism more effective.

A further opportunity for the backbencher will be during debates. During Mrs Thatcher's premiership the most significant backbench speeches came from those she had just removed from the front bench. Sir Geoffrey Howe's speech shortly after his departure is a good example. If such a speech voices opposition and if others share that view then it is obviously of greater significance than the inevitable opposition from the other side of the House.

Most politicians are ambitious; none would want to see their own Government defeated. These two factors limit the extent of backbench opposition. Further, MPs are answerable to their constituents who might take a dim view of opposition. A government may not wish to call the backbencher's bluff, but the backbencher certainly does not hold all the cards.

In conclusion, it is not possible to say whether the position of the present Conservative Government – which very much needs to listen to its own backbenchers, who can indeed be a more effective opposition – is representative of modern British Parliaments. The effect of four consecutive Conservative Governments together with policies that challenge the views of some Conservatives have perhaps created an unusual situation. However, one might predict that if John Major's Government does not survive until 1997, it will be because of the opposition behind him rather than from the other side of the House.

7 LEGISLATURE II – THE HOUSE OF LORDS

7.1 Introduction
7.2 Key points
7.3 Recent statutes
7.4 Analysis of questions
7.5 Questions

7.1 Introduction

The House of Lords is a non-elected chamber. It plays a part in the legislative process but ultimately its powers are very limited. Nevertheless many argue that the quality of debate in the House of Lords is high and the House can sometimes effectively challenge the Commons.

The reform/abolition of the House of Lords has been on the political agenda for many years but other than the Life Peerages Act 1958 which has very much revitalised the House no significant attempts at reform have been successful.

7.2 Key points

a) *The composition of the House of Lords*

   i) The Lords Spiritual: Archbishops of Canterbury and York, the Bishops of London, Durham and Winchester, and the next 21 diocesan bishops of the Church of England in seniority of appointment.

   ii) The Lords Temporal:

   - Hereditary peers and peeresses in their own right of England, Scotland, Great Britain and the United Kingdom.
   - Life peers created under the Life Peerages Act 1958.
   - Lords of Appeal in Ordinary.

b) *The functions and work of the House of Lords*

   The 1968 Government White Paper *House of Lords Reform* referred to seven functions of the House of Lords.

   i) Its appellate role as the supreme court of appeal.

   ii) The provision of a forum for free debate and matters of public interest.

   iii) The revision of Public Bills brought from the House of Commons.

   iv) The initiation of Public Bills.

   v) The consideration of subordinate legislation.

7 LEGISLATURE II – THE HOUSE OF LORDS

    vi) The scrutiny of the activities of the Executive.

    vii) The scrutiny of private legislation.

c) *House of Lords' reform*

    i) The Parliament Act 1911
- A Bill certified by the Speaker as a Money Bill should receive the Royal Assent and become an Act of Parliament without the consent of the House of Lords if, having been sent up from the House of Commons at least one month before the end of the session, it had not been passed by the Lords without amendment within one month of its being sent up.
- Any other Public Bill, except one for extending the life of Parliament, could become an Act of Parliament without the consent of the House of Lords if it had been passed by the House of Commons in three successive sessions, two years having elapsed between its Second Reading and its final passing in the House of Commons, and if it had been sent up to the House of Lords at least one month before the end of each of the three sessions.
- The maximum duration of a Parliament was reduced from seven years to five.

    ii) The Parliament Act 1949
- Amends the Parliament Act 1911 by reducing the number of sessions in which a Bill must be passed by the House of Commons from three to two, and reducing the period between the Second Reading and final passing in the House of Commons from two years to one.

    iii) Life Peerages Act 1958
- This Act empowers the Crown to create life peers who vote in the House of Lords. The on-going result of the Act is that the House of Lords has become rejuvenated and appointments are made from people with wide ranging experience in different walks of life. The role of the House of Lords as a debating chamber is consequently significant.

    iv) The Peerage Act 1963
- This Act enables hereditary peers, other than those of first creation, to renounce their titles for life by disclaimer. The peerage remains dormant and devolves upon the heir in the normal manner on the renouncer's death. A person who has disclaimed a peerage is entitled to vote in Parliamentary elections and is eligible for election to the House of Commons.

    v) The Parliament (No 2) Bill 1969

In November 1968 the Labour Government published a White Paper, *House of Lords Reform*, which was later embodied in the Parliament (No 2) Bill 1968–69. Its main proposals were as follows:
- The reformed House of Lords was to be a two-tier structure comprising voting peers and non-voting peers.
- Succession to a hereditary peerage was no longer to carry the right to a seat in the House of Lords, but existing peers by succession would have

CONSTITUTIONAL LAW

the right to sit as non-voting members during their life time, or might be created life peers to enable them to continue in active participation as voting members.
- Voting peers were expected to play a full part in the work of the House and be required to attend at least one-third of the sittings. They would be subject to an age of retirement. Non-voting peers would be able to play a full part in debates and in committees, but would not be entitled to vote.
- The voting House would initially consist of about 230 peers, distributed between the parties in such a way as to give the government a small majority over the Opposition parties, but not a majority of the House as a whole when those without party allegiance were included.
- The reformed House would be able to impose a delay of six months from the date of disagreement between the two Houses on the passage of non-financial public legislation. After this delay a Bill could be submitted for Royal Assent by resolution of the House of Commons.
- The Lords would be able to require the House of Commons to reconsider subordinate legislation, but would not be able to reject it outright.
- A review would be made of the functions and procedures of the two Houses once the main reform had come into effect.

The Bill was abandoned on April 17, 1969.

d) *Conclusion*

i) Reform of the House of Lords has been a focus for political debate for many years.

A majority argue for its reform rather than abolition tacitly acknowledging the important role a second chamber has in scrutinising the activities of government.

ii) The current debate on 'a written constitution for the United Kingdom' includes a proposal for the House of Lords to become an elected chamber – see Charter 88.

7.3 Recent statutes

As with the House of Commons students need to consider the many recent political issues, usually controversial, that have involved the House of Lords. Examples here could indicate the effectiveness or otherwise of the House in exercising its role within the Constitution.

War Crimes Act 1991.

7.4 Analysis of questions

The House of Lords is a popular topic for examiners. Questions demand a knowledge of the role and functions of the House and may in addition require the student to consider the relationship between the House of Commons and the House of Lords or the implications of reform of the House of Lords. The tendency to write in a highly descriptive way everything known about the topic must be resisted.

7 LEGISLATURE II – THE HOUSE OF LORDS

7.5 Questions

QUESTION ONE

'While a second chamber is needed to serve a number of legislative purposes the present House of Lords is restricted by its composition from exercising its powers effectively.' (Wade and Bradley).

Discuss.

University of London LLB Examination
(for External Students) Constitutional Law June 1986 Q4

General Comment

The usual House of Lords question. As always don't write everything you know about the House of Lords and don't be tempted to simply turn out the traditional (and now largely discredited) criticisms of the Lords. Remember that while the undemocratic nature of its composition is a major criticism of the House, it is also one of its greatest assets.

Skeleton Solution

- Introduction; the need for a second chamber.
- The criticisms of the hereditary and life peerage systems.
- The advantages which flow from the undemocratic nature of the composition of the House of Lords.
- The factors limiting the effective exercise of the powers of the House.

Suggested Solution

For many years there has been opposition to the continued existence of the House of Lords as the second chamber in our present bicameral parliamentary system. Nevertheless the fact remains that a second chamber is needed to assist in the legislative process and the House of Lords performs the functions of a second chamber extremely well.

However, despite the success of the House of Lords in performing its functions it can be argued that the House is nevertheless restricted by its aristocratic and unrepresentative composition from exercising its powers effectively. In a democracy, it may be argued all legislators should be directly accountable to the people at elections or at least accountable indirectly, for example, by election by the House of Commons. Their Lordships, however, take their seats in the legislature either because they are hereditary peers or because they have been created life peers under the Life Peerages Act 1958. The former are criticised on the grounds that high office should be awarded to those who earn it on merit and not by accident of birth, and as most hereditary peers are Conservative this leads to a permanent Conservative majority in the House. The life peers are criticised because of the considerable powers of patronage left in the hands of the Prime Minister to reward party loyalists and retiring ministers with seats in the Upper Chamber. It is also thought by some that since the members of the House of Lords do not represent any body of constituents they speak for a small privileged section of the community.

But criticism of the composition of the House of Lords is often ill-founded and uninformed. It can be argued that the composition of the House does not directly affect the effectiveness of the chamber – quite the opposite. The quality of members and speeches is often very high. Debates are well informed. Those upon whom peerages are conferred are usually persons with considerable experience of politics, public service or industry, or who have otherwise made their mark in public or intellectual life. They bring to the House a wide range of expertise. The hereditary element also provides many young peers and because the Lords do not have any constituencies to consider they can devote more time to their parliamentary duties and do not have to worry about re-selection or re-election. In many respects therefore the membership of the House of Lords is far superior to that of the House of Commons. The only difficulty is the undemocratic nature of their appointment.

It is the consciousness of their undemocratic nature of appointment which is the major impediment to the effectiveness of the House. While the Parliament Acts 1911 and 1949 did have a direct effect on the effectiveness of the House of Lords – for example, the House no longer has power over money matters and governments no longer depend on the favour of the Lords for their continuation in office – nevertheless under the Parliament Acts their Lordships do retain the power to amend non-money Bills. Although the House of Lords cannot impose its will on the Commons in legislation, it can effectively delay Government Bills for one year. But the Lords are reluctant to exercise their suspensory powers over legislation which they still retain. If they interfere with government business they may lay themselves open to allegations of seeking to frustrate the wishes of the people as expressed through their democratically elected government.

This makes the House of Lords extremely vulnerable. How can they act as a check on the House of Commons in such circumstances? The Government can brush aside opposition in the House of Lords 'because they don't represent the people', and the threat of abolition or reform is always present. Their Lordships are well aware of this. This is perhaps one reason why in spite of their inbuilt Conservative majority they have always shown restraint when dealing with Labour government legislation. Recent events have shown however that the reports of the impotence of the House of Lords have been exaggerated and that, given the right circumstances, its effectiveness and efficiency is not altogether impaired by these legislative and political constraints.

When the threat of abolition is lifted, as it usually is under a Conservative Government, their Lordships can be very effective in carrying out their constitutional functions. The Lords retain a high degree of political independence inherent in their undemocratic character. They do not have to rely upon the continued support of a political party for their seats in the legislature and while the majority of hereditary peers may be Conservative, a Conservative Government is not guaranteed a majority in the House. They vote according to their conscience, not the demands of the Whips. Where the government has a heavy legislative programme, amendment or delay in the Lords can seriously threaten the legislative timetable for that particular session and the government will be forced to take notice and attempt a compromise with the Lords. If compromise fails and the government implements the procedure under the Parliament Acts, even a one year delay may prove fatal to the government's plans.

But such opposition is possible only where the House of Lords retains popular support for its action, where, for example, the government is acting unconstitutionally

7 LEGISLATURE II – THE HOUSE OF LORDS

or outside the terms of its mandate. In other situations their Lordships may be reluctant to seriously oppose the government's wishes. The fear of abolition or public censure would be decisive.

Therefore while the effectiveness of the House of Lords in respect of its legislative functions and powers is relatively unimpeded and in many respects enhanced by the anachronistic and undemocratic nature of its composition, its effectiveness as a check upon the House of Commons, and thus in reality upon the government of the day, is limited.

QUESTION TWO

Outline the constitutional problems and benefits, if any, that would arise if the House of Lords were abolished.

University of London LLB Examination
(for External Students) Constitutional Law June 1985 Q3

General Comment

This question involves discussion of the role of the House of Lords as the second chamber in our bicameral parliamentary system and the constitutional problems and benefits which would arise if the Lords were abolished in favour of an unicameral parliamentary system. Don't write everything you know about the House of Lords and don't be tempted to simply turn out the traditional (and now largely discredited) criticisms of Lords as justification for their abolition. Remember, the House of Lords plays a vital function as a revision chamber and helps relieve the pressure of work on the already overburdened House of Commons. Events in recent years have also shown that the House of Lords is the only effective check on a Government which dominates the House of Commons. It is doubtful whether any real benefits would arise from the abolition of the House of Lords. Reform yes, abolition no.

Skeleton Solution

- Introduction: arguments for reform/abolition of the House of Lords.
- The problems caused by adopting a unicameral parliamentary system. The position of the Judicial Committee; role of the House as a revision chamber for Public Bills; inability of Commons to deal adequately with all Bills passed; need for fundamental change in House of Commons procedure; role of Lords as a check on the Executive; need for written Constitution/Bill of Rights.
- Benefits of abolition: saving of costs; space; forcing of change and reform of House of Commons procedures.

Suggested Solution

For many years there has been opposition of some sort or another to the continued existence of the House of Lords as the second chamber in our present bicameral parliamentary system. The argument is that as presently constituted the House of Lords is undemocratic, outdated and unsuitable in a modern society. Some therefore favour reform, so that, for example, its composition becomes more democratic and its powers perhaps increased so that it can act as a more effective check on the House of Commons, (and thus, in reality, on the government of the day), than it does at present. Others, however, wish to go further still and see the abolition of the second chamber in favour of a unicameral parliamentary system.

If the House of Lords were abolished certain constitutional problems would undoubtedly result. Whether these problems would be insuperable is a matter of opinion. What cannot be denied, however, is that despite the problems regarding its composition, the fact remains that the House of Lords does perform a valuable service within the present parliamentary system and if abolished many of its functions would still have to be performed by some other body, presumably the House of Commons. In 1968, the Government White Paper *House of Lords Reform* referred to seven functions of the House of Lords. An examination of each of these functions serves to illustrate some of the problems that might result from abolition.

Firstly, the House of Lords acts as the final court of appeal for the whole of the United Kingdom in civil cases and for England, Wales and Northern Ireland in criminal cases. If the House were abolished therefore a new 'supreme' court would have to be established to take its place, unless of course the Court of Appeal were to become the final appeal court for England and Wales. However, as the judicial work of the House is separate from its other functions and only involves the Judicial Committee – drawn from the Lord High Chancellor, the Lords of Appeal in Ordinary and Lords who hold or have held high judicial office – the separation of the Judicial Committee from the rest of the House of Lords or its replacement by some new body would not perhaps cause too great a constitutional problem.

Secondly, the House provides a forum for free debate on matters of public interest, Wednesday in particular being traditionally set aside for special debate on a wide range of subjects. Apart from the fact that these debates are usually of a very high standard; a standard that would perhaps never be reached in the Commons, even if the time were available, this loss would not pose any great constitutional problem.

Thirdly, and perhaps most importantly, the House acts as a revising chamber for Public Bills brought from the House of Commons. About one half of the time of the House of Lords is devoted to the consideration of Public Bills. The majority of this time is spent on revising Bills which have already passed the Commons, where the great majority of government legislation is introduced. The House of Commons does not have the time to fully debate all the legislation it has to pass each session and the use of procedures for the curtailment of debate, such as the guillotine, often means that Bills are passed by the Commons without really being considered at all. A second chamber is therefore required to examine and revise such Bills. If the second chamber is abolished then the procedures of the House of Commons for enacting legislation will have to be changed if the present standard and volume of legislation is to be maintained. This could be achieved by Membership of the House of Commons becoming full-time and by making even more use of committees. However, even then the volume of legislation may still prove to be too great, necessitating either a shortening of the procedure by which a Bill is enacted or making more use of subordinate legislation, which some would argue is already over used as it is. Certainly some fundamental changes would have to be made to the proceedings of the House of Commons and these may prove unacceptable to many of the present MPs.

Also it must be remembered that the House of Commons, because of the distortion produced by our electoral system, is largely controlled by a government which does

7 LEGISLATURE II – THE HOUSE OF LORDS

not represent even 50 per cent of the electorate. A second chamber is thus required to at least delay substantially controversial legislation which may be unpopular with the majority of the people of the country. If the second chamber is abolished then the only way to control a government with an absolute majority in the House of Commons may be to have either a written Constitution or a Bill of Rights containing entrenched clauses, perhaps requiring a referendum for amendment.

The House of Lords also initiates Public Bills. While the more important and controversial Bills almost invariably begin in the House of Commons, Bills which are relatively uncontroversial in party political terms are regularly introduced in the House of Lords. If abolished, these Bills will have to be wholly dealt with by the Commons thus adding to its already overburdened workload. Similarly, the subordinate legislation and the private legislation at present dealt with by the House of Lords would also fall to be wholly dealt with by the Commons if the second chamber were abolished.

The arguments in favour of a unicameral Parliament are mainly political and it is doubtful whether any real practical benefit would result from the abolition of the House of Lords. Certainly it is doubtful that the loss of the Lords could ever be compensated. However, there are benefits of sorts which would flow from abolition, such as the saving of money and the making available of more space in the Palace of Westminster. Abolition would also have to result in the widespread reform of the House of Commons if any semblance of a parliamentary democracy is to be maintained. Such reform may be viewed as a substantial benefit. However, the main fear, and indeed the most likely consequence of the abolition of the House of Lords, is that it will simply serve to strengthen the Executive control of the Legislature.

QUESTION THREE

'Paradoxically, the House of Lords is an essential and valuable second chamber.'

Critically assess this statement.

University of London LLB Examination
(for External Students) Constitutional Law June 1991 Q3

General Comment

A question inviting one to consider the shortcomings and advantages of the second chamber. It is advisable to deal with the two issues separately, citing specific examples.

Skeleton Solution

- Examine common criticisms of the House of Lords; membership, unelected, powers.
- Consider its contribution to scrutiny of the executive, and the legislative process.

Suggested Solution

The quotation under discussion assumes that, in the normal course of events, a body such as the House of Lords would not normally be able to function properly as the second legislative chamber, but that, despite its theoretical shortcomings, it performs that task very well. This answer will first address itself to those aspects of the House of Lords that one might suppose render it unable to play such an important constitutional role.

Firstly its membership. None of the members of the House of Lords is elected. All members are there either through appointment, birth, or by virtue of the office they hold. The institution is, therefore, an affront to democracy. Peers in theory represent no-one but themselves, or the interests of those exercising the power of appointment, and as such are not accountable to the people despite the influence they might have over the law making process. It is added that peers are paid a daily attendance fee and this is an unnecessary extra burden on the taxpayer. The Commons is short of space and could make use of the room currently used by the Lords.

Secondly, there is the argument that one elected chamber is enough. To have a second (particularly in a unitary system) is simply a confusion. If there are faults in the way the House of Commons operates at present that should be dealt with by reform of the House of Commons. For example, the introduction of a system of proportional representation and/or the adoption of a really effective system of select committees to scrutinise the Government's activities and with the powers necessary to exercise a great deal more influence than at present over the Government. Rather than being 'controlled' by a Second Chamber, the Government could be controlled by a written constitution containing some entrenched clauses, perhaps requiring a referendum for amendment.

Thirdly, the House of Lords has a majority of Conservative Party supporters who, although they may seldom attend, can always be relied upon to turn up and vote in favour of that party's legislation (or opposition to legislation). These are the so-called 'backwoodsmen'.

Despite all of the foregoing, the House of Lords continues to be a respected and valuable part of the British constitution. Why should this be? There are a number of reasons.

The House provides a forum for free debate on matters of public interest. Wednesday is traditionally set aside for special debates on a wide range of subjects. Debates may be initiated either by the Government, Opposition, backbench or independent Members. Once a month, from the beginning of the Session until the Spring Bank Holiday recess, there are two 'Short Debates', limited to two and a half hours each. The right to initiate such debates is confined to backbenchers and crossbenchers and the subjects for debate are chosen by ballot.

The House of Lords serves a valuable purpose in scrutinising Bills passed by the House of Commons, with about one half of the time of the House of Lords devoted to the consideration of Public Bills. This process is especially important because, unlike the Commons, the Lords have nothing corresponding to the guillotine and there is therefore no effective machinery for curtailing debate. Also the Lords have no provision for the selection of amendments for debate and therefore all amendments tabled may be debated. To some extent the House of Lords can compensate for inadequate scrutiny of legislation by the House of Commons. The powers of the House of Lords to thwart the wishes of the House of Commons are, of course, limited by the provisions of the Parliament Acts 1911 and 1949, under which certain Public

7 LEGISLATURE II – THE HOUSE OF LORDS

Bills may be presented for the Royal Assent without the consent of the Lords; see the War Crimes Act 1991.

The House of Lords does not stand idle at the start of a parliamentary session waiting for legislation to work its way up from the House of Commons. Bills which are relatively uncontroversial in party political terms have been introduced in the House of Lords with a fair degree of regularity. These include the Wildlife and Countryside Bill (1980–81 Session), the National Heritage Bill, Data Protection Bill and the Health and Social Services and Social Security Adjudications Bill (1982–83 Session). By convention all Consolidation Bills (Bills which do not alter the law but replace a number of Acts dealing with a particular subject by a single Act) and most Bills to give effect to changes in the law proposed by the Law Commissions, are introduced in the Lords.

Unlike Members of the House of Commons, Members of the Lords are free to introduce Private Members' Bills into the House and there is usually sufficient time for them to be debated. However if they are passed there is no guarantee that time will be found for them in the House of Commons. The fact that the Lords have no constituents makes it easier for them to discuss measures proposing controversial changes in the law in this way. The Lords thus played a significant part in reforming the law relating to homosexuality and abortion.

Their Lordships also contribute to the scrutiny of delegated legislation. The powers of the House of Lords over delegated legislation were not curtailed by the Parliament Acts and are therefore the same as those enjoyed by the House of Commons. When a resolution of each House approving the instrument is required, the House of Lords always has an opportunity to debate the instrument. In the case of negative instruments, any Member may move a motion to annul the instrument and while in the Commons time often cannot be found to debate such motions, in the Lords there is no such difficulty.

The government departments will have representatives in the House of Lords who can be questioned about policy by peers in the same way that ministers can be questioned in the House of Commons. Each day up to four Oral or 'Starred Questions' may be asked of the Government and are taken as first business. No Lord may ask more than two Questions on any day nor may he have more than three Questions on the order paper at any time. Supplementary Questions may be asked by any Member, but there may not be a debate. 'Unstarred Questions' are taken at the end of business. The Lord asking the Question makes a speech, and a debate may take place before the Minister makes his reply, which concludes the proceedings. Private Notice Questions may be asked on matters of urgency. It is for the Leader of the House or as a last resort for the House itself, to decide what constitutes a matter of urgency. The process of question time in the House of Lords therefore provides a valuable adjunct to the procedure in the House of Commons.

In conclusion, it is submitted that there is one further argument in favour of the retention of the House of Lords, namely that the House of Commons, because of the distortion produced by our electoral system, is largely controlled by a government which does not represent even 50 per cent of the electorate. A Second Chamber, (and one with greater powers than the present House of Lords) is thus required to at least substantially delay controversial legislation which may be unpopular with the majority of the people of the country. During the 1980s, with its succession of Conservative governments with large majorities, it was the House of Lords that inflicted over 100 defeats upon the Government in votes on various controversial pieces of legislation. The Labour Party in opposition was virtually powerless, given the nature of the parliamentary process.

8 PARLIAMENTARY PRIVILEGE

8.1 Introduction
8.2 Key points
8.3 Recent cases
8.4 Analysis of questions
8.5 Questions

8.1 Introduction

For a Member of Parliament to carry out his duties to his constituents properly he must be free to raise matters without the fear of being sued for slander or libel. Parliamentary privilege allows him to do so within the confines of Parliament itself. There is, of course, the risk of abuse and, in any event, the counter argument that those attacked may not have a chance to defend themselves.

It is sometimes said that the rules of parliamentary privilege constitute a clear case of 'power without responsibility', but it has to be accepted that over the years parliamentary privilege has been essential to the exposure of injustices and malpractices which the restrictive English libel laws might otherwise have allowed to continue unchecked.

As with most of constitutional law it is a matter of striking the right balance; in this area the need for freedom of speech in Parliament has to be respected and, perhaps, all that needs to be changed to achieve the balance is for Parliament itself to be much more willing to impose heavy penalties on those Members who are deemed to have abused this privilege.

8.2 Key points

It is important that students understand the following issues regarding parliamentary privilege:

a) *Definition*

Parliamentary privilege is defined by Erskine May in *Parliamentary Practice*, 21st edition, as:

' ... the sum of the peculiar rights enjoyed by each House collectively as a constitutional part of the High Court of Parliament and by members of each House individually, without which they could not discharge their functions, and which exceed those possessed by other bodies or individuals.'

b) *Privileges of the House of Commons*

i) 'Ancient and undoubted rights and privileges'

At the opening of each Parliament, the Speaker formally claims from the

CONSTITUTIONAL LAW

Crown for the Commons 'their ancient and undoubted rights and privileges'. These are:

- Freedom of Speech in Debate

The right is guaranteed in article 9 of the Bill of Rights 1688 which provides:

'the freedom of speech and debates or proceedings in Parliament ought not to be impeached or questioned in any court or place out of Parliament.'

No Member may be made liable in the courts for words spoken in the course of parliamentary proceedings.

What is said in Parliament cannot be used to support a cause of action in defamation which has arisen outside Parliament: *Church of Scientology of California* v *Johnson-Smith* [1972] 1 QB 522.

In *Pepper* v *Hart* [1993] 1 All ER 42 the court took account of extracts from *Hansard* to assist in statutory interpretation. Emphasis was, however, made of the need to give effect to Parliament's intentions, rather than to undermine the independence of MPs.

What are proceedings in Parliament? Remarks made in debate, discussions in committee, parliamentary questions and answers, and votes are clearly within the definition. Other words spoken within the precincts of Parliament unconnected with parliamentary proceedings are not protected: *Rivlin* v *Bilainkin* [1953] 1 QB 485.

As indicated in section 8.4 Analysis of questions, a likely point for consideration in the examination question is what is 'a proceeding in Parliament'. In this regard it should be noted that this may cover matters said outside the parliamentary chamber. Students should note the following statement from Viscount Radcliffe in *Attorney-General for Ceylon* v *De Livera* [1963] AC 103 in which he was considering what was meant by a proceeding in Parliament:

'the answer given to that somewhat more limited question depends upon the following consideration, in what circumstances and in what situations is a member of the House exercising his "real" or "essential" function as a member ... the most that can be said is that, despite reluctance to treat a member's privileges as going beyond anything that is essential, it is generally recognised that it is impossible to regard his only proper functions as a member as being confined to what he does on the floor of the House.'

Particular problems have frequently arisen regarding the status of communications between MPs and Ministers: *Case of GWR Strauss MP* (1957–58) HC 227. Such communications may only enjoy qualified privilege under the law of defamation: *Beach* v *Freeson* [1972] QB 14.

Letters from members of the public to MPs enjoy only qualified privilege under the law of defamation: *R* v *Rule* [1937] 2 KB 375.

Communications between MPs and the Parliamentary Commissioner for Administration are accorded absolute privilege in the law of defamation: Parliamentary Commissioner Act 1967, s10(5).

The fair and accurate reporting of parliamentary proceedings is protected by qualified privilege at common law: *Wason* v *Walter* (1869) LR 4 QB 73; *Cook* v *Alexander* [1974] QB 279.

Fair and accurate extracts from, or abstracts of, papers published under the authority of Parliament enjoy qualified privilege in the law of defamation: Parliamentary Papers Act 1840.

- Freedom from arrest

The immunity only applies to civil arrest and extends while Parliament sits and for 40 days before and 40 days after: *Stourton* v *Stourton* [1963] P 302.

The immunity does not protect Members from arrest on criminal charges.

- Freedom of access to Her Majesty whenever occasion shall require; and that the most favourable construction should be placed upon all their proceedings.

ii) Other privileges

The other privileges of the House of Commons, not expressly claimed by the Speaker include:

- The right of the House to regulate its own composition

The House retains the exclusive right to determine by resolution when a writ for the holding of a by-election shall be issued.

The House maintains the right to determine whether a Member is qualified to sit in the House and can declare a Member's seat vacant on grounds of legal disqualification or for any other reason it thinks fit.

The House may expel a Member whom it considers unfit to sit: the *Case of Gary Allighan MP* (1947) HC 138.

- The right to take exclusive cognisance of matters arising within the precincts of the House

The House maintains the right to control its own proceedings and regulate its internal affairs without interference from the courts: *Bradlaugh* v *Gossett* (1884) 12 QBD 271.

If a statute is to bind the House it must do so clearly: *R* v *Graham-Campbell, ex parte Herbert* [1935] 1 KB 594.

iii) The right to punish both Members and non-members for breach of privilege and contempt

The House has the power to maintain its privileges and to punish those who break or commit contempt of the House.

Contempt of the House is a very wide concept. Erskine May describes it as:

' ... any act or omission which obstructs or impedes either House or Parliament in the performance of its functions, or which obstructs or impedes any member or officer of such House in the discharge of his duty, or which has a tendency, directly or indirectly, to produce such results may be treated as a contempt even though there is no precedent of the offence.'

Thus while the House cannot create new privileges, except by statute, there is no complete list of behaviour which constitutes contempt.

Complaints of breach of privilege may be raised by a Member or in the House by the Speaker. If the Speaker rules that a prima facie case has been made out a motion is proposed that the matter be referred to the Committee of Privileges.

The Committee of Privileges comprises 15 senior Members of the House. It is the master of its own proceedings. It can compel the attendance of witnesses and the production of documents; failure to comply being a contempt. There is no requirement of legal representation.

The Select Committee on Parliamentary Privilege in 1967 recommended that persons directly concerned in the Committee's investigations should have the right to attend its hearings, make submissions, call, examine and cross-examine witnesses, and be legally represented and apply for legal aid.

Offenders may be reprimanded or admonished or committed to prison. Members may be suspended or expelled from the House.

iv) The right of impeachment (now obsolete).

c) *The courts and parliamentary privilege*

The House of Commons claims to be the absolute and sole judge of its own privileges and maintains that its judgment cannot be called into question by any other court. The courts do not agree. They maintain the right to determine the nature and extent of parliamentary privilege when adjudicating upon the rights of individuals outside the house. This disagreement has given rise to constitutional conflict: *Stockdale* v *Hansard* (1839) 9 Ad & E 1; *Case of the Sheriffs of Middlesex* (1840) 11 Ad & E 273.

d) *MPs as representatives of outside interests*

If a Member agrees to represent an outside interest group in Parliament, is a threat by that group to remove support from the Member a breach of privilege?

 i) It is improper for a Member to enter into any arrangement fettering his complete independence by undertaking to press some particular point of view on behalf of an outside interest whether for reward or not: *Case of WJ Brown MP* (1947).

 ii) It is improper to attempt to punish a Member financially because of his actions as a Member: *Case of the Yorkshire Area Council of National Union of Mineworkers* (1975).

e) *Privileges of the House of Lords*

The privileges of the House of Lords are similar to those enjoyed by the House of Commons.

f) *The Nolan Report*

The Nolan Report (see comment in chapter 6) recommended that the House should:

8 PARLIAMENTARY PRIVILEGE

i) require agreements and remuneration relating to parliamentary services to be disclosed;
ii) expand the guidance on avoiding conflicts of interests;
iii) introduce a new code of conduct for members;
iv) appoint a Parliamentary Commissioner for standards;
v) establish a new procedure for investigating and adjudicating on complaints in this area about members.

Controversy has arisen amongst Members of Parliament as to:

i) the extent to which Parliamentarians should enjoy outside interests; and
ii) whether consultancies and other paid work should be reviewed by a body other than Parliament.

8.3 Recent cases

The important principle-making cases are referred to in the key points section. While there are occasions today when particular MPs are reported to the Committee of Privileges, they are reported for breaches established by these cases. While students should note headline making cases, they should only serve as further examples of existing principles.

Pepper v *Hart* [1993] 1 All ER 42.

Prebble v *Television New Zealand Ltd* [1994] 3 WLR 970.

8.4 Analysis of questions

This is an important subject and a question on this area in nearly every examination paper can be expected. The question can either be a general essay question requiring a critical discussion of the topic or a problem solving exercise; if the latter, the popular question requires you to consider whether what a particular MP has said about someone comes within the meaning of a 'proceeding in Parliament' so as to be protected by parliamentary privilege and/or whether what a particular newspaper writes about an MP comes within the meaning of qualified privilege so as, once again, to be protected from attack.

8.5 Questions

QUESTION ONE

The House of Commons has too wide a jurisdiction to punish contempts and breaches of privilege.

Discuss.

University of London LLB Examination
(for External Students) Constitutional law June 1984 Q5

General Comment

This is a straightforward essay question requiring the student to show the relationship of Parliament to the courts as regards parliamentary privilege.

CONSTITUTIONAL LAW

Skeleton Solution

Parliamentary privilege:

- courts decide what privileges exist;
- Parliament deals with breaches of such privileges.

Suggested Solution

Parliamentary privilege is part of the law and custom of Parliament evolved by the two Houses in order to protect their freedom to conduct their proceedings without improper interference by the Sovereign, the courts, or the public. The privileges enjoyed by the House of Commons include those 'ancient and undoubted privileges' claimed by the Speaker at the beginning of each new Parliament such as freedom of speech in debate, freedom from civil arrest and freedom of access via the Speaker to the Sovereign. There are also those privileges enjoyed by the House in its corporate capacity such as the right to regulate its own composition and the right to regulate its own proceedings. These special rights, powers and immunities conferred by parliamentary privilege are justified as being essential for the conduct of the business and the maintenance of the authority of the House.

Parliamentary privileges are part of the common law in so far as their existence and validity are recognised by the courts. But they are enforced not by the courts but exclusively by Parliament. By virtue of its inherent right to control its own proceedings and maintain its dignity, the House of Commons in protecting its privileges may punish those who violate them or commit contempt of the House. Breach of privilege consists of either an abuse of a particular privilege by a Member or any conduct which interferes with one of the privileges of Parliament. Contempt is a much wider concept and consists of any conduct which tends to bring the House into disrepute or detract from its dignity. No matter whether the offence is styled a breach of privilege or a contempt, or both, the penal powers of the House are the same. Offenders may be reprimanded or admonished by the Speaker. Members may be suspended or expelled. Officials of the House may be dismissed and any Member or stranger may be committed to prison for the duration of the Parliamentary session. However, in discussing the jurisdiction of the House to punish for breach of privilege and contempt a distinction must be drawn between the two.

In the past questions of privilege have been a source of considerable conflict between the Commons and the courts. Indeed, the House still asserts that it is the absolute and sole judge of the extent of its own privileges and has invoked its historical status as part of the High Court of Parliament in claiming that its judgments are not examinable by any other court. But this is a claim to which the courts do not fully accede. While the courts recognise the control which the House has over its own proceedings, in *Stockdale* v *Hansard* (1839) the court maintained the right to determine the nature and the limits of parliamentary privilege when adjudicating upon the rights of individuals outside the House. The court also affirmed that the Commons cannot create new privileges by resolutions of the House, only by statute. Therefore, while the jurisdiction of the House of Commons to punish for breaches of privilege is wide, in the sense that the privileges are enforced exclusively by the House, nevertheless there are limitations, notably the court's power to determine

8 PARLIAMENTARY PRIVILEGE

whether the privilege arises and if so its scope and effect. In such cases privilege forms a part of the common law and is subject to it.

But while the House cannot by resolution enlarge the scope of its own privileges, it has not closed the categories of contempt. Therefore, while the courts may assert their jurisdiction to decide the existence and extent of privileges of the House, what constitutes a contempt of the House is essentially a matter which only the House can decide. If a contempt issue arises relating to the internal proceedings of the House, the courts will decline to interfere, and whether in relation to matters inside or outside the House, the courts have always recognised the power of the House to imprison for contempt. It is accepted today that where the cause of committal stated in the return to the writ is insufficient in law, the court may review. But if no cause for committal other than the simple statement of contempt of the House is shown in the return, the court will not make further inquiry into the reasons for the committal. Therefore the jurisdiction of the House of Commons to punish for contempt is very wide. The House has power to commit persons for contempt for whatever conduct it adjudges to amount to contempt, provided that the cause of the contempt is not stated.

QUESTION TWO

Jones is an MP for the constituency of Westhampton which for some time has suffered from a deterioration in relations between the police and the immigrant community. Recently Jones received a letter from a constituent complaining that he had been beaten up by one PC Plod for no reason whatsoever other than the fact that he was black. (This allegation was completely untrue.) Jones decided this was an opportunity to get to grips with the race relations problem and wrote three letters: one to a minister in the Home Office; one to the Westhampton Weekly; and one to the Community Relations Officer of the Local Authority. All the letters repeated the allegation as if it was pure fact. Jones also repeated the allegation in a question to the Secretary of State for the Home Office made during parliamentary question time and the question was reported in the Daily Garble the next day. Jones has also recently been offered a post with the Equality for Immigrants Association in which he is to be paid £5,000 per annum and he is expected to always support measures furthering the interests of the Association.

PC Plod has recently issued writs against the constituent, the Daily Garble and Jones complaining he has been libelled. Furthermore, the Speaker of the House has become aware of the offer of employment made by the EIA.

Discuss the foregoing in the light of the law relating to parliamentary privilege.

Written by the Editors

General Comment

A typical question on the major aspect of parliamentary privilege, namely freedom of speech, requiring a discussion of the relationship of the privilege with the tort of defamation.

CONSTITUTIONAL LAW

Skeleton Solution

Introduction

- Outline nature and basis of parliamentary privilege.
- State types of privilege raised by question, ie freedom of speech, freedom from interference.
- State that the question raises following:

  Is letter from constituent privileged?

  Are letters from Jones privileged?

  Is report by Daily Garble protected by qualified privilege?

  Is employment with EIA against freedom from interference?

Letter from constituent

- Probably not absolutely privileged: *Rivlin* v *Bilainkin* (1953).
- May attract qualified privilege – *R* v *Rule* (1937) – but is he acting maliciously?

Letters from Jones – which ones fall within meaning of 'proceeding in Parliament'?

- Question in house – yes: *Church of Scientology* v *Smith* (1972); *Case of GWR Strauss MP* (1957–58).
- Letter to Home Office – yes: *Attorney-General for Ceylon* v *De Livera* (1963).
- Letter to Westhampton Weekly – no.
- Letter to Community Relations Officer – no.

Daily Garble report

Probably attracts qualified privilege: s7 Defamation Act 1954; *Cook* v *Alexander* (1974); *Beach* v *Freeson* (1972).

The offer of employment

Jones is restricted in how he can act and also is receiving a payment. Accordingly this offer probably does interfere with his freedom as an MP and would be a contempt: *Case of DFS Henderson MP* (1945); *Case of WJ Brown MP* (1947).

Suggested Solution

In order for MPs to function properly they must be able to carry out their duties freely and without fear of being sued for defamation. Such protections come within the ambit of parliamentary privilege. This question raises two particular privileges as far as Jones is concerned: freedom of speech and freedom from interference. It is also in the public interest that constituents in their complaints to Members of Parliament and newspapers reporting parliamentary matters should also receive a degree of protection from the possibility of being sued for libel. This question also demands a discussion of the extent to which such persons are protected by qualified privilege.

Turning firstly to the letter to Jones from the constituent, in *R* v *Rule* (1937) the appellant wrote a letter to the MP containing defamatory statements about a police officer and a magistrate. It was held that such a letter may attract qualified privilege, ie so long as the author was not motivated by malice he could not be sued for

8 PARLIAMENTARY PRIVILEGE

defamation. Further in *Rivlin* v *Bilainkin* (1953) it was suggested that if such a letter concerned matters currently being discussed by Parliament it might be absolutely privileged. On the facts of the instant case since the allegation by the constituent is completely untrue it is difficult to see how he can be said not to be acting maliciously and, therefore, he is likely to be held liable to PC Plod.

As regards the actions by Jones, whether he is absolutely privileged depends on whether they fall within the meaning of 'proceedings in Parliament'. Clearly the question raised in the House of Commons must be a 'proceeding in Parliament' and would be privileged: *Church of Scientology* v *Smith* (1972). In the *Attorney-General for Ceylon* v *De Livera* (1963) Viscount Radcliffe stated that it was not only proceedings on the floor of the House that were covered by the expression 'proceedings in Parliament'. His Lordship considered that an MP was protected whenever he was carrying out his 'real' or 'essential' functions as an MP.

It would seem that the letter to the Minister for the Home Office would come within the 'real' or 'essential' functions of Jones and, therefore, be privileged. Support for this can be found in the *Case of GWR Strauss MP* (1957–58). In this case Strauss wrote to the Paymaster General about a nationalised industry. The Select Committee held this letter to be privileged although the matter was then referred to the full House of Commons which decided it was not privileged. However, it is now felt that it would be deemed to be privileged.

On the basis of the above, however, it is doubtful whether the letters to the Westhampton Weekly and the Community Relations Officer can be deemed 'proceedings in Parliament' and would not, therefore, be privileged.

The Daily Garble has reported a 'parliamentary proceeding' namely the question in the House. The Defamation Act 1954 preserves the right of newspapers to accurately and fairly report such proceedings. Such reporting attracts qualified privilege and, since there is no suggestion of malice by the Daily Garble, it will be protected from the defamation action by PC Plod: *Cook* v *Alexander* (1974).

Finally the offer of employment by the Equality for Immigrants Association has to be considered. Jones is to be paid £5,000 for always supporting measures that further the interests of the Association. Two cases fall to be considered in deciding whether this arrangement would be in breach of the privilege against interference.

In the *Case of DFS Henderson* (1945) Henderson asked an MP for help in his negotiations with the Ministry of Agriculture. He offered to pay 100 guineas to the MP's local association if the negotiations were successful. Was this a bribe and, therefore, a contempt of Parliament? It was held that since the payment was not to the MP personally and also because the MP's permission to make such a payment was sought beforehand that there was no contempt. However, such a practice was deemed to be generally objectionable. And in the *Case of WJ Brown* (1947) the MP had been elected General Secretary of the Civil Service Union on condition that it did *not* affect his political independence and that he did *not* have to represent the views of the union. Brown fell out with the Union who voted to remove him as its General Secretary. Brown complained that the Union was trying to interfere with his independence as an MP and was, therefore, in contempt. It was held that Brown had voluntarily placed himself in his position and the actions of the Union could not amount to a contempt.

CONSTITUTIONAL LAW

In Jones' case he clearly is receiving a direct payment and, further, is limiting his political independence because he would have to vote in support of measures in the interests of the EIA whether he agreed with them or not. It is likely, therefore, that the Speaker would report him to the Committee of Privileges if he accepted the employment and that he would be held to be in contempt. Whilst the Committee has powers to expel and fine Members of Parliament it is often the case that MPs are let off with little more than a stern warning.

QUESTION THREE

Bulldog is a Member of Parliament. He received unsolicited mail from several constituents alleging that a company operating in the constituency had been guilty of gross negligence resulting in financial loss to those constituents. Bulldog raised the matter with the company but received no satisfactory response. He then raised the question of the company's negligence during a debate in the House of Commons. He also sent copies of the letters of complaint to the responsible Minister and had a meeting with that Minister at the Minister's private home during which Bulldog again accused the company of negligence. Bulldog also raised the matter at a public meeting in his constituency. He has since found out that the allegations were not true and has received a letter from the company's solicitors alleging defamation.

To what extent will the doctrine of parliamentary privilege protect him against the threatened defamation action?

Written by the Editors

General Comment

A question requiring the student to identify whether each of the three situations in which Bulldog makes the false allegation against the company can be deemed a 'proceeding in Parliament' so as to come with the parliamentary privilege of freedom of speech and, accordingly, amount to a full defence to an action for defamation.

Skeleton Solution

- Open by explaining what parliamentary privilege is and its legal effect, dealing in particular with the particular privilege of freedom of speech.
- Explain the importance and meaning of 'proceeding in Parliament'.
- Go on to consider each of the situations in which the alleged defamatory remarks have been made and conclude whether or not they are covered by privilege.

Suggested Solution

At the beginning of a parliamentary session the Speaker of the House of Commons claims for Parliament and all its members all those 'ancient and undoubted rights and privileges' that Parliament has traditionally enjoyed. These privileges include such matters as freedom from civil arrest and freedom to regulate Parliament's internal affairs (eg the ordinary licensing laws of the country do not apply inside Parliament – see: *R v Graham-Campbell, ex parte Herbert* (1935). However the most important of these privileges is freedom of speech in debates and other 'proceedings in Parliament'. What is covered by the privilege cannot be called into question in any

8 PARLIAMENTARY PRIVILEGE

court outside Parliament. Parliament itself has its own Committee on Privileges which can take its members to task if the privilege is abused. But no-one outside Parliament can bring an action for defamation against a Member of Parliament if what he says comes within the ambit of a 'proceeding in Parliament'. This has been defined as applying whenever a Member of Parliament is carrying out his 'real or essential functions' as an MP (see *Attorney-General for Ceylon* v *De Livera* (1963)). This question demands an examination of each of the occasions that Bulldog made the false allegation in order to see whether all or any of those occasions can be properly regarded as 'a proceeding in Parliament' so as to attract the defence of parliamentary privilege.

As regards the letters from the constituents it appears from the case of *Rivlin* v *Bilainkin* (1953) that since the letters do not concern parliamentary proceedings they cannot attract absolute privilege but they can attract qualified privilege (see *R* v *Rule* (1937). Accordingly unless the company can show malice then the writers are protected from an action of defamation against them for passing the accusation on to Bulldog and, further, Bulldog would be protected when passing the accusation on by sending the letters to the Minister.

Bulldog raises the matter again on the floor of the House during a parliamentary debate. This is clearly 'a proceeding in Parliament' and would be absolutely privileged (see: *Church of Scientology* v *Johnson-Smith* (1972). But what about the repetition of the allegation outside Parliament at the Minister's house? As indicated above the case of *Attorney-General for Ceylon* v *De Livera* makes it clear that the privilege is not confined to proceedings within the House of Parliament. Since he is reporting a matter of public concern to the responsible minister I consider that it would be held to be a situation where Bulldog is carrying out his 'real' or 'essential' role as an MP, and would be deemed a 'proceeding in Parliament' and, therefore, absolutely privileged.

Lastly we have to consider the repetition of the allegation at the public meeting in Bulldog's constituency. It is extremely doubtful that such meeting could be described as a 'proceeding in Parliament'. His remarks would, therefore, attract neither absolute nor qualified privilege. He may have the defence of fair comment but I would advise him to offer a public apology to the company as soon as possible in the hope that a financially damaging action for defamation may thereby be avoided.

QUESTION FOUR

'The sole justification for the present privileges of the House of Commons is that they are essential for the conduct of its business and the maintenance of its authority.' (Sir Barnett Cocks)

Discuss.

University of London LLB Examination
(for External Students) Constitutional Law June 1989 Q3

General Comment

An essay question requiring a critical discussion of how far parliamentary privileges are justified today.

CONSTITUTIONAL LAW

Skeleton Solution

- Introduction – original necessity for privilege and examples of privileges.
- Examine privileges in detail pointing out whether they remain essential – freedom of speech, freedom from civil arrest, right to regulate composition and proceedings and to punish those in contempt or breach of privilege.
- Conclusion.

Suggested Solution

Many of the privileges of Parliament have their origins in the sixteenth and seventeenth centuries at a time when the House of Commons was striving to prove its independence and to prevent interference with its members and proceedings by the Monarch and others outside Parliament. The privileges were originally developed to safeguard the position of MPs individually and that of the House as a whole. Today the privileges established during these centuries still exist but a select committee in 1967 commented that some were no longer required as they had become obsolete and suggested reforms, which have still not been implemented.

At the beginning of each new Parliament the Speaker claims 'ancient and undoubted privileges' which consist of freedom of speech in debate, freedom from civil arrest and freedom of access via the Speaker to the Sovereign. The Commons also enjoys privileges in its corporate capacity such as the right to regulate its own composition, the right to take exclusive cognisance of matters arising within the precincts of the House and the right to punish both Members and non-members for breach of privilege and contempt.

Perhaps the most important of the privileges of the Commons is that of freedom of speech. It was enshrined in the Constitution by article 9 of the Bill of Rights 1688 and provides 'Freedom of Speech and debates or proceedings in Parliament should not be questioned in any court or place outside of Parliament.' Practically this means that no criminal prosecution can be launched nor can any civil action for defamation be commenced in respect of words uttered or written during 'debates and proceedings in Parliament.' There is debate over the meaning of the phrase 'proceedings in Parliament' (*Strauss* case (1957–58)) but it seems that for anything said in the House in the course of Parliamentary business (such as debates or committee hearings etc) the MP has immunity. Potentially MPs could abuse this privilege by knowingly making false statements in the House but it was considered that this danger was outweighed by the public interest in ensuring that MPs could speak freely when carrying out Parliamentary business. It should be noted that if an MP does abuse his privilege it is open to the House itself to punish him for contempt of Parliament or to expel him from the House as unfit (*Allighan* (1947)).

The privilege of freedom of speech also prevents those outside Parliament attempting to dictate to MPs how they should speak in debate and/or vote. Although it is acknowledged that MPs may maintain business and other interests outside Parliament there is a register of Members' interests in which each MP is supposed to declare his other activities. Article 9 has been used to stop such outside commitments being used to force an MP into a particular course of action in the Chamber (*Yorkshire Area Council of the National Union of Mineworkers* case (1975)).

8 PARLIAMENTARY PRIVILEGE

In these ways the privilege of freedom of speech remains important to the Houses of Parliament.

By contrast the privilege of freedom from civil arrest is obsolete and is long overdue for repeal. It provides that for the forty days before, during a session and for the forty days after it an MP may not be subject to civil (not criminal) arrest. Although this was needed when the usual method of enforcing a debt was to incarcerate the debtor in a debtors' prison which, in the absence of the immunity, could have effectively disenfranchised large numbers of voters it is no longer required when arrest in civil proceedings is rare indeed.

Freedom of access via the speaker to the sovereign is today merely a formality but the Common's powers to regulate its own composition and internal proceedings remain relevant. Election petitions are no longer determined by the Commons itself, but by an election court made up of High Court judges, but the Commons still determines when to move a writ for a by election to fill any vacancies which arise. It may also declare that a member is unfit and expel him from the House. The House regulates its own proceedings and the courts will not take cognisance of these procedures even when these conflict with statute as in *Bradlaugh* v *Gossett* (1884), where an MP was refused permission by the Commons to make his oath of allegiance in a form permitted by statute. The court's refusal to interfere in Parliament's internal procedure is exemplified in *Pickin* v *British Railways Board* (1974) where the fact that notices had apparently not been given by promoters of a private Bill so as to satisfy orders of the House of Lords did not lead to the invalidity of the Act of Parliament subsequently passed. This attitude is one aspect of the doctrine of Parliamentary sovereignty and there has been criticism of the fact that the courts do not intervene in such cases.

One aspect of Parliament's right to regulate its own conduct is its jurisdiction to punish breach of privilege and contempt of Parliament. Breach of privileges, consists of abuse of privilege by a member or of any conduct by any one MP or non member which interferes with one of the privileges of Parliament. Contempt is a wider concept and consists of conduct which tends to bring the House into disrepute or detract from its dignity. Whether the offence is breach of privilege or contempt, the penal powers of the House are the same. Members may be reprimanded or admonished by the Speaker or Members may be suspended or expelled. Officials of the House may be dismissed or a Member or stranger may be committed to prison for the duration of the Parliamentary Session. The Select Committee on Parliamentary Privileges recommended that the punitive powers of the Commons and Lords be curtailed and although no such reform has been formally made, in practice the Commons seems reluctant to do more than give a reprimand to outsiders found to be in contempt (even where as in 1986 the Committee of Privileges had recommended that a lobby correspondent be expelled for six months with his paper, The Times, being allowed no substitute for that period). The most severe penalty it uses in respect of MPs is suspension.

The procedure by which complaints of breach of privilege or contempt of Parliament are made is open to criticism. At present a Member may complain to the Speaker and the Speaker may refer the matter to a Committee of Privileges. This committee can compel attendance of witnesses and production of documents. Failure to comply

CONSTITUTIONAL LAW

is a contempt. The Select Committee on Parliamentary Privileges in 1967 recommended that persons directly concerned in the Committee's investigation should have the right to attend the hearings, make submissions, call and examine witnesses. Also legal aid, with leave of the Committee, should be granted. These recommendations were not implemented.

Furthermore even when the Committee of Privileges has reached its conclusion on the evidence that decision is not binding on the House which may reject it (eg *Strauss* (1957–58)). This state of affairs can hardly be justified in cases where the Commons might take a harsher point of view without hearing the evidence. However normally the Commons as a whole take a more lenient view than the Committee.

It does seem that this area is ripe for reform but such reform is unlikely to materialise in the near future as it is not seen by political parties as a priority.

QUESTION FIVE

What reforms, if any, should be made to the privileges of the House of Commons?

University of London LLB Examination
(for External Students) Constitutional Law June 1991 Q5

General Comment

It is desirable to set out the main privileges and then deal with the more significant privileges in detail. Most of the answer will be concerned with the privilege of free speech as this is currently the most contentious. In some cases it is desirable to point out that privileges need not be reformed because they are not being abused in practice.

Skeleton Solution

- List the main privileges.
- Explain freedom of speech, possible abuses, reform of its scope.
- Consider freedom from arrest; little need for this any more.
- Other privileges considered briefly.

Suggested Solution

The principal privileges claimed from the Crown for the Commons are freedom of speech in debate, freedom from arrest, freedom of access to Her Majesty whenever occasion shall require, the right to have the most favourable construction placed upon all their proceedings, the right of the House to regulate its own composition, the right to take exclusive cognisance of matters arising within the precincts of the House, the right to punish both Members and non-members for breach of privilege and contempt, and the right of impeachment.

a) *Freedom of speech*

Freedom of speech is of fundamental importance to the freedom and indeed the power of Parliament. If Members could be attacked by the public or the Executive

8 PARLIAMENTARY PRIVILEGE

for speaking their minds they might be so intimidated as not to be able to carry out their deliberative and legislative functions properly. The right is guaranteed in article 9 of the Bill of Rights 1688 which provides:

'The freedom of speech and debates or proceedings in Parliament ought not to be impeached or questioned in any court or place out of Parliament.'

The effect of article 9 is that no Member may be made liable in the courts for words spoken in the course of parliamentary proceedings. If a Member were to be sued for defamation in respect of something said during the course of parliamentary proceedings, the writ should be struck out as declaring no cause of action. If the matter did come to trial the court must hold that the Member is protected by absolute privilege in the law of defamation. This protection extends to both civil and criminal liability. Nor can what is said in Parliament be used to support a cause of action in defamation which has arisen outside Parliament; see *Church of Scientology* v *Johnson-Smith* (1972).

It has not been seriously suggested that this particular parliamentary privilege be removed, but reliance upon it by Members has from time to time been criticised. The danger is that Members will make statements in the House under the cloak of privilege that they would not dream of repeating outside. The reputations of others can be damaged without any right of compensation. The MP Geoffrey Dickins was heavily criticised when he threatened to reveal the name of a doctor who had allegedly raped an eight year old girl, but against whom the police had declined to take proceedings due to lack of evidence. As was pointed out, the danger in such cases is that the individual named may have his career ruined by such statements, without ever having been convicted of the alleged offence in a court of law. It is submitted that such abuses of privilege are best dealt with, not by reforming the scope of the privilege, but by relying upon the Speaker of the House to properly regulate the conduct of debate in the House. It is conceded, however, that one aspect of this privilege that could be clarified is the scope of the expression 'proceedings in Parliament'. Remarks made in debate, discussions in Committee, Parliamentary Questions and Answers, and votes are clearly within the definition. Other words spoken within the precincts of Parliament unconnected with parliamentary proceedings are not protected. There are 'grey areas' however, as illustrated by the so-called 'Strauss affair' (1957–58), which concerned a letter written by Strauss, a Labour MP, to the Paymaster General complaining about the way in which the London Electricity Board disposed of their scrap cable. The Paymaster General denied responsibility on the ground that the matter concerned day to day administration rather than policy, and he passed the letter to the Board. The Board took exception to Strauss' allegations and threatened to sue him for libel unless he withdrew and apologised. Strauss raised the threat as a question of privilege and the matter was referred to the Committee of Privileges. The Committee reported that in writing his letter Strauss was engaged in a proceeding in Parliament for the purposes of article 9 and that the Board, in threatening to sue, were in breach of parliamentary privilege. However when the Report of the Committee was debated in the House, on a free vote it rejected the findings of the Committee. The House resolved that Strauss' letter was not a proceeding in Parliament. See further *Rost* v *Edwards* (1990).

CONSTITUTIONAL LAW

b) *Freedom from arrest*

Immunity from arrest is now of little importance and in 1967 the Committee on Parliamentary Privilege appointed to review the law of parliamentary privilege recommended its abolition. The immunity only applies to civil arrest and extends not only while Parliament sits, but also for 40 days before and after. The immunity does not protect Members from arrest on criminal charges, nor from detention under regulations made under the Defence of the Realm Acts in time of war. In 1940, for example, the Commons Committee of Privileges was of opinion that there had been no breach of privilege when Captain Ramsay, a Member, had been detained under regulations made under the Emergency Powers (Defence) Act 1939. There is little basis for the continued existence of the privilege.

c) *The right of the House to regulate its own composition*

Within the scope of this privilege fall a number of matters which are important as matters of principle, but which are of little significance in everyday terms. The privilege, which encompasses the right to determine disputed elections, the right to determine by resolution when a writ for the holding of a by-election shall be issued, the right to determine whether a Member is qualified to sit in the House, and the right to expel a Member whom it considers unfit to sit, has been used sparingly. Provided these powers are not used oppressively, it is submitted that they are not in need of any substantive reform.

d) *The right to punish for breach of privilege and contempt*

The House has the power to maintain its privileges and to punish those who break them or commit contempt of the House. All breaches of privilege are contempts of the House but not all contempts involve the infringement of the existing privileges of the House. Contempt of the House is a very wide concept. Perhaps the most questionable aspect of this system is the fact that the House sits as victim, prosecutor and judge when dealing with offenders. It is noteworthy that in proceedings before the European Commission on Human Rights it was held that the jurisdiction of the Maltese House of Representatives, to punish those alleged to have been in breach of its privileges, contravened article 6 para 1 of the European Convention on Human Rights.

QUESTION SIX

Critically assess the respective roles of the House of Commons and the courts in regulating Parliamentary privilege.

University of London LLB Examination
(for External Students) Constitutional Law June 1993 Q8(b)

General Comment

A wide-ranging question, requiring the examinee to look at privilege from the angles of the House of Commons (by character prejudiced angles) and of the courts (by character independent angles). But assessment of those angles should take place in the context of the historical development of privilege, which at least gives a kind of rational basis to Parliament's exclusive claims in several important areas. Critical analysis should be supported by reference to appropriate academic research.

Skeleton Solution

- Definition of parliamentary privilege and problems of control.
- Internal proceedings of the House and risk of abuse of collective power.
- Roles of Speaker and Privileges Committee.
- Manner of hearing for alleged contemnors.
- Scope of privilege of free speech under article 9 Bill of Rights 1688.
- Internal discipline and absence of judicial review.
- Vagueness of concept of 'proceedings in Parliament' and case for and against codification.

(Other reform proposals are considered at appropriate points during the solution.)

Suggested Solution

Parliamentary privilege is part of the common law which grants certain exemptions from the law to MPs in order that they may perform their functions. By its nature privilege is difficult to subject to normal processes of parliamentary and judicial review. There is the added complication that parliamentary privilege was won after an historic conflict between the legislature and an absolute monarchy (the latter at times supported by the judges). This explains the traditional sensitivity of the relationship between the legislature and the judiciary on the matter of privilege, raising fears for the Rule of Law.

Dicey argued for equality under the law, but the internal proceedings of the House of Commons are not subject to judicial review. Control, if any, must be exercised by the Commons itself, principally through the Speaker and the select committee on parliamentary privilege. The danger is that the House, collectively, may act as judge and jury in its own cause on a matter concerning an individual MP's rights to represent the constituency which elected him, eg as in the House's expulsion for political reasons of the radical Charles Bradlaugh: *Bradlaugh* v *Gossett* (1884). Since no judicial review is available over such a decision, the only remedy for an expelled member is to petition the House which expelled him: *Case of the Sheriffs of Middlesex* (1840).

The House also claims exclusive rights to punish 'strangers' (non-MPs) for breaches of MPs' individual privileges and for contempt of the whole House. These are dealt with either by rulings from the Speaker or by reference to the Committee of Privileges, consisting of 15 MPs from all parties chosen for their expertise in parliamentary law and their long experience of the life of the Commons. But MPs not on the Committee as well as academic observers, have expressed fears about the degree of discretion delegated to the Speaker and the Committee by the whole House. The methods used to deal with 'offenders' are far removed from 'due process of law'.

For example, the accused may be arrested by the Sergeant-at-Arms (the enforcement officer of the House) and brought before a private hearing of the Committee. The accused has no right to legal representation and may be cross-examined by a panel of QCs. The accused has no right to call evidence or to cross-examine the witnesses against him. The Committee reports to the whole House on whether the offence is proven and, if so, what penalty (including, in theory, imprisonment) should be imposed. There is no right of appeal to the courts against conviction or sentence and no opportunity for judicial review over the way the decision was reached.

It is not surprising that authorities such as the late Professor de Smith condemned privilege hearings as a 'travesty of justice' in which biased MPs acted as judges in their own cause. He argued cogently that, with a modern independent judiciary, such privileges were not necessary and that the House's jurisdiction over punishable contempts and breaches of privilege should be transferred to the courts so that these matters are subject to due process of law.

Similarly it has been argued that the House no longer needs the absolute rights to freedom of speech granted in respect of 'proceedings in Parliament' by article 9 of the Bill of Rights 1688. Such freedom has the potential to become a licence to defame, to be used irresponsibly by publicity-seeking members. Whilst the House, through the Speaker, has the power under its internal standing orders to discipline members who abuse the right, it appears that the House has been very reluctant to exercise such discipline, at least over an MP who criticises the conduct of outsiders. When an MP criticises the behaviour or integrity of a fellow MP this is usually taken more seriously and the speaker will demand a retraction and issue warnings about the need for 'parliamentary language in respect of the honourable members of this House'. Some MPs, eg Labour MPs Brian Sedgemore and Tam Dalyell in the 1980s, were suspended from sittings of the House because of their refusals to retract accusations against particular MPs (who were also Government Ministers).

Patricia Leopold ([1981] PL 30) suggests that the House should introduce new safeguards on this matter, eg new conventions which oblige MPs to give advance notice to the person they intend to criticise, and to use all other methods to establish the truth of particular rumours/allegations before ventilating them under the cover of privilege. Others have argued that the absolute privilege under article 9 should be replaced by the defence of qualified privilege, giving MPs the same degree of protection as given to everyone else by the law of defamation.

In the absence of such reform judicial control will be haphazard and uncertain, mainly because of the difficulty of defining precise limits to the concept of 'proceedings in Parliament': see the inability of the Judicial Committee of the Privy Council to reach a decided view on this point in the reference arising from the *Strauss* case (1957–58). Only a bold judge would feel able to give the benefit of any doubt to the citizen when faced with a claim to privilege, eg Popplewell J in declaring that the register of MPs' Interests was not privileged in *Rost* v *Edwards* (1990). Miss Leopold ([1990] PL 475) commends this 'robust' attitude but argues that the matter is too important to be left to haphazard development of the common law, contending that the area of privilege requires codification on lines of Australia's Parliamentary Proceedings Act 1987. However, although codification might end the uncertainty of judicial review, a jealous and suspicious Parliament might also take the opportunity to define its privileges as widely as possible, leaving no chance for judges to give the kind of decision Popplewell J gave in *Rost* v *Edwards*.

9 THE EXECUTIVE

9.1　Introduction
9.2　Key points
9.3　Recent developments
9.4　Analysis of questions
9.5　Questions

9.1 Introduction

The Executive includes the monarchy, ministers, central government, the Civil Service, armed forces and the police. The monarchy is bound by convention and executive functions are largely exercised by ministers. With the advent of the Cabinet, policies decided by government form the basis of legislation passed by Parliament. The Prime Minister enjoys enormous powers because of his position as head of the Cabinet.

9.2 Key points

a) *The Prime Minister*

   i) Formal position of the Prime Minister
   - The office of Prime Minister is a de facto institution recognised by statute but governed mainly by convention.
   - The office of Prime Minister is invariably held together with the office of First Lord of the Treasury: Ministerial and Other Salaries Act 1975.
   - On the creation of the Civil Service Department in 1968 the Prime Minister became Minister for the Civil Service.

   ii) Choosing a Prime Minister
   - The choice of Prime Minister is a matter for the Queen alone in the exercise of the Sovereign's personal prerogative.
   - By convention however the Queen should choose that person who is able to command the support of the majority in the House of Commons.

   iii) Functions of the Prime Minister
   - Formation of the government: Ministers are appointed by the Queen on the advice of the Prime Minister. All ministers must be or become members of one or other House of Parliament. There may be up to 95 holders of ministerial office in the House of Commons: House of Commons Disqualification Act 1975.
   - Formation of the Cabinet: The choice of Conservative Cabinet is a matter entirely in the Prime Minister's discretion, although his choice will be influenced by political expediency. The Labour Shadow Cabinet is elected.

- Presiding over Cabinet meetings: The Prime Minister presides over full Cabinet meetings and also over meetings of the most important committees of the Cabinet. The Prime Minister decides the agenda for Cabinet meetings and controls discussion within the Cabinet. At the conclusion of a Cabinet meeting no formal vote is taken on the policy decided; it is for the Prime Minister to sum up the consensus opinion. The Cabinet Secretariat is directly responsible to the Prime Minister and the allocation of functions between Cabinet, committees of the Cabinet and individual departments is controlled by him.
- The organisation and control of central government: The Prime Minister decides how government functions should be allocated between departments and may create, amalgamate or abolish government departments. The Prime Minister may also take an interest in the affairs of particular departments and intervene personally in major issues and take decisions without consulting Cabinet.
- Powers of patronage: By convention the Prime Minister advises the Queen on the granting of peerages and other honours and on appointments to certain high offices of state.
- Advising the Sovereign: The Prime Minister is the main channel of communication between the Cabinet and the Sovereign, and it is his duty to keep the Queen informed on matters of State.
- Presentation and defence of government policy: Prime Minister's interventions in debate always attract media attention. The Prime Minister also controls government communications and the dissemination of information.

b) *The Cabinet*

   i) Composition of the Cabinet

   The number of ministers in the Cabinet is the sole choice of the Prime Minister. Usually it comprises between 18 and 23 members. The composition of the Cabinet is also a matter for the Prime Minister's discretion. However by convention and custom certain ministers are always members of the Cabinet.

   ii) Conventions relating to Cabinet government
   - The Queen must act on the advice of Her Ministers.
   - The Cabinet must always tender unanimous advice.
   - The Cabinet must obtain and maintain a majority in the House of Commons on all major matters of policy.
   - The Cabinet must produce a 'Queen's Speech' at the opening of each session of Parliament, stating the legislation which it proposes during that session.
   - The 'mandate' doctrine requires the government's statement in the Queen's speech to be consistent with the policy on which they were elected.

   iii) Cabinet committees

   A complicated system of Cabinet committees exists to facilitate the discussion and formulation of policy options and to co-ordinate the activities of the various government departments, with regard to policy.

    iv) The Cabinet Secretariat

In 1917 a Secretary to the Cabinet was appointed to service Cabinet and Cabinet committee meetings, take minutes and circulate details of conclusions reached in Cabinet. The Secretariat is headed by the Permanent Secretary to the Cabinet Office who is directly responsible to the Prime Minister.

    v) Prime Minister's Policy Unit

The Prime Minister maintains a Policy Unit in Downing Street, independent of the Cabinet Office.

    vi) Cabinet secrecy

As all ministers must support government policy it is desirable that the process by which such policy decisions are made be kept secret, unless the Prime Minister decides otherwise, therefore secrecy is attached to discussions in Cabinet, Cabinet papers and the proceedings of Cabinet committees.

c) *Prime ministerial or Cabinet government?*

    i) The Cabinet is the engine house of government. Administrative action is co-ordinated and legislative initiatives sanctioned in the Cabinet. Cabinet can therefore exert significant control over Parliament.

However, the special position enjoyed by the Prime Minister has led some authorities to the conclusion that Cabinet government has now given way to Prime Ministerial government.

A Prime Minister is, however, dependent on the support of Cabinet members which once withdrawn makes continued office untenable. This was the position when Margaret Thatcher resigned following the party vote on the leadership contest. It had originally been her intention to continue to the final ballot but she was advised against this action by ministers.

    ii) The power of Prime Minister relative to the Cabinet depends upon several factors:

- The personality of the particular Prime Minister.
- The standing of the Prime Minister both in Parliament and in the Party.
- Whether the Prime Minister is minded to take full advantage of the conventional powers available to the holder of the office.

d) *Collective responsibility*

The doctrine of collective responsibility involves two rules:

    i) The rule that the government must resign if it loses the support of the House of Commons.

The Prime Minister and his ministers are collectively responsible to Parliament for the conduct of national affairs. If the Prime Minister loses support in Parliament he must resign or seek a dissolution of Parliament.

ii) The rule that the government must speak with one voice.
- All members of the government share in the collective responsibility of the government, and ministers may not publicly criticise or dissociate themselves from the government policy.
- A Cabinet Minister who feels unable to agree with his colleagues should resign.
- The rule is closely related to that of Cabinet secrecy. As all ministers must support government policy it is desirable that the process by which such policy decisions are made be kept secret.
- The rule increases party discipline and unity within the government and also serves to strengthen the authority of the Prime Minister in relation to his colleagues.

e) *Agreements to differ*

Occasionally it may be politically impossible for the Cabinet to maintain a collective front.

i) The National Government 1932: The Liberal members of the National Government only agreed to remain in the government on condition that they were allowed to speak and vote against it on the question of the imposition of tariffs.

ii) The Labour Government 1975: The Labour Cabinet 'agreed to differ' on the question of the United Kingdom's continued membership of the European Community.

f) *Individual responsibility*

Ministers are responsible to Parliament for their own actions, omissions and mistakes as well as for those of the officials in their departments. Normally criticism should be directed at the minister rather than at any civil servant who may be at fault. This principle is said to help preserve the anonymity, and therefore the objectivity and efficiency, of the Civil Service.

i) Ministerial responsibility for departmental maladministration

Two questions arise from the minister's departmental responsibility:
- Is the minister obliged to accept responsibility for every piece of maladministration within his department?
- If maladministration is found to have occurred is the minister under a duty to resign?

ii) Situations in which a minister must accept responsibility

In a debate on the Crichel Down Affair 1954, the Home Secretary stated his views as to when a minister must accept responsibility and not blame his civil servants:
- A minister must protect a civil servant who has carried out his explicit orders.
- A minister must defend a civil servant who acts properly in accordance with the policy laid down by the minister.

- Where an official makes a mistake or causes some delay, but not on an important issue of policy and not where a claim to individual rights is seriously involved, the minister acknowledges the mistake and he accepts the responsibility although he is not personally involved.
- Where action has been taken by a civil servant of which the minister disapproves and has no previous knowledge, and the conduct of the official is reprehensible, there is no obligation on a minister to endorse what he believes to be wrong or to defend what are clearly shown to be errors of his officers. He remains, however, constitutionally responsible to Parliament for the fact that something has gone wrong, but this does not affect his power to control and discipline his staff.

iii) Is there a duty to resign?

There is no suggestion that a minister has to resign if he does accept responsibility. Whether a minister has to resign or not depends upon a variety of political factors including:

- the temperament of the minister;
- the attitude of the Prime Minister; and
- the mood of the party and the tone of the Opposition.

Note the recent tendency to confine responsibility to 'policy' rather than 'operation' of policy.

g) *The courts and ministerial responsibility*

While the courts cannot enforce the convention of ministerial responsibility they are prepared to acknowledge its existence: *Carltona Ltd* v *Commissioners of Works* [1943] 2 All ER 560.

9.3 Recent developments

An up-to-date knowledge of political affairs as they affect the role of the Prime Minister and government ministers is important.

The resignation of Prime Minister John Major, thus precipitating a leadership election in which he successfully stood, in an attempt to silence a faction within the party who were constantly challenging his style of leadership and his position on Europe.

The Scott Enquiry Report, due to be published in 1996.

9.4 Analysis of questions

Questions are essay type and often test students' knowledge of the conventions of ministerial responsibility. A good understanding of the function of Parliament and accountability of government is required.

9.5 Questions

QUESTION ONE

'Parliamentary experience of recent years has demonstrated that collectively Members (of the House of Commons) can exercise the political will necessary to provide the

CONSTITUTIONAL LAW

parameters within which the Government can govern, albeit of necessity in a limited and generally negative way.' (Norton)

Discuss.

University of London LLB Examination
(for External Students) Constitutional Law June 1990 Q1

General Comment

A difficult question that requires students to identify ways in which MPs can influence and hold to account the government.

Skeleton Solution

Parliamentary accountability – the extent to which government is truly accountable for its actions:

- conventions of accountability;
- committee system;
- ombudsman;
- Debate, question time.

Conclusion: separation of powers; Legislature's control over the Executive.

Suggested Solution

The starting point of the constitution is the representation of the electorate in Parliament, which is the supreme and sovereign law maker. Developed from this is the notion that the electorate thereby makes its preferred choice of government. However, for obvious practical reasons, elections cannot be held every year, nor can referendums be held on all points of importance that arise during a government's term of office. Thus, the accountability of government directly to the electorate is only periodic and it is this situation that gives rise to the fear of the possibility of an 'elective dictatorship', with a carte blanche to govern in whichever way it pleases for the term of its office.

To a certain extent this is an ill founded fear since the final reckoning will ultimately come with the dissolution of Parliament. Of more concern, however, is the situation that arises where, for the most part, a government's policies and style of government finds general approval, but where particular measures are potentially constitutionally threatening.

In such circumstances, government becomes indirectly accountable to the representatives of the electorate in Parliament and as such Parliament is termed the 'watchdog' of Executive action. Since the Commons is the elected chamber and the focus of most political activity, without dismissing the important work of the Lords, it must clearly be the area where the ground rules of governmental activity are laid down.

Thus in purist theory, the political arm of the Executive is collectively responsible to Parliament in general and to the House of Commons in particular. The idiomatic traditions of Parliament provide the forum for the supervision of government. The

9 THE EXECUTIVE

experience of recent years has brought much attention to bear on how effective these complex constraints and restrictions are when the Commons is effectively dominated by the party that holds office.

Before considering in detail the general parliamentary restrictions on government activity, it must be made clear that the mere fact that a party commands a majority in the House does not guarantee a majority of votes. Even where the whip system that urges members to comply is in strict operation, a member cannot be forcibly compelled to vote with the government. Although the price of such rebellion might be suspension from the parliamentary party, such defiance often has a profound political consequence and may be the prompt for revision of legislation when the action is taken in concert.

As well as such purely political considerations, the application of conventions relating to the accountability individually and collectively of ministers establishes a further set of checks which are enforced through Parliament. The intense political embarrassment caused by ministerial or departmental misfeasance usually finds its focus in parliamentary questions or debates, where, on serious issues, the choice of either a convincing explanation or resignation is expected to be forthcoming.

Similarly, where decisions are made at Cabinet level, ministers are held collectively to account to Parliament. As De Smith observes, if a minister dissents he should resign first, and then publicly distance himself from the subject in contention. However, the purist theory lacks a little in substance, since a suspension of the convention is possible and the government attitude seems to be enshrined not a little in Mr Callaghan's remark that ' ... I certainly think the doctrine should apply, except in cases where I announce that it does not.' This indeed indicates the extent of the 'flexibility' of our unwritten constitution.

Parliament, if it feels so inclined, may censure the government with a motion of no confidence where the government is held to be collectively responsible. Of convention, such a motion, if it were successful, would prompt the resignation of the government. In recent years, however, Mrs Thatcher was censured on specific issues without subsequently leaving office. Once again it is the 'flexible' constitution at work. The significance of such a motion is to be viewed more in terms of a political tactic and a method of attracting media attention.

A more direct and effective control of government is the need for parliamentary approval for the financing of government initiatives. Since Parliament holds the country's purse strings, the government must inspire enough confidence in the Commons, at least to provide funding for new policies. The structure of government finance is necessarily complex, but the parliamentary system is structured so as to cope with these rigours. Central to this system is the Public Accounts Committee, which, although reflecting the parliamentary representation of the parties, has such a non-partisan reputation that it is, by convention, chaired by a member of the Opposition. Although it primarily seeks out financial irregularities, it also monitors extravagant spending and imprudent contractual transactions.

Extensive powers of discovery and enquiry were conferred on the Treasury and Civil Service Committee, which was set up in 1979, to the extent that scrutinising Treasury policy is within the Committee's brief. In such ways Parliament tacitly defines the parameters within which the Executive can finance its policies.

Aside from these financial controls, the standing orders and procedures of the Commons provide adequate opportunities for confrontation of the government by the opposition and their own back benchers on contentious issues. Debating opportunities on the Queen's speech, budget and on Opposition Days, motions of censure and others and emergency debates take on more significance with the eye of the country fixed on television.

The committee system now mirrors the departmental organisation of central government with the setting up of Select Committees to examine the expenditure, administration and policy of various designated government departments. Their powers are the same as those of the Treasury and Civil Service Committee and are brought together under the auspices of the Liaison Committee. The force of the House's authority and powers to punish for contempt are behind these committees.

The teeth of the Defence Select Committee were tested during the 'Westland Affair' (1986) when it sought to discover the names of civil servants who were responsible for the leaking of a letter from the Solicitor General. Although the government achieved a compromise, the Committee never conceded that in law there were any governmental restraints on the exercise of its functions.

The Departmental Select Committee system is generally regarded as a forum for more in-depth and informed discussion than is available elsewhere in Parliament. Furthermore, their unanimous, but often powerfully critical reports, such as that of the Foreign Affairs Committee on government proposals to raise fees for overseas university students, have certainly had effects on Executive policy. However, the paucity of free debating time means that only a handful of the reports have had full discussion on the floor of the House of Commons.

Parliament's role as the arena for airing criticism of the government has been significantly augmented by the advent of television cameras. Certainly the parliamentary proceeding that most captivates the imagination of the electorate is Question Time, when the government at least appears to be under the most stringent attack. The extent to which the request for oral or written answers to questions to any minister is actually laying down the parameters of government, rather than political point scoring, is somewhat questionable. However, it is clear that the electoral fortunes of a party or MP may be decided in the cut and thrust of these brief sessions, something of which the government is clearly aware. However, De Smith's view that 'a question to a minister is rather a method of ventilating a grievance than of securing a remedy' is perhaps the most realistic approach.

In addition to the practical limitations of parliamentary questions as a method of scrutinising the government, certain questions may be refused if they lie outside the sphere of competence of a minister. Answers may not be forthcoming if the matter is sub judice, or simply because an answer would cost more than £250, the current ceiling for expenditure on parliamentary answers.

A final method available to members to ensure the maintenance of the standards of government is by directing the Parliamentary Commissioner for Administration to investigate alleged maladministration. However, this function is one that is seldom exercised collectively, and therefore merits no detailed discussion.

Thus, having explored the way in which members might scrutinise the Executive, we must assess the truth of Norton's assertions. In our parliamentary system, strong reliance is placed upon adherence to conventions. The effect of disapproving motions relating to conventions of responsibility cannot be denied; resignations in the 1988–89 parliamentary session underline this. However, the change in attitude towards, for example, the motion of censure, demonstrates that reliance on convention as a method of Executive control is unsatisfactory, particularly when a government commands a sizeable majority in the Commons.

Equally, there are limits on the extent to which control of the government can be exercised by intermittent rebellions of back bench members, who stand to lose their status within the parliamentary party and with the electorate.

Financial control holds out the most practical promise as delineating the parameters of government, but once again is subject to the control of the majority party in the House, which is almost always subject to strict party discipline.

It is therefore in the arena of the debating floor and during Question Time, which, due to its high media profile, is of great significance in terms of public opinion, that the democratic check on the executive finds its strongest weapon. Where MPs collectively know that public opinion supports them against government policy, even back benchers of the party in power may find a reservoir of courage to criticise and rebel.

Conversely, the committee system is increasingly being regarded as the part of the Commons where much of the serious work goes on. With its smaller and more informed membership, and its greater opportunities for detailed and lengthy scrutiny, as well as the tendency of committees to be less partisan or concerned with political point scoring, this forum has become in many ways a powerhouse of the democratic process. Opportunities exist not only to criticise, but to make searching enquiries of the way in which the process of government is carried on.

It is difficult to envisage, however, what Norton's conception of a positive way of providing the parameters within which government can govern would amount to. Obviously, the doctrine of the separation of powers prevents excessive interference by the legislature in Executive functions. Thus, the positive function of members must be to maintain and enforce the constitutional safeguards against abuse of Executive power. Since these safeguards are largely in the nature of conventions, then following the general view that they are adhered to since their breach would result in political embarrassment, Parliament's only significant function is to heighten the electorate's awareness of government threats to the constitution. It is arguable that this role is better performed by the media, although it cannot compel ministers to account. More importantly parliamentary committees can extract information in a way that need not be as self-consciously populist as the methods employed on the floor of the House of Commons.

In the final analysis, any weaknesses or limitations in the methods available to members who wish to lay down the parameters for good government have to be put down to the inherent weaknesses of our constitution. Additionally, it must be remembered that excessive interference in Executive functions by the legislature is constitutionally undesirable.

CONSTITUTIONAL LAW

QUESTION TWO

To what extent, if at all, is it true to say that the conventions of individual and collective ministerial responsibility are twins and yet incompatible?

University of London LLB Examination
(for External Students) Constitutional Law June 1986 Q6

General Comment

This question involves discussion of the conventions of collective and individual responsibility and comment upon the inter-relationship between them, in particular the overlaps which seem to exist in their application.

Skeleton Solution

- Introduction – the doctrine of responsible government.
- Collective responsibility; the content and application of, and the justification for, the convention.
- Individual responsibility; the content and application of, and the justification for, the convention.
- The possibility for conflict in the application of collective and individual responsibility.

Suggested Solution

Democracy requires that those who govern should be responsible to those whom they govern. The convention of ministerial responsibility seeks to achieve this aim. It has two aspects. Firstly, the collective responsibility of the government as a whole to Parliament and, secondly the individual responsibility of ministers to Parliament for decisions, taken in their departments, whether by themselves or by their civil servants.

The doctrine of collective responsibility involves two rules. Firstly, it is accepted that the government must resign if it loses the support of the House of Commons. The Prime Minister and his ministers are collectively responsible to Parliament for the conduct of national affairs. If the Prime Minister loses support in Parliament he must resign or seek a dissolution of parliament. The rule does not mean that the government must resign whenever it is defeated on any issue. There has to be a clear-cut defeat for the government on a matter of policy.

Secondly, the doctrine of collective responsibility involves the rule that the government must speak with one voice. All members of the government share in the collective responsibility of the government, and ministers may not publicly criticise or dissociate themselves from government policy. The essence of collective responsibility is that the Cabinet should be seen to be in agreement: a Cabinet Minister who feels unable to agree with his colleagues should resign. The constitutional justification for the rule is that the answerability of the government to Parliament would be severely impaired if individual ministers were able to say that they personally did not agree with decisions taken in Cabinet. Ministers, including non-Cabinet members, are normally bound therefore not to differ publicly from Cabinet decisions nor to speak or vote against the government in Parliament. The rule increases party discipline

9 THE EXECUTIVE

and unity within the government, strengthens the government in Parliament and reinforces the secrecy of decision making within the Cabinet thereby minimising public disagreement between both ministers and departments of state. It also serves to strengthen the authority of the Prime Minister in relation to his colleagues.

The convention of individual responsibility requires that ministers are responsible to Parliament for their own actions, omissions and mistakes as well as for those of the officials in their departments. This principle is said to help preserve the anonymity and therefore the objectivity and efficiency of the civil service. Thus, Government Bills are introduced into Parliament by the departmental ministers, who are responsible for the proposals they contain. In debates concerning the work of individual departments, the minister concerned is expected to reply to the criticisms raised and usually seek to defend the department. Ministers are also expected to meet the reasonable requests of members for information concerning their departments and answer questions relating to their departments at question time.

It can be seen therefore that in many respects the relationship between individual and collective responsibility is very close and to this extent they may be viewed as twins. However, there is also in some respects a high degree of incompatibility between the two. For instance, if responsibility for making of policy decisions lies collectively with the whole government, is it not inconsistent to hold the departmental minister individually responsible for the implementation of that policy? Many of the decisions announced by a minister will have been taken or approved in Cabinet or by Cabinet committees and to this extent the doctrine of collective responsibility will attach to them. Similarly, while a departmental minister may have the authority to make decisions relating exclusively to the sphere for which he is responsible, on many matters he may have to consult with other departments, for example the Treasury. Should that minister then be held responsible for the consequences? Conversely, if a minister is facing censure in Parliament as a result of his departmental policies, he may be individually responsible and accountable to Parliament, but he can nevertheless expect to receive the support of his governmental colleagues by bringing collective responsibility into play.

Of course, both individual and collective responsibility are rules of convention governed largely by political expediency and in consequence their practice may bear little relation to their theory. While their theory therefore may give an impression of incompatibility, the practical application of these conventions, looked at in their political context and judged on their particular facts, may explain the apparent incompatibility.

QUESTION THREE

'If a mistake is made in a Government Department the Minister is responsible even if he knew nothing about it.' 'A Minister cannot be blamed for a mistake made if he did not make it himself.'

Consider these contrasting views.

University of London LLB Examination
(for External Students) Constitutional Law June 1989 Q4

CONSTITUTIONAL LAW

General Comment

A straightforward question on individual responsibility.

Skeleton Solution

- Discuss individual responsibility giving examples which are relevant.
- A lot depends on the attitude of PM of the day.
- Contrast Crichel Down criteria with recent examples of resignations.

Suggested Solution

In any democratic state it is a requirement that the people who govern should be responsible to those whom they govern. In the UK, for instance, responsibility is collective ie the government as a whole is responsible to Parliament and responsibility is individual ie individual ministers are responsible to Parliament for decisions taken by them or their civil servants in their departments. The principle of individual ministerial responsibility developed historically before the doctrine of collective responsibility. Collective and individual responsibility are rules of convention and as such are flexible concepts since conventions are rules of political practice regarded as binding by those to whom they apply but everyone recognises that they are subject to exceptions. Neither of the two quotations is an accurate statement of the requirements of individual ministerial responsibility, which it is wellnigh impossible to formulate in a way which indicates in every case what the outcome will be for a Minister who has made a mistake or whose department has in some way failed.

A Minister is responsible for his or her personal acts whether or not he or she is a member of the Cabinet. Responsibility will also include general conduct in the relevant department and any acts or omissions done in the name of the department. The responsibility may be legal or political or a combination of these. It seems that the meaning of responsibility and the persons or bodies to whom it is owed will vary according to the circumstances.

One of the practical expressions of individual ministerial responsibility is that a Minister is required to answer questions in Parliament with regard to the conduct of officials in his department although questions may be disallowed because of the sub judice rule or because of national security. It is true that a Minister need not accept responsibility if an official has committed a dishonest act, exceeded his authority or disobeyed instructions. He cannot, however, totally absolve himself and he will be required to explain in public what has happened. In this sense the Minister will – whether he is to blame or not – have to 'carry the can'. The Minister must also, of course, when required, explain government policy in relation to his department. In the event that the Minister's replies fail to satisfy MPs or the Lords a motion to reduce the Minister's salary or to censure him may result, but because of party discipline these are rare. In order to consider the truth or otherwise of the quotations it is now necessary to consider some precedents in detail categorising them, if possible, under one of the quotations.

Perhaps one of the clearest examples of a Minister resigning because of a mistake, even though he knew nothing of it at the time it occurred, is that of Sir Thomas Dugdale who resigned as Minister of Agriculture as a result of the Crichel Down

Affair in 1954: In doing so he took responsibility for alleged maladministration by Senior Civil Servants without his knowledge. Some commentators have sought to explain this resignation on the basis that compulsory purchase was involved, (a matter about which the electorate were extremely sensitive at the time) but it certainly stands as a most stringent example of the 'rule' in force, particularly since the maladministration affected only one family and was a matter of embarrassment rather than one where severe loss either financial or in terms of physical wellbeing was concerned.

Lord Carrington's resignation in 1982 as Secretary of State for Foreign Affairs together with those of the other Foreign Office Ministers who resigned with him can also be seen as an example of the first quotation in that it could be argued that Lord Carrington was poorly advised during the negotiations with Argentina over the Falkland Islands but personally made no mistake. On the other hand one could argue that he himself was culpable in that the department's failure to predict the invasion was an indication that it was inefficient or ill run and that in his position he should himself have been better informed and better able to foresee the invasion.

In recent times a rather different attitude has been taken in relation to mistakes by civil servants; whereas formerly the Minister maintained the anonymity of the civil servant and would take responsibility in certain recent cases the blame has been laid squarely at the feet of civil servants (who have sometimes been disciplined) whilst ministers have felt no compunction to resign. An example of the 'rule' set out in the second quotation is the Maze Prison breakout which was followed by resignation of civil servants but no ministerial departures.

If the first quotation is correct then a fortiori it would be expected that any Minister himself making a mistake would have to take responsibility for it and very likely resign. If one examines some recent resignations and calls for resignation one can see that ministerial mistakes do not necessarily result in resignation.

The second quotation also tends to imply that a Minister who personally makes a mistake will be 'blamed'; and the concomitant of this would very likely be resignation. If one examines recent cases one can see that there is no hard and fast rule. Some mistakes by Ministers lead to resignations others merely to calls by the Opposition for resignation. Whether a Minister survives a mistake seems to depend upon factors such as whether he nevertheless retains the confidence of the Prime Minister and the Cabinet, the view of the backbenchers of his own party and the level of public outcry. For instance Sir Leon Brittan initially survived calls for his resignation as Secretary of State for Trade and Industry over allegations that he had misled the Commons about a letter from British Aerospace to the Government during the Westland Helicopter Affair in 1986. His survival was due to the continued support of Prime Minister and Cabinet. However when his behaviour (in authorising a leak to the press of a letter sent by the Law Officers to Michael Heseltine and then arguably covering up what had been done) came to light, several weeks later not even the Cabinet's support could protect his position when the Conservative backbenchers withdrew their support from him and he was forced to resign. In December 1988 Edwina Currie resigned as a Health Minister after over enthusiastic and somewhat misleading comments on the level of salmonella infection in poultry production. Her fault was to alienate poultry producers who had suffered severe financial loss and the Government was forced to mount a costly compensation scheme. The remarks cost

Mrs Currie her job but was she simply unlucky? Had there been some other important news story on the day of her remarks perhaps the media and the public would have overlooked them entirely – they would not then have been a 'mistake' and there would have been no resignation.

A lot depends, therefore, on the attitude of the Prime Minister of the day, the Cabinet and backbenchers and the attitude of the public to the particular mistake. The two contrasting views expressed in the question, are neither taken singly nor together a sufficient explanation of the difficult and subtle convention of individual ministerial responsibility.

QUESTION FOUR

'There are no conventions about ministerial responsibility. Ministers simply do what they, or the Prime Minister, want to do.'

Discuss.

Writen by the Editors

General Comment

A difficult question to answer well. Students need not only to give an account of the conventions of individual and collective responsibility, but also to have a good understanding of developments in British politics in the last 15 years, and then be able to give examples to show that much depended on the Prime Minister's attitude.

Skeleton Solution

- The conventions of individual and collective responsibility to Parliament – a statement of the traditional position with examples.
- An analysis of the more recent tendency for ministers to resign dependent on the factors such as the mood of the country, the support of the PM and the attitude of the minister concerned, with examples.

Suggested Solution

Democracy requires that those who govern should be answerable to those whom they govern. The convention of ministerial responsibility seeks to achieve this aim. It has two aspects. Firstly, the collective responsibility of the government as a whole to Parliament and, secondly the individual responsibility of ministers to Parliament for decisions taken in their departments whether by themselves or by their civil servants.

The doctrine of collective responsibility involves two rules. Firstly, it is accepted that the government must resign if it loses the support of the House of Commons. The Prime Minister and his ministers are collectively responsible to Parliament for the conduct of national affairs. If the Prime Minister loses support in Parliament he must resign or seek a dissolution of Parliament. The rule does not mean that the government must resign whenever it is defeated on any issue. There has to be a clear cut defeat for the government on a matter of policy or a vote of no confidence.

Secondly, the doctrine of collective responsibility involves the rule that the government must speak with one voice. All members of the government share in the

9 THE EXECUTIVE

collective responsibility of the government, and ministers may not publicly criticise or dissociate themselves from government policy. The essence of collective responsibility is that the Cabinet should be seen to be in agreement. A Cabinet Minister who feels unable to agree with his colleagues should resign. The constitutional justification for this rule is that the answerability of the government to Parliament would be severely impaired if individual ministers were able to say that they personally did not agree with the decision taken in Cabinet. Ministers, including non-Cabinet members and Parliamentary Private Secretaries are normally bound therefore not to differ publicly from Cabinet decisions nor to speak or vote against the government in Parliament. The rule increases party discipline and unity within the government, strengthens the government in Parliament and reinforces the secrecy of decision making within the Cabinet thereby minimising public disagreement between both ministers and the departments of State. It also serves to strengthen the authority of the Prime Minister in relation to his Cabinet colleagues.

The convention of individual responsibility requires that ministers are responsible to Parliament for their own actions, omissions and mistakes as well as for those of their officials in the department. This principle is said to help preserve the anonymity and therefore the objectivity and efficiency of the civil service. Thus, Government Bills are introduced into Parliament by the departmental ministers, who are responsible for the proposals they contain. In debates concerning the work of individual departments the minister concerned is expected to reply to the criticisms raised and usually seeks to defend the department. Ministers are also expected to meet the reasonable requests of members for information concerning their departments and answer questions relating to their departments at question time.

Both individual and collective ministerial responsibility are rules of convention governed largely by political expediency. It may therefore be true to observe that as regards responsibility, ministers simply do what they, or the Prime Minister, want to do. So long as they do not get into political difficulty no other sanction is available to compel compliance. The whole purpose of conventions is to introduce flexibility into the Constitution and ministerial responsibility, particularly individual responsibility, is perhaps one of the best examples of conventional flexibility in contemporary constitutional practice.

If one were to start with the classic exposition of individual ministerial responsibility stated by Maxwell-Fyfe in the Crichel Down debate and then contrast it with modern practice it is quite obvious that a fundamental change has taken place regarding the situations in which the minister must accept responsibility and not publicly blame the civil servant. For example, the Secretary of State for Northern Ireland distinguished between defects of policy for which he was responsible and defects in the operation of that policy for which he was not when IRA prisoners broke out of the Maze Prison. The minister escaped political difficulties so one must assume that this now represents the current conventional practice.

One can of course defend this change on the grounds that as the minister within the new super departments relies more upon the expertise of his civil servants, the increased profile of the civil servants in decision making should be reflected in the civil servant accepting more public responsibility when things go wrong. Convention is merely adapting itself and evolving to meet this change; individual responsibility being still regulated by a set of rules which in appropriate circumstances will have to be obeyed, as Lord Carrington found out after the invasion of the Falkland Islands. One should also be wary of confusing ministerial resignations with the convention of individual responsibility. Resignation has never fallen under the convention and thus has always depended to a large extent upon the attitude of the individual minister and the Prime Minister in particular, but the attitude of fellow ministers and of government backbenchers also plays a role. The position of Leon Brittan, Secretary of State for Trade and Industry, during the Westland Affair in 1986 is an instructive example. Leon Brittan faced criticisms and calls for his resignation on two occasions and was finally forced into resignation. The first criticism was of an alleged breach of collective responsibility when the Secretary of State allegedly indicated to a senior executive of British Aerospace that it would be in the public interest if that company withdrew from the European Consortium (the inference being that it was in the national interest for the rival US rescue by Sikorsky Helicopters to go through) a breach of collective responsibility as the government's declared policy was one of neutrality. A letter was sent by British Aerospace to the Prime Minister to complain and the Secretary of State under close questioning in the House of Commons denied all knowledge of such a letter.

This misjudgment gave rise to calls for his resignation, but the Cabinet closed ranks to protect the Minister. Finally the Secretary of State was forced into resignation when it was discovered that without authority from the Law Officers he had authorised the leaking to the press of a letter addressed by them to Michael Heseltine, former Secretary of State for Defence. The Prime Minister and Cabinet again tried to close ranks to protect Mr Brittan but the Conservative backbenchers 1922 Committee resolved that it could no longer support his tenure of office and he was thus forced to resign.

Similarly with collective responsibility. Breach usually results in resignation but in some situations a breach will involve no adverse consequence. There may even be waivers of collective responsibility. During the period of the Labour government in the 1970s waivers were granted in respect of the Referendum on EC Membership in 1975 and the European Assembly Elections in 1978. In both cases these were necessitated by the precarious position of the government which was split over the issue. The essence of convention is flexibility and occasional breaches and waivers of collective responsibility do not remove the underlying convention. Its continued existence can be seen in the resignation of Michael Heseltine, Secretary of State for Defence, during the Westland Affair in 1986.

There is in many respects a degree of incompatibility between collective and individual responsibility. For example, if responsibility for the making of policy decisions lies collectively with the whole government, is it not inconsistent to hold the departmental minister responsible for the implementation of that policy? Many of the decisions announced by a minister will have been taken or approved in Cabinet or by Cabinet Committee and to this extent the doctrine of collective responsibility will attach to them. So why should the Prime Minister when things go wrong be able to divert attention from the government by passing responsibility to the departmental Minister. Undoubtedly this happens and once again it is accommodated within the flexible confines of convention. If the convention of collective responsibility is serving a purpose then some sanction will follow its breach. But again so long as no political difficulties ensure, so what.

Therefore it may be true to say that ministers simply do what they, or the Prime Minister, want to do. But there are conventional rules relating to ministerial responsibility which in appropriate circumstances will have to be obeyed if political difficulties are not to follow for those in breach.

10 THE EUROPEAN CONVENTION AND A BILL OF RIGHTS

10.1 Introduction
10.2 Key points
10.3 Recent cases
10.4 Analysis of questions
10.5 Questions

10.1 Introduction

The civil liberties we enjoy in the United Kingdom are described as residual. That is to say we are free to do what we like as long as it is not against the law. This position can be contrasted with the position in countries with a written Constitution where individual freedoms are usually defined and protected in a 'Bill of Rights'.

Legislation which curtails freedom includes, for example, public order legislation, laws on obscenity, laws to protect national security and so on. By the same token some legislation confers rights eg race relations and sex equality.

Traditionally the courts have viewed their role as being to protect liberty. Note, however, that under the doctrine of parliamentary sovereignty the government is often able to pass legislation which cannot be challenged by the courts and some pressure groups – eg Liberty – see significant inroads being made into our traditional freedoms.

10.2 Key points

a) *Why do we need a Bill of Rights?*

   i) The common law is inadequate to protect human rights; it lays down negative as opposed to positive rights. For example there is no positive right to freedom of speech but merely a number of rules about what cannot be said, ie defamation, obscenity, etc.

   ii) Whilst rights are given to the individual by the common law and statute an individual would have to search through a host of cases and statutory provisions to find out what his civil rights were; much better for such rights to be contained in one document which would be enshrined in Englishmen's minds much as basic rights contained in the American Constitution are known by all United States citizens.

   iii) There is no written Constitution. In countries with such a written Constitution the courts are free to strike down legislation which is in breach of the Constitution. In the United Kingdom the concept of parliamentary sovereignty means that Parliament can do no wrong; so long as an Act receives the approval of both Houses of Parliament and the assent of the monarch the

10 THE EUROPEAN CONVENTION AND A BILL OF RIGHTS

courts are bound to apply it even if it does interfere with what elsewhere would be basic civil liberties: *Pickin* v *British Railways Board* [1974] AC 765.

iv) The inability of the courts to control Parliament has become increasingly important in the light of the fact that government cannot be kept in check by Parliament. The government of the day by reason of the majority vote system in Parliament can force any measure through the House of Commons and the House of Lords can only delay legislation, it cannot veto it.

v) Whilst the United Kingdom is a signatory to the European Convention on Human Rights 1953 it has no binding effect in the United Kingdom and, furthermore, on a number of occasions the United Kingdom has been found to be in breach of the Convention, eg telephone tapping by police in *Malone* v *United Kingdom* [1985] 7 EHRR 14.

b) *The European Convention on Human Rights as an aid to interpretation*

In *R* v *Secretary of State for the Home Department, ex parte Brind* [1991] 2 WLR 588 the House of Lords was not prepared to accept that there should be a presumption that Parliament intended to legislate in conformity with the European Convention on Human Rights. In *Harman* v *Secretary of State for the Home Department* [1982] 2 WLR 338 Lord Scarman saw a need to interpret the law consistently with the provisions of the Convention, but Lord Diplock, in the same case, disagreed. In *Derbyshire County Council* v *Times Newspapers Ltd* [1993] 1 All ER 1011 the House of Lords declined to rely on the Convention (article 10) in reaching a decision.

c) *Should we simply adopt the European Convention or produce a completely new document?*

One preferred view is to simply adopt the European Convention. To do otherwise would mean that there would be two documents guaranteeing basic civil liberties, one English and one European. There would be a danger of conflict, contradiction and confusion. However there are arguments against this approach as follows:

i) The European Convention is over 40 years old. It was mooted and designed in the years immediately following the end of the second World War. Can it really be said to be relevant to what is today a very different world?

ii) It is drafted in very general terms; our judges are used to specifically worded statutes which they can and do interpret literally. Would our judges be able to deal with such generally worded provisions which would require more than a mere literal interpretation? And if they were so able would they be accused of making law and thereby come into conflict with the legislature?

iii) The Convention itself is not ideal. For example the right to 'liberty and security of the person' (article 5) is expressly subject to a number of exceptions allowing, for example, the lawful detention of persons for the prevention of infectious diseases, of persons of unsound mind, of alcoholics, of vagrants and of drug addicts. Article 11 which protects the 'right of freedom of assembly' etc is subject to restrictions – in particular governments can argue 'national security' as a legitimate reason for denying such a freedom. Finally article 15 allows a government 'in time of war or other public emergency' to ignore certain of the Convention's provisions. What is a 'public emergency' can be a very subjective matter!

iv) Furthermore, some of the Convention's ideals may be against popular political thinking at any given time. For example the right to 'peaceful enjoyment of possessions' would seem to militate against public taxation.

Perhaps the answer would be to adopt the European Convention but with amendments to bring it in line with modern requirements.

d) *How could any Bill of Rights Act be 'entrenched'?*

i) The problem

Generally Parliament cannot bind its successors. Accordingly it cannot pass 'unrepealable' Acts. See *Vauxhall Estates* v *Liverpool Corporation* [1932] 1 KB 733 and *Ellen Street Estates Ltd* v *Minister of Health* [1934] 1 KB 590.

Thus in theory it would be impossible to pass a Bill of Rights which could be 'entrenched' for evermore.

ii) The answer

However, there are many statutes that could not, in practice, be repealed eg Commonwealth of Australia Act 1901, Act of Union with Scotland Act 1706, European Communities Act 1972.

Surely a Bill of Rights Act could not in fact be repealed? Would such a repealing Act get the Royal Assent and, if it did, would the courts be prepared to obey such a repealing statute?

e) *The European Convention on Human Rights in practice*

There are a number of cases which have gone to the European Court which have, subsequent to the Court's decision, had an impact on United Kingdom law. *Attorney-General* v *Times Newspapers Ltd* [1974] AC 273 influenced the law on contempt; and a series of cases on corporal punishment, eg *Tyrer* v *United Kingdom* [1978] 2 EHRR 1, *Campbell and Cosans* v *United Kingdom* [1982] 4 EHRR 293 had an impact on the right of schools to administer corporal punishment. It is important to understand the influence these and other examples have on the development and reform of United Kingdom law.

f) *Recent developments*

Britain is the only country in the EU that neither has its own Bill of Rights nor has adopted into its own law the European Convention. The move into Europe has operated to highlight what many believe to be a deficiency in our constitutional law. Accordingly in recent years there has been an increased and renewed clamour by pressure groups and certain judges for something to be done in this regard.

The major developments are as follows:

i) In 1988 a pressure group known as Charter 88 was established to press for constitutional change. A submission was presented to the United Nations arguing that the Common law was no longer sufficient to ensure the continuing protection of the fundamental rights and freedoms that would be enshrined in a Bill of Rights. It argued that 'over the past five years there have been so many violations of Convention rights ... that the credibility of the British Governments arguments against a bill of rights has been completely undermined.' Charter 88 advocated the introduction of a written constitution setting out the relationship between the lawmakers (Parliament); the government and the judiciary; and adopting the European Convention on Human Rights. It also argued in favour of a new system for electing MPs and selecting judges and generally for much more openness in government.

ii) One of the major criticisms of Charter 88 was the British Government's insistence on secrecy. This was highlighted in the 'Spycatcher' case (*Attorney-General* v *Guardian Newspapers (No 1)* [1987] 1 WLR 1248) in which the Government sought an injunction on preventing the publication in Britain of a book by an ex civil servant even though it had been freely published in other countries throughout the world. The House of Lords initially granted the injunction (it was later lifted) but only by a bare majority of three to two. The case was of importance as regards the question of a Bill of Rights because one of the dissenting judges, Lord Bridge, stated that the case had changed his mind about the need for a Bill of Rights. He stated that he had not previously seen the need to introduce such a Bill but the case illustrated that the freedom of speech that would be protected by a Bill of Rights (eg article 10 of the European Convention) was no longer capable of being protected by the Common law.

iii) In 1989 a Private Member's Bill was introduced into the House of Commons by Richard Shepherd which would have made the European Convention on Human Rights part of English law. However, the Bill was defeated by a narrow majority.

iv) In 1991 the civil liberties organisation, Liberty (previously known as the National Council for Civil Liberties) published its own proposals for a Bill of Rights known as 'A People's Charter'. This advocates the introduction of constitutionally enshrined freedoms by the adoption of the European Convention on Human Rights and attempts to deal with the problem of 'entrenchability' (see paragraph (c) in key points above) by arguing in favour of the setting up of a human rights committee comprising MPs elected from Parliament by way of proportional representation. This committee would have the power to vet proposed legislation to see if it accorded with 'Convention' principles and, further, by a two thirds majority would have the power to overturn a decision of the courts on the constitutionality of a proposed measure.

10.3 Recent cases

Campbell v *United Kingdom* (1992) The Times 1 April.

R v *Secretary of State for the Home Department, ex parte Brind* [1991] 2 WLR 588.

Derbyshire County Council v *Times Newspapers Ltd* [1993] 1 All ER 1011.

CONSTITUTIONAL LAW

10.4 Analysis of questions

The question of whether the United Kingdom should pass its own Bill of Rights is one that has been raised periodically by various pressure groups over the last two decades. Its appearance as a question on the examination paper has very much corresponded with years in which the cry for the introduction of a Bill of Rights has been louder than usual. Any European agreement on a Social Charter is likely to result in renewed cries for the introduction of such a Bill and, accordingly, you can expect a question on this area over the next few years. Any such question will usually be in the form of an essay requiring the candidate to talk about the following:

a) The need for, and effect of, a Bill of Rights.

b) Whether such a Bill should simply incorporate the European Convention on Human Rights or should the United Kingdom adopt a completely new document.

c) How, if at all, it could be ensured that any Bill of Rights Act passed is not repealed in the future.

10.5 Questions

QUESTION ONE

Argue the case for and against the adoption of the European Convention on Human Rights and its protocols as a Bill of Rights for the United Kingdom.

University of London LLB Examination
(for External Students) Constitutional Law June 1986 Q9

General Comment

This question requires a good knowledge of the arguments for and against the adoption of the European Convention on Human Rights as a Bill of Rights. A knowledge of Lord Wade's Bill to incorporate the Convention into United Kingdom domestic law would also be useful.

Skeleton Solution

- Introduction: the existing constitutional safeguards for protecting human rights in the United Kingdom.
- The European Convention on Human Rights: the objects of the Convention and the machinery for enforcement.
- The arguments in favour of adopting the Convention as a Bill of Rights for the United Kingdom.
- The arguments against adopting the Convention: the problem of parliamentary sovereignty; politicising the judiciary.
- Lord Wade's Bill to incorporate the Convention into domestic law.

Suggested Solution

The United Kingdom Constitution is unwritten in the formal sense and accordingly lays great emphasis on the virtues of the common law and the legislative supremacy of Parliament. It relies heavily on the political process to ensure that Parliament

10 THE EUROPEAN CONVENTION AND A BILL OF RIGHTS

does not override the basic rights and liberties of the subject, nor remove from the courts the adjudication of disputes between the citizen and the state arising out of the exercise of executive power.

This traditional British approach to individual liberties is considered by many to be outdated and incapable of protecting individual rights from executive encroachment. The critics advocate the creation of a new Bill of Rights for the United Kingdom. Accordingly, in 1978 a select committee of the House of Lords was established to consider whether a Bill of Rights was desirable and, if so, what form it should take. The committee, while doubting that a Bill of Rights was desirable, nevertheless held unanimously that if there were to be a Bill of Rights, it should be a Bill to incorporate the European Convention of Human Rights into United Kingdom law. There have been more recent attempts to raise public awareness and instigate political debate, notably by Charter 88 and Liberty. In 1989 a Private Member's Bill was introduced with the aim of making the European Convention on Human Rights part of United Kingdom law, but it was defeated.

The European Convention on Human Rights (see Beddard, *Human Rights and Europe*, 2nd ed, 1980), prepared under the auspices of the Council of Europe, entered into force in September 1953. The Convention is a treaty under international law and its authority derives solely from the consent of those states who have become parties to it. The Convention declares certain human rights which should be protected by law in each state and provides political and judicial procedures by which alleged infringements of these rights may be examined at an international level. Every state party to the Convention has a duty to ensure that its domestic law conforms to the Convention, but a state is under no duty to incorporate the Convention itself within its domestic law. While about half the states who are parties to the Convention have incorporated it within their domestic law, others, including the United Kingdom, have not incorporated the Convention. Successive British governments have maintained that human rights are already adequately protected by law in the United Kingdom.

Those who argue in favour of adopting the European Convention as a Bill of Rights for the United Kingdom point out that human rights are not adequately protected under our present law and that further constitutional protection for human rights is therefore necessary. In support of their case they point to the ever increasing role of the state in economic and social affairs and the widespread public disillusionment with the parliamentary process and the 'undemocratic' electoral system which produces a legislature dominated and controlled by the executive. As evidence of their case they point to the 'incremental' erosion of civil liberties exemplified recently by the Criminal Justice and Public Order Act 1994. There is also concern at the record of the United Kingdom under the European Convention on Human Rights and dissatisfaction with the performance of the courts in dealing with disputes between the citizen and the state: see *Malone v Metropolitan Police Commissioner* (1979). With the executive every day assuming more statutory powers and in so doing eroding our common law liberties, so it becomes more vital to provide safeguards against the abuse of those powers.

Assuming that some form of Bill of Rights is needed in the United Kingdom, incorporation of the European Convention would probably be the easiest and most acceptable option available to the government. There is no dispute as to the rights

CONSTITUTIONAL LAW

protected. The Convention omits economic and social rights, over which considerable political controversy might arise, and is confined to certain basic rights and liberties which the framers of the Convention considered would be generally accepted in the liberal democracies of Western Europe. Incorporation of the Convention would also avoid the frequent humiliation suffered by the United Kingdom government before the European Court of Human Rights when, in the glare of international publicity, it is found in breach of its international obligations under the Convention. These foreign 'judges' would no longer be able to interfere with our law and instead breaches of the convention would be dealt with before our own municipal courts.

However, to be fully effective incorporation would have to enable the British courts to apply the Convention if necessary in preference to existing rules of statute or common law and this will entail grafting onto the present Constitution an added power in the courts to give redress to the individual even against an Act of Parliament. Such an attempt would raise issues concerning the relationship of the courts to the political process, including the special difficulties inherent in the attempt by a supreme Parliament to bind itself.

There are therefore formidable legal and political problems in the incorporation of the European Convention as a new Bill of Rights for the United Kingdom (see Jaconelli, *Enacting a Bill of Rights, the Legal Problems*, 1980). It is extremely difficult to bring about any enactment of fundamental rights that may not be violated by ordinary process of legislation, and what is the value in having a Bill of Rights that cannot bind future Parliaments? Also, is it desirable to have constitutional change likely to give greater power to the judiciary? Some argue that, in reviewing administrative decisions, the courts are already inclined to interfere in political disputes and should not be encouraged to extend this to the review of legislative decisions: political decisions should be made by democratically elected politicians, not by judges.

The House of Lords in 1979 did in fact approve a Bill proposed by the Liberal peer Lord Wade, that sought to incorporate the European Convention in United Kingdom law and provide a compromise which both enabled the United Kingdom to give better effect to its existing obligations under the Convention, and respond positively to the domestic movement for the greater protection of human rights. However the Bill failed to receive government support in the House of Commons, as did another attempt in 1989. It remains to be seen therefore whether future decisions of the European Court of Human Rights will influence government thinking in favour of incorporating the Convention.

QUESTION TWO

What differences, if any, would incorporation of the European Convention on Human Rights into British law make to the British Constitution?

University of London LLB Examination
(for External Students) Constitutional Law June 1987 Q9

General Comment

Although this question is phrased rather generally students should concentrate on the effects of incorporation on the sovereignty of Parliament and the role of the judiciary in interpreting and enforcing a Bill of Rights in the United Kingdom.

10 THE EUROPEAN CONVENTION AND A BILL OF RIGHTS

Skeleton Solution

- Introduction. The need for a Bill of Rights.
- Mechanism for incorporation of the European Convention on Human Rights into United Kingdom law.
- Effects of incorporation on the Constitution. The sovereignty of Parliament; the role of the judiciary.

Suggested Solution

Recently there have been increasing demands for the enactment of a Bill of Rights in the United Kingdom to safeguard the fundamental rights and freedoms of the individual. As the executive becomes more powerful, controlling the legislature and interfering more and more in the lives of the citizen, some protection, it is argued, becomes necessary. The State has become prosecutor and judge in its own cause. Because of this the common law negative freedoms we enjoy are under constant attack and the judges are powerless to check the legislative supremacy of that agent of the executive, Parliament. The Criminal Justice and Public Order Act 1994 was a controversial measure and seen by many as a further erosion of freedom of expression and protest. In most countries there is a written Constitution which is not just a sacred piece of paper but a statement that the people are the ultimate source of power, that the state and its legislature and its civil servants and laws are the servants of the people. It is argued that the enactment of a Bill of Rights in the United Kingdom will help to reassert the supremacy of the individual over the state.

To achieve this the simplest and perhaps most obvious answer is to look to the European Convention on Human Rights. The United Kingdom is a party to the Convention and successive British governments both socialist and conservative have allowed citizens to petition the European Commission of Human Rights and seek enforcement of the rights and freedoms set out in the Convention in international law. Why not go one step further and incorporate the European Convention into domestic law so that its provisions may be enforced and applied by British judges in British courts? But if such incorporation did take place would it make any difference to the operation of the British constitution as regards the protection of fundamental rights and freedoms? Probably not.

This is because the enactment of a Bill of Rights in the United Kingdom involves the consideration of a theoretically insurmountable problem, the sovereignty of Parliament. A Bill of Rights is a piece of paper. It has no practical value unless it can be enforced against those having the power to take away the rights and freedoms of the citizen. But the United Kingdom Parliament is sovereign. There are no legal restraints on its legislative powers. This absence of legal restraint has three aspects: Parliament is legally competent to legislate upon any subject matter; no Parliament can bind its successors or be bound by its predecessors; and once Parliament has legislated no court or other person can pass judgment upon the validity of the legislation.

Parliament may therefore make or unmake any law. There is no area or subject matter outside the scope of its legislative powers. Parliament is also unable to limit its own legislative powers for the future. Parliament cannot bind its successors and a later Parliament is always, in theory at least, able to expressly repeal the legislation made by an earlier Parliament. Also, under the doctrine of implied repeal as expressed in *Vauxhall Estates* v *Liverpool Corporation* (1932) the provisions of an earlier Act can always be repealed by implication by provisions in a later Act which are inconsistent with those in the earlier Act. Further, in *Ellen Street Estates Ltd* v *Minister of Health* (1934) it was also held that Parliament cannot, by a statement in an earlier Act, effectively provide that the provisions of that Act cannot be repealed by implication by inconsistent provisions in a later Act. The role of the courts is also limited with regard to Acts of Parliament. For example the case of *Pickin* v *British Railways Board* (1974) illustrates the point that once it is established that an Act has received the consent of the House of Commons, the assent of the House of Lords (or that it has been passed under the provisions of the Parliament Acts 1911-1949), and the assent of the Sovereign all the courts can do is apply it subject to their limited powers of statutory interpretation.

It can be seen therefore that even if the present Parliament enacts a Bill of Rights for the United Kingdom a later Parliament intent on restricting or abolishing the rights and freedoms contained in it may do so either by express enactment or even impliedly by the enactment of a later statute which conflicts with its provisions. The courts will be powerless to intervene. So long as Parliament remains sovereign there can be no entrenchment of legislation against future amendment or repeal. Only Parliament can limit its own sovereignty and such limitations must have been enacted in the form of statute. However no Parliament can bind its successors. Therefore whatever limitations are imposed upon the sovereignty of Parliament by one statute may be repealed by a subsequent Act. Therefore in theory at least it may be true to say that even if enacted, a Bill of Rights could be repealed tomorrow and the existence of the Bill will make no difference to this aspect of our Constitution.

However in theory there are means by which limitations can be placed upon the sovereignty of Parliament. For example some statutes such as the Statute of Westminster 1931 contain limitations as to the scope and subject matter of parliamentary legislation. Others such as the Colonial Laws Validity Act 1865 contain limitations as to the manner and form of future legislation. The civil liberties organisation Liberty has attempted to deal with the problem of entrenchability by arguing that a human rights committee should have power to vet proposed legislation to see if it accords with the principles of a Bill of Rights. The real check upon the sovereignty of Parliament however in practice remains public opinion. The government always knows that it will have to face a General Election within a few years and this stark reality may have a restraining effect upon their legislative proposals and deter any attempted government tampering with the Bill of Rights. Of course these informal restraints are present and operating already to curtail executive power and in this respect the presence of a Bill of Rights will make little difference.

One difference that would be made to the British Constitution by the incorporation of the European Convention on Human Rights into British law concerns the role of the judiciary. A Bill of Rights would involve a shift of power from elected and accountable Members of Parliament to judges who are neither elected nor accountable. These judges will be involved not just in making interim policy choices about what the law should be, pending action by the Legislature, but in making final policy choices which some would argue they cannot be trusted to do. It will turn judges into legislators. Judges whose job it is to know and apply the law will be asked to create and form the law. In this respect it may be doubted that British court procedure is the best environment in which to thoroughly analyse the kind of problematic political questions such a Bill of Rights will raise.

QUESTION THREE

'In a country such as the United Kingdom which has an unwritten constitution based largely on parliamentary sovereignty, it is by no means clear that the enactment of a Bill of Rights is desirable, or that such a Bill could be protected from amendment or repeal.'

Discuss.

University of London LLB Examination
(for External Students) Constitutional Law June 1990 Q4

General Comment

A question dealing with the two major matters always raised in this topic: (1) 'Is it needed?'; and (2) 'How can it be entrenched?'

Skeleton Solution

- What is a Bill of Rights?
- How, if at all does it improve an an unwritten condition?
- Could it be repealed in the future in the light of case law, namely *Vauxhall Estates*, etc?

Suggested Solution

The notion of a bill of rights is that a document consisting of fundamental rights for citizens may be given the full force of law and invested with such constitutional significance that the creation and application of laws and the actions of administrative bodies must conform with its content and spirit. In countries that have experienced the turmoil of revolution or that have gained independence from imperial powers a bill of rights is frequently the highest source of constitutional law. It is a measure of the significance attached to such documents that the terms 'constitution' and 'bill of rights' are often used interchangeably in common parlance.

However, the United Kingdom has a bill of rights in name only. The Bill of Rights 1688, although providing certain guarantees against arbitrary legal penalties, deals primarily with the respective powers of the monarchy and Parliament. There are certain other guarantees of personal rights embodied in municipal and European Union legislation, but there is no single piece of legislation, let alone one that has the legal supremacy of, say, the American Constitution. This is not to say, however, that there is no demand for one. The Westminster model of democracy may be a reassurance against monarchic dictatorship, but the mechanism and nature of executive government, coupled with the 'first-past-the-post' electoral system is not an effective prophylactic against other forms of dictatorship and the piecemeal erosion of civil liberties. In recent years, both of the main opposition parties have called for constitutional reform.

Since it is obvious that such political situations are not entirely unprecedented or beyond the conception of those who are concerned with such matters, why, we must ask, has no bill of rights been passed into law? There are three, or more, possible reasons; that it is undesirable, unnecessary or impracticable.

Before delving deeper into these assertions one might make some general observations as to the 'British conception' of the protection of rights. One assumes that somehow we have managed without a bill of rights and since we do not apparently live in a state that constantly restricts our freedom, someone must have thought out a system that guarantees our rights. Jurists have expressed the opinion that general statements of principle, that, in the words of the American Constitution are 'self-evident', have no greater guarantee than the earnest goodwill of the judiciary and Parliament. The experience of many former Commonwealth countries which were given Westminster style government and a bill of rights, confirms the fallibility of a bill of rights without the right sentiment in the hearts of those who must govern by it. However, it does also emphasise the fragility of a reliance on benevolent paternalism.

It is not simply the experience of less established democracies that fuel these suspicions. Under the Republican administration in America, the appointment of averred opponents of the existing content of the Constitution has led to an increase in concern about civil liberties issues such as abortion and the freedom of expression. The issue of Supreme Court 'packing' lends credibility to the notion that a general declaration of the rights of the individual is open to illiberal as well as liberal interpretation. Such an argument may be even stronger in the United Kingdom where the impartiality of judges has been questioned on occasions when there is a serious assertion of civil liberties.

Conversely, it may be suggested that by investing the courts with more power as a consequence of their role in the interpretation of such a constitutional document, the pursuit of a coherent 'rule of law' may inspire them to follow more liberal lines. Such a view may be reinforced by the perceptible changes in the review of administrative actions and attitudes towards conflicts between British legislation and EU obligations.

It is this attitude that draws us to the primary argument for the undesirability. The most vehement critics of justiciable rules intended to protect civil liberties hold up the spectre of 'rule by judges'. A bill of rights for the United Kingdom would be undemocratic, they assert. The argument runs that although a bill of rights is designed to protect the rights of the general public, a bill of rights would also, however, fetter politicians, the democratic representatives of the people, from carrying out their mandated obligations, without constant concern as to whether their legislative actions will fall foul of the judiciary who are not democratically accountable.

This argument rather smacks of the assertion that we should not have a bill of rights because the electorate may not like the consequences, which may be true. Alternatively, it may reveal the possibility that politicians find the idea undesirable because it may lead to considerable inconvenience and an unwelcome limitation on their legislative power.

Whichever the reason it is certain that, at the present time, there is by no means a consensus as to the desirability of a bill of rights and in a parliamentary democracy

10 THE EUROPEAN CONVENTION AND A BILL OF RIGHTS

such as ours it is mandatory that a majority of politicians are in agreement before there is any possibility of this sort of constitutional change.

Some jurists consider that, although legal safeguards of individual rights are necessary, adequate mechanisms already exist. If their contention is correct then a bill of rights is undesirable because it is superfluous. This belief is primarily fuelled by various international treaties to which the United Kingdom is party. The principal example must be the European Convention on Human Rights, which provides a forum for the review of particular human rights violations and a court which may adjudicate on alleged breaches of the Convention. The parameters of the Treaty are wide, although not all-embracing; however its application is slow, to say the least, resulting in only a small proportion of the petitioners satisfying the Commission, which processes applications for hearings in the European Court of Human Rights, that no adequate legal remedy exists in national law. Furthermore, as was discovered in *Malone* v *United Kingdom* (1985), national courts cannot apply the Convention directly, and need not even take it into account. This is as a result of the failure of the British Parliament to enact the Convention as municipal legislation.

Certain of the obligations created by our membership of the European Union, such as article 119 of the Treaty of Rome, which prevents certain types of employment discrimination on the basis of gender, have, as Lord Denning observed in *Macarthys Ltd* v *Smith* (1981), the full force of law. However, Community measures apply principally to the commercial aspects of life, and, as such, do not deal with other freedoms and rights in equal need of protection. Moreover, there is nothing, at least theoretically, to prevent Parliament, even at this late stage, from revoking or refusing to implement its European obligations.

If we can therefore accept that there is a vacuum in this area of constitutional law and that at some point in the future a majority of Parliament will be in favour of passing a bill of rights, we must examine its potential status in law. Obviously, as a simple Act of Parliament it would have the status of all Acts of Parliament; namely it would be good and binding law unless and until it was repealed, and as such all would have to abide by it. However, it would be up to the normal democratic processes to safeguard the Act itself and in circumstances where a new Parliament consisted of those who saw this bill of rights as unnecessary or undesirable, it could lose its status at the stroke of the legislative pen.

Thus, a simple Act of Parliament could not provide the monolithic certainty that one would expect of a cornerstone of the constitution, at least so far as the legal theory goes. Thus, one is faced with the problem of entrenching a bill of rights for the United Kingdom. The experience of earlier Parliaments who have sought, by drafting clauses against repeal, to challenge the concept that no Parliament can bind its successors, shows us, as in the cases of *Vauxhall Estates* v *Liverpool Corporation* (1932) and *Ellen Street Estates Ltd* v *Minister of Health* (1934) that a later Parliament, simply by stating something different, can implicitly repeal an earlier Act. Even if we could assume the judiciary would treat our Bill of Rights with the same reverence as the European Communities Act 1972, which seeks to have all legislation construed in accordance with its provisions, the situation would be doubtful. It seems that entrenchment would require something more than good draftsmanship, since even the requirement for a weighty majority of Parliament to modify or abolish this document could itself be set aside by Parliament.

It would therefore seem that nothing short of a complete restructuring of the constitutional tenets of the United Kingdom would give the desired effect, namely that Parliament was made less supreme than a constitutional document enshrining rights. But how may one Parliament surrender the sovereignty of all future Parliaments even in the name of a constitutional form of 'perestroika'. Perhaps the abolition of the Lords would provide an opportunity to move the legal goal posts, by adding the proviso that subsequent Parliaments were subject to the bill of rights. However, in theory, there would be nothing to prevent this itself from being overturned.

It soon becomes clear that when one pursues constitutional theory to its bitter end, ultimately one concludes that the constitution is as it is and its flexibility means that democratic change may be made, but constitutional guarantees cannot be written in stone. Such an attitude may be seen to be at the same time a truism and an absurdity. It is the nature of the British, and other constitutions that they have been created and added to by historical forces and certain documents have become, by dint of the democratic will and the writings of jurists, sacrosanct, such as the Bill of Rights 1688 or the Reform Bill 1832. There is nothing but a continuing respect for the democratic forces that created them and for the certainty that they provide, through the passing ages, to keep them from repeal, and should the democratic will exist then these may be swept away. It is clear from the constitutional changes in the Soviet Union, for example, that rules of the constitution, however monolithic and theoretically entrenched, may in practice always be discarded.

Assuming that the legislature are willing and the general public support such a measure, a bill of rights could be passed and would remain in force as long as it was still desired. It is likely that a government that would not respect the will of the electorate would certainly not be too concerned about the constitutional niceties of entrenchment, even if it were possible.

QUESTION FOUR

Critically assess the following statement that 'the case for a Bill of Rights rests on the belief that it would make a distinct and valuable contribution to the better protection of human rights'.

University of London LLB Examination
(for External Students) Constitutional Law June 1988 Q6

General Comment

The question seems to be inviting discussion on the issue of whether human rights are adequately protected by the British Constitution as it stands at present, or whether the enactment of specific legislation is called for. Thus some consideration of the protection offered under domestic legislation and the common law is called for. Thought should be given as to how an effective Bill of Rights might be introduced, and to the question of its contents.

10 THE EUROPEAN CONVENTION AND A BILL OF RIGHTS

Skeleton Solution

- Explain the protection offered under English law – statutory provisions – common law decision.
- Shortcomings of both – examples of breaches of human rights under the ECHR by the United Kingdom government.
- Problems of the contents of a Bill of Rights – problems of implementation.

Suggested Solution

The question invites discussion of the merits and demerits of a Bill of Rights being enacted. One could commence by pointing out that there is already a Bill of Rights on the statute book, that of 1688, but of course that legislation was not concerned with the rights of individuals so much as the relationship between Parliament and the Crown. Whilst the Bill of 1688 may have been effective to prevent individuals being subject to arbitrary prerogative power as exercised by the monarch in person, it did little to protect the individual citizen from the excesses of governmental power exercised under the guise of parliamentary sovereignty; indeed one might well contend that one of the failings of the 'Glorious Revolution' was to place too much power in the hands of the legislature, and thereby the government.

There have been a number of attempts to introduce a Bill of Rights aimed at strengthening the protection of individual rights under English law. One attempt took the form of a Private Member's Bill introduced by Sir Edward Gardner, the Human Rights and Fundamental Freedoms Bill (1986), which sought to incorporate the European Convention on Human Rights into English law. The Bill very narrowly failed in the Commons*, but there was clearly considerable parliamentary support for such a measure. Another attempt in 1989 also failed.

The statement under consideration suggests that a Bill of Rights could make a distinct contribution to the better protection of human rights, thus prompting the question, distinct from what?

Under English law, individual rights are protected by either statute or common law. Examples of statutory protection are provided by the Race Relations Act 1976, Sex Discrimination Act 1975, and the Police and Criminal Evidence Act 1984. At common law decisions such as *Christie* v *Leachinsky* (1947), under which a police officer was required to inform a suspect of the grounds for an arrest, or *Entick* v *Carrington* (1765) under which the courts invalidated the practice of issuing general search warrants, have undoubtedly contributed to the protection of individual rights and liberties. Can it be said that this combined protection is so inadequate that a formal Bill of Rights is needed?

The problem with 'equal rights' or 'civil liberties' legislation is that such measures are always at the mercy of successive Parliaments. As a consequence of parliamentary sovereignty they can always be amended or repealed. Further, it can be argued that when Parliament places individual liberties on a statutory basis it can draft them in terms that make them more limited in operation than they were at common law. More generally, successive Parliaments have fought shy of granting United Kingdom citizens positive statutory rights, such as the right to free expression, the right to information, and the right to privacy.

The failings of the common law are that it is sporadic in nature. The judiciary can only develop individual rights at common law if cases are brought before them. Whether or not this occurs is a haphazard affair, not the best way in which to tackle such a serious matter. In any event, any decision of the courts can be nullified by subsequent parliamentary action in the form of new legislation, which can even be retrospective if necessary. The courts have not always responded when called upon by litigants to defend or develop human rights. Mr Malone's arguments for a right to privacy fell upon deaf ears in *Malone* v *Metropolitan Police Commissioner* (1979), the Vice-Chancellor concluding that as there was no English law governing the matter of telephone tapping, he would be usurping the function of Parliament by holding that such action did amount to an invasion of the plaintiff's right to privacy regarding his communications.

On the basis of the above, Charter 88, amongst others, has contended that a Bill of Rights is needed in the British Constitution because individual rights are not adequately protected at present by statute and common law. Those who contend that human rights are not violated by the United Kingdom can be referred to the succession of findings against the United Kingdom by the European Court of Human Rights under the European Convention. See *Malone* v *United Kingdom* (1985); *Tyrer* v *United Kingdom* (1978). Furthermore, the courts are reluctant to use the European Convention on Human Rights as an aid to interpretation, or to use the Convention to 'fill in the gaps' in United Kingdom statutes: see *R* v *Secretary of State for the Home Department, ex parte Brind* (1991); *Derbyshire County Council* v *Times Newspapers Ltd* (1993).

Matters in relation to which the British government, and by implication the British Constitution, has been found wanting are: the law of contempt; the law relating to telephone tapping; the rights of prisoners to communicate with lawyers; the rights of prisoners to be legally represented in prison disciplinary proceedings; detention without trial under the Prevention of Terrorism legislation; corporal punishment; and restrictions upon adult homosexuals in Northern Ireland.

If it is accepted that a human rights measure is needed, the next question that needs consideration is its content. Most of those who support the introduction of a Bill of Rights point to the European Convention on Human Rights as a suitable model, but how valuable would this be?

Three matters in particular should be borne in mind. First the Convention is selective in the rights it seeks to protect, it contains no reference to a right to education, health care, or employment. It reflects a 'Western' view of individual rights, as opposed to a 'Socialistic' view. Secondly, the Convention includes many limitations upon the rights set forth, and does allow signatory states to derogate from some of its provisions in certain circumstances. For example the Convention does provide for freedom of association, but goes on to recognise that governments can limit this right if it is in the national interests to do so, thus the Civil Service Unions involved in the 'GCHQ' union ban dispute were not able to pursue their case under the Convention. Thirdly, a Bill of Rights can only be effective if it is protected to some extent from repeal or amendment by subsequent governments, and if subsequent legislation is applied only to the extent that it does not conflict with the Bill of Rights. To prevent changes being introduced by a subsequent Parliament would involve a major constitutional change in the nature of parliamentary sovereignty,

10 THE EUROPEAN CONVENTION AND A BILL OF RIGHTS

with a marked increase in the powers of the judiciary. The controversy surrounding the status and effect of the European Communities Act 1972 provides an example of the difficulties that could be encountered. Many would feel that human rights are not in sufficient peril in the United Kingdom to justify such a constitutional upheaval.

* Debated on 6 February 1987; although it attracted 94 votes in support and only 16 in opposition, it was lost on the technical requirement that there had to be 100 MPs supporting the measure.

QUESTION FIVE

'Civil liberties will not be given adequate protection unless and until the European Convention on Human Rights is incorporated into English law'.

Discuss.

University of London LLB Examination
(for External Students) Constitutional and Administrative Law June 1992 Q6

General Comment

This is a standard discussion question on the Bill of Rights. The European Convention on Human Rights and its current relation to the UK need discussing as well as the pros and cons of incorporation.

Skeleton Solution

- How civil liberties are protected here.
- The European Convention.
- Arguments in favour of incorporation.
- Lord Scarman's views.
- Problem of entrenchment.
- Changed role of judiciary.
- Current safeguards.
- European Convention's limitations.

Suggested Solution

The basic rights and liberties of United Kingdom subjects are not contained in or protected by a single document. Traditionally, reliance has been placed upon the political process, particular legislation (eg Race Relations Act 1976) or the powers of the courts to ensure that an individual's rights are not usurped. Those who consider this protection insufficient most frequently call for the incorporation of the European Convention on Human Rights to guarantee civil liberties.

The European Convention, which was prepared under the auspices of the Council of Europe, came into force in 1953. It is a treaty and has been incorporated by about half the signatories (eg Austria, Belgium, Germany), but not by the United Kingdom. However each signatory has a duty to ensure that its domestic law conforms with the Convention. Thus, although it does not give rights and remedies in English law, the Convention has considerable influence.

Would incorporation make a difference? At present the European Convention affords some direct protection to United Kingdom citizens in that rights can be enforced by the European Court of Human Rights in Strasbourg. The process is long and slow and comes after all domestic remedies have been exhausted, but nevertheless has led to over 100 changes to United Kingdom laws, regulations or administrative practices (according to Robertson, *Freedom, the Individual and the Law* (1989)). For example, *Dudgeon* v *UK* (1981) led to the lifting of the prohibition on homosexuality in Northern Ireland; *Sunday Times* v *United Kingdom* (1979) altered the contempt laws.

However, it can be argued that this long route to the European Court of Human Rights could be short-circuited by incorporation. It would also reduce the embarrassment of the United Kingdom's frequent appearances in Strasbourg (although recourse to the Court would, of course, remain). It can further be argued that incorporation would show a commitment to civil liberties.

These arguments have powerful advocates. Lord Scarman (in *English Law: The New Dimension* (1974)) challenged the assumption that English law substantially complies with our international obligations and that incorporation would therefore add little. He pointed out that it is not just laws, but regulations and policies that must comply – and the frequency of the United Kingdom's visits to Strasbourg suggests they do not. For example, *Republic of Ireland* v *United Kingdom* (1978) concerned the policies which allowed maltreatment of terrorist suspects in Northern Ireland.

Incorporation, desirable or not, creates its own problems. Firstly, there is the problem of entrenchment. Parliament cannot bind its successors so that, without more, the Act incorporating the Bill of Rights would have no greater strength or status than any other Act. By the doctrine of implied repeal, a later and conflicting Act would impliedly repeal the Act's provisions (eg *Vauxhall Estates* v *Liverpool Corporation* (1932)). In practice, of course, some Acts are effectively entrenched (eg The Statute of Westminster 1931 and arguably the European Communities Act 1972) in that repeal would be a political impossibility and that could be the same for a Bill of Rights.

Secondly, a domestic court would have to replicate the powers of the European Court to the extent of challenging laws made by Parliament. How could this be achieved? Should the judiciary be given such powers? Would it not politicise the judges? Certainly it would completely alter the constitutional balance of the UK.

Thirdly, the argument suggests that civil liberties are currently insufficiently protected. There are several statutes covering aspects of civil liberties (eg Sex Discrimination Act 1975, Police and Criminal Evidence Act 1984). At common law there are decisions which have contributed to the protection of civil liberties, such as *Entick* v *Carrington* (1765) (on the issue of general search warrants) and *Christie* v *Leachinsky* (1947) (informing a suspect of the grounds of arrest). Together they have afforded some protection but clearly in a piecemeal fashion.

A fourth point relates to the Convention itself. Contrary to what some may believe, it is a very selective document. Not only does it not refer to, for example, employment, education or health care, it also allows limitations to be set. In the GCHQ case (*Council for Civil Service Unions* v *Minister for the Civil Service* (1984)) the union could not pursue its case under the Convention since their threatened freedom of association conflicted with 'national interests'.

10 THE EUROPEAN CONVENTION AND A BILL OF RIGHTS

There are too many variables for a simplistic answer. However, one can conclude that a Bill of Rights is at least of symbolic value, that it has been incorporated elsewhere without problem and that it would focus attention on civil liberties when laws are made rather than when civil liberties have been challenged.

QUESTION SIX

In AV Dicey's view, individual rights are best protected under the common law. To what extent does the record of the United Kingdom under the European Convention of Human Rights uphold or deny this view?

University of London LLB Examination
(for External Students) Constitutional Law June 1993 Q6

General Comment

It is important to note the emphasis of the question which is rather more narrow than might appear at first glance. It is tempting to run through all the well-rehearsed arguments for and against incorporation of the Convention on Human Rights, but the examiner wishes the student to concentrate on a particular issue: would a UK citizen's individual rights be better protected under incorporation than at existing common law? Note the reference to Dicey and try to commence the discussion with reference to Dicey's Rule of Law and the emphasis he gave to judge-made law as the basis for constitutional rights.

Skeleton Solution

- Dicey's concept of judge-made constitutional rights.
- UK's position under the European Convention on Human Rights (ECHR).
- Violations of the ECHR by UK law (useful reference can be made to academic research on this point).
- Effect on sovereignty of Parliament of incorporation of ECHR.
- Alternative views on UK's record under ECHR.
- Existing common law use of ECHR to resolve ambiguous domestic law.
- Position where domestic law is unambiguous and the need for an elected body to have the last say on contentious issues of policy.
- Conclusions.

Suggested Solution

In Dicey's exposition of the theory of the Rule of Law emphasis was placed on the role of the judge as defender of civil liberties; indeed Dicey went as far as to assert that the British Constitution, in its aspects relating to basic rights and freedoms, was a judge-made one. Historically Parliament built on the foundations laid by the common law. Since 1952 successive British governments have ratified the European Convention on Human Rights (ECHR) and since 1965 individual United Kingdom citizens have been permitted to petition the European Court of Human Rights at Strasbourg to obtain remedies for breaches of the Convention by UK governments. The experience has been cited by many authorities as evidence that English common law, as adapted by statute law on a piecemeal basis, no longer provides adequate protection of individual rights, and that therefore incorporation of the Convention into domestic law so as to give United Kingdom judges greater powers to protect fundamental freedoms is urgent and necessary.

In a devastating critique, Anthony Lester QC ([1984] PL 46) argues that the United Kingdom has the worst record of violations of the European Convention:

'... no other country which belongs to the Convention has been faced with so many cases of such importance'.

His catalogue includes cases involving inhumane treatment of prisoners generally and of terrorist suspects in particular; inadequate safeguards against invasion of privacy; unfair sex and race discrimination, especially in the fields of employment and immigration law; inhumane punishments for school children (cane in English schools, tawse or strap in Scottish schools); nationalisation without fair compensation; oppressive interference with free speech through the laws of contempt of court and confidentiality; and so the list goes on. In all these examples the government of the day was usually obliged to enact new laws to comply with the ECHR rulings, but Lester argues cogently that such slow reform could be avoided if the Convention were directly enforceable by UK judges, who would be able (and indeed obliged) to adapt common law and statute law to comply with the jurisprudence of the ECHR and the precedents set by ECHR, which would become the supreme court for the United Kingdom on human rights.

Naturally incorporation would involve setting limitations to the powers of Parliament, but Lester argues that a mature Parliament should be able to accept constraints on its sovereignty so far as those constraints are necessary to protect human rights: 'The Convention sets those limits in relation to fundamental rights and freedoms, protecting minorities against the tyranny of elected majorities, and ordinary men and women against the misuse of administrative and judicial discretion.'

Even if one accepts the latter view for the sake of argument, there is still a large bone of contention at the heart of Lester's analysis and reasoning. It concerns the issue of whether individual rights would be better protected under an incorporated Convention. At first sight Lester's catalogue of British inadequacies would appear conclusive, but in fact his case is rather misleading. Although it is true that the United Kingdom has the worst record of violations, this should be set in the context that the United Kingdom allowed the right of individual petition as long ago as 1965, whereas others of the 1952 signatories allowed their citizens such access much later, eg France in the early 1980s, so that the inadequacies of the French system are only now coming to light (bearing in mind the typical wait of four to five years before a case reaches judgment at ECHR).

Another factor which could be used to counter Lester's argument is that United Kingdom judges already take account of the ECHR when interpreting ambiguous common law and statute law; indeed it has been said that it is mandatory for judges to do so when deciding how to resolve conflicts at common law: see per Butler-Sloss LJ in *Derbyshire County Council* v *Times Newspapers Ltd* (1993). Indeed, the Law Lords went further afield than the Court of Appeal by taking account of the American Constitution! This signifies how alert and willing the senior judges are when it comes to protection of human rights in the face of out-of-date common law or statute laws. In the *Derbyshire* case both the Court of Appeal and the House of Lords held that

10 THE EUROPEAN CONVENTION AND A BILL OF RIGHTS

local authorities could not sue for libel in respect of their reputation for administration because otherwise such a right of action would stifle legitimate public criticism of their activities and impose an unnecessary restriction on freedom of expression in a democratic society. Lord Keith, in the leading judgment, managed to reach his conclusion without finding the need to rely upon the European Convention: 'I find it satisfactory to be able to conclude that the common law of England is consistent with the obligations assumed by the Crown under the treaty in this particular field.' Who needs the ECHR to give a ruling of this kind when common law is capable of giving it? As Lord Denning often said in his career on the bench, common law is capable of evolving from precedent to precedent so as to move with the times and to meet the needs of society.

Of course such reconciliation of English law with the obligations under ECHR is not possible if statute law is unambiguous: see *R v Secretary of State for the Home Department, ex parte Brind* (1991). But, as Lord Ackner pointed out in that case, that is the price for preserving a degree of national self-government and independence, and to ensure that the people are ruled by their elected legislature and not by the unelected (and very unrepresentative) judiciary. Further, it would be rare for a government to legislate so as to flout international opinion and domestic wishes; the practical and political constraints on a sovereign legislature are usually sufficient to deter such behaviour. The United Kingdom has survived for centuries without an American-style Supreme Court and a European-style Bill of Rights and, when violations of human rights are compared on a fairer and more scientific basis than in Lester's critique, the United Kingdom probably emerges with a reasonably good record, a place to which many still wish to emigrate.

11 PUBLIC ORDER

11.1   Introduction
11.2   Key points
11.3   Recent cases and statutes
11.4   Analysis of questions
11.5   Questions

11.1 Introduction

There are many legal restrictions on our freedom to assemble and associate together. Such restrictions represent the political view of the extent to which a civil liberty should be restricted in the interests of social order and involves a balancing exercise which often results in emotive arguments between those who prioritise public order on the one hand and those who fear excessive state controls on the other.

Historically governments have reacted to threats to social order by introducing measures which are restrictive. Recent problems in Britain ranging from violence on football terraces to serious disorder in urban areas have resulted in the introduction of legislation which has increased police powers – the Police and Criminal Evidence Act 1984 – and recast the law relating to public order – the Public Order Act 1986 and the Criminal Justice and Public Order Act 1994. These two Acts taken together are a significant step towards the codification of the law on public order but other significant measures coexist alongside them. It is therefore important to understand what restrictions exist to fully understand what freedoms we do in fact enjoy.

The demonstration is an important political weapon which can result in government policy being changed, eg the reform of local taxation which introduced the 'poll tax'. One of the priorities of government is to maintain public order, and a balance has to be drawn between the right to protest and the existence of legal controls to prevent the breakdown of public order – see Lord Denning's speech in *Hubbard* v *Pitt* [1976] QB 142.

11.2 Key points

Common law

a) *Breach of the peace*

Section 40 of the Public Order Act 1986 specifically retains the common law powers to deal with or prevent a breach of the peace and s17(5) and (6) of the Police and Criminal Evidence Act 1984 preserve common law powers of entry to deal with breaches of the peace.

A precise definition of breach of the peace is difficult to give, but it must involve an element of actual or apprehended violence to person or property. A police officer who has either witnessed a breach of the peace, or who has reasonable

11 PUBLIC ORDER

grounds for believing that a breach of the peace is about to occur, can arrest an offender without warrant: see *R* v *Howell* [1982] QB 416; *R* v *Chief Constable of Devon and Cornwall, ex parte CEGB* [1982] QB 458; *Moss* v *McLachlan* (1984) 149 JP 167. In *Duncan* v *Jones* [1936] 1 KB 218 the power was used to effectively prevent a public meeting. In *Moss* v *McLachlan* (1985) 149 JP 167 flying pickets were turned back on the basis that a breach of the peace was 'imminent'.

b) *Entry into meetings*

While there is no doubt that the police have a right to be present in public places where there are fears of public disorder, there did exist some uncertainty as to their powers in respect of private premises where they had reason to believe a breach of the peace was imminent: see *Thomas* v *Sawkins* [1935] 2 KB 249.

Statutory powers

c) *Obstruction of the police*

Under the Police Act 1964 any person who assaults the police in the execution of their duty or resists or wilfully obstructs the police in the course of their duty is guilty of an offence. Policing inevitably involves the exercise of discretion. In the context of public order the issue is the extent to which the police can lawfully intervene. See *Duncan* v *Jones* [1936] 1 KB 218; *Piddington* v *Bates* [1960] 3 All ER 660.

d) *Obstruction of the highway*

Under the Highways Act 1980 a person is guilty of an offence if he wilfully obstructs the free passage of the highway. To initiate a meeting which results in such an obstruction can result in conviction, even in circumstances where the highway was not completely blocked: see *Arrowsmith* v *Jenkins* [1963] 2 QB 561; *Hirst and Agu* v *Chief Constable for West Yorkshire* [1987] Crim LR 330.

e) *Public Order Act 1986*

The Public Order Act 1986 provides a framework of controls which apply to processions and demonstrations and enacts a range of offences to deal with conduct of varying seriousness.

i) Public order offences

The Public Order Act 1986 abolishes the Common law offences of riot, rout, unlawful assembly and affray. It also abolishes the statutory offence of threatening behaviour under the Public Order Act 1936. These it replaces with an expanded range of public order offences – riot, violent disorder, affray, threatening behaviour and disorderly conduct.

Section 1 – riot. The offence of riot is retained for the most serious public order offences.

- Twelve or more persons must be present together and the difficult concept of common purpose is retained. This is to underline the seriousness of violent behaviour when committed collectively.

- A person of reasonable firmness must, as a result of the incident, fear for his personal safety. This hypothetical person need not actually be present at the scene at the time of the riot..
- Each of the persons present using unlawful violence is guilty of an offence. Unlawful violence is defined in s8.
- The consent of the DPP is necessary for a prosecution with underlying policy implications.

Section 2 – violent disorder. The offence of violent disorder is intended to deal with a range of situations from major public disorder to minor group disturbances eg football hooliganism. It is a lesser offence than riot.

- Note the similarities with riot, ie the use or threat of unlawful violence and the fact that a person of reasonable firmness present at the scene should fear for his personal safety (although again this hypothetical person need not actually be present). See *R* v *Hebron* [1989] Crim LR 839.
- The number of persons present need only be three.
- The consent of the DPP is not necessary for a prosecution.

Section 3 – affray. This redefined offence is directed at those who use or threaten violence towards others as individuals.

- A person of reasonable firmness must fear for their personal safety.
- The offence anticipates the following sort of conduct – fighting outside pubs or football grounds and also on private premises. See *R* v *Davison* [1992] Crim LR 31.

Section 4 – threatening behaviour. This section replaces s5 of the Public Order Act 1936.

- The concept of threatening abusive or insulting words or behaviour is retained and words can be verbal or in writing.
- There must be an intention to provoke unlawful violence or a person must believe that unlawful violence will be used against him. See *R* v *Horseferry Road Magistrates' Court, ex parte Siadatan* [1990] Crim LR 598.
- Much of the old case law will continue to be relevant. See *Brutus* v *Cozens* [1973] AC 854; *Jordan* v *Burgoyne* [1963] 2 All ER 225.

Section 5 – this section introduces a new offence of causing harassment, alarm or distress.

- The offence applies to disorderly behaviour and a person who sees or hears the conduct must be likely to be caused 'harassment, alarm or distress'. The objective here is to protect the vulnerable.
- Defences are: (i) that the accused had no reason to believe that any such person was present; (ii) that the conduct was reasonable; and (iii) that the accused was inside a dwelling and had no reason to believe anyone outside could see or hear them.

Sections 17–23 – racial hatred. The sections deal with a variety of circumstances in which racial hatred is likely to be stirred up.

- As with s4, conduct must be threatening, abusive or insulting. The consequence must be the stirring up of racial hatred.
- The same interpretative conditions will apply to 'threatening', or 'abusive' or 'insulting' as with s4. See *Jordan* v *Burgoyne* [1963] 2 QB 744.

Racial hatred is defined in s17. See too *Mandla* v *Lee* [1983] 2 AC 548.

ii) Processions and demonstrations

A more comprehensive legal framework is laid down by the Public Order Act 1986 for the control of public processions and public meetings.

Section 11 – this section requires advance notice to be given to the police of public processions.

- By and large this section is intended to cover planned marches, including commemorative marches and excluding instances where it is not practicable to give notice, ie a spontaneous march.

Section 12 – authorises 'a senior police officer' to impose conditions as to time, place or route on a public procession.

- There must be belief that serious public disorder or damage to property will result or that the objective is intimidation.

Section 13 – authorises the chief constable to apply to the council for an order prohibiting all marches for three months.

- The ban is a blanket ban and not aimed at specific groups. Clearly the chief constable must believe that serious public disorder would result in the event that the march was allowed to proceed.
- The ban is subject to the consent of the Home Secretary.
- The ban is subject to judicial review: *Kent* v *Metropolitan Police Commissioner* (1981) The Times 15 May.

Public assemblies are defined in s16, and the conditions on public assemblies are virtually the same as for public processions.

f) *Public Order Act 1936*

Section 1 of the Act makes it an offence to wear a uniform signifying membership of a political organisation. See *O'Moran* v *DPP* [1975] QB 364.

g) *Picketing*

Pickets can be in breach of both the civil and criminal law. Under s15 of the Trade Union and Labour Relations Act 1974 remedies are available for illegal picketing. In addition pickets find themselves in breach of the Public Order Act (as above).

h) *Additional powers*

There are additional powers available to the state to suppress anti-social behaviour which would be relevant in a public order context – see the Police and Criminal Evidence Act 1984 and the Prevention of Terrorism (Temporary Provisions) Act 1989.

CONSTITUTIONAL LAW

i) *Criminal Justice and Public Order Act 1994*
   i) Removing trespassers

   Section 61 repeals s39 of the Public Order Act 1986 and gives police new powers to 'remove trespassers on land'.

   Trespass was already criminalised by s39 of the 1986 Act, but it proved difficult to enforce.

   Section 61 is more tightly drawn and covers cases where permission to be on land has been withdrawn, reduces the number of vehicles required for a dispersal order to be made from 12 to six, extends definition of 'land' to include common land, and gives police powers to confiscate vehicles not willingly removed.

   ii) Aggravated trespass

   Section 68 – 'A person commits an offence if he trespasses on land in the open air and, in relation to any lawful activity which people there assembled are doing or are about to engage in, does anything that is intended by him to have the effect of:
   a) intimidating those persons so as to deter them from engaging in that activity; or
   b) obstructing that activity; or
   c) disrupting that activity.'

   iii) Trespassory assemblies

   Sections 70 and 71 insert new sections into s14 Public Order Act 1986 concerning the regulation of assemblies in progress.

   A chief constable can apply to the local authority for an order banning a trespassory assembly on the grounds that it may give rise either to serious disruption to the life of the community, or where the land or a building or monument on it, is of historical, architectural, archaeological or scientific importance and significant damage to the land, building or monument may occur.

   These provisions cover places to which the public has no, or limited, rights of access. The ban is for up to four days and needs the consent of the Secretary of State.

   iv) Squatters

   Sections 75 and 76 – Lawful owners and occupiers of property now have access to quicker and effective remedies against squatters. They can go to court immediately and apply for an interim possession order. If granted, squatters will have 24 hours to leave premises. Failure to do so will be an offence.

   v) Unauthorised campers

   Section 77 – Local authorities now have the power, where people are for the time being residing in a vehicle or vehicles on a highway or any unoccupied land, or on any occupied land without the occupier's consent, to give a direction that those persons must leave, taking vehicles and property with them. Failure to comply is a criminal offence.

Note: Section 80(1) repeals a provision in the Caravan Sites Act 1968 which required local authorities to provide sites for gipsies. They are still empowered to do so, but are no longer required to.

vi) Raves

Sections 63–67 – A rave is defined as a gathering in open air of 100 or more persons (whether or not they are trespassers), at which amplified music is played during the night which, by reason of its loudness and time at which it is played, is likely to cause serious distress to inhabitants of the locality.

If a police officer reasonably believes that two or more people are planning a rave and that ten or more are waiting for it to begin or attending such a gathering, dispersal orders may be made requiring them to leave.

Powers of entry and seizure of vehicles and sound equipment are given.

Police officers are also empowered to turn people within a five-mile radius away before sufficient numbers gather.

vii) Intentional harassment, alarm or distress

Section 154 takes its place as s4A of the Public Order Act 1986.

An offence is committed where a defendant, with intent to cause a person harassment, alarm or distress (a) uses threatening, abusive or insulting words or behaviour, or disorderly behaviour, or (b) displays any writing, sign or other visible representation which is threatening, abusive or insulting, thereby causing that person, or another person, harassment, alarm or distress.

viii) Racial hatred

Section 155 makes publishing or distributing racially offensive material (s19 Public Order Act 1986) an arrestable offence.

ix) Burden of proof

As with the Public Order Act 1986, the burden of proof in many sections of the Act is on the defence, not the prosecution – contrary to article 6 of the European Convention on Human Rights which states: 'Everyone charged with a criminal offence shall be presumed innocent until proved guilty according to law.'

11.3 Recent cases and statutes

R v *Morpeth Ward Justices, ex parte Ward and Others* [1992] Crim LR 497.

Criminal Justice and Public Order Act 1994.

11.4 Analysis of questions

Questions can be problem or essay. Included below are examples of each. A knowledge of the Public Order Act 1986 is essential and a methodical application of

CONSTITUTIONAL LAW

the provisions of the Act to any problem will earn marks. An essay question may require a broader if limited knowledge of the social background to the Act's introduction. The Criminal Justice and Public Order Act 1994 gives police further powers and must be understood alongside existing provisions.

11.5 Questions

QUESTION ONE

What difference, if any, has the Public Order Act 1986 made to English law?

> University of London LLB Examination
> (for External Students) Constitutional Law June 1987 Q8

General Comment

A relatively straightforward question concerning the Public Order Act 1986. Students should know the changes introduced by this Act and compare the new provisions with those existing at common law and under the Public Order Act 1936. A question like this is now unlikely to be set, but it is included for revision purposes on the provisions of the 1986 Act.

Skeleton Solution

- Introduction. General provisions of the Public Order Act 1986.
- Abolition of common law riot, rout, unlawful assembly and affray. Introduction of statutory riot, violent disorder and affray.
- Provisions relating to processions. Sections 12 and 13.
- Provisions relating to assemblies. Section 14.
- Provisions relating to racial hatred.
- Causing fear or provocation of violence. Causing harassment, alarm or distress.
- Miscellaneous provisions.

Suggested Solution

The Public Order Act 1986 was passed on 7 November 1986. Some provisions of the Act came into force on 1 January 1987. Most of the rest of the Act came into force on 1 April 1987. The Act firstly repeals certain provisions of the Public Order Act 1936. Secondly it abolishes the common law offences of riot, rout, unlawful assembly and affray. Third, it introduces new statutory offences to replace some of the common law offences abolished or statutory offences repealed. Fourth, it amends or repeals other statutory provisions including those concerning racial hatred. Fifth, it introduces new powers in relation to offences committed at or in connection with football matches. Sixth, it introduces miscellaneous provisions in relation to tampering with goods on sale and also mass trespass.

One of the main differences made to the law under the new Act is that the ancient common law offences of riot, rout, unlawful assembly and affray have been abolished and replaced by three statutory offences: riot, violent disorder and affray. The basis of these offences is no longer breach of the peace but fear for personal safety on the part of a person of reasonable firmness present at the scene.

11 PUBLIC ORDER

As regards the Public Order Act 1936 this is largely repealed. Section 3 has been repealed and replaced by a new provision of greater scope and effect and has been extended to certain public assemblies. As was already the case under the old 1936 Act, s12 of the 1986 Act gives the police the power to impose conditions on certain processions and under s13 the chief officer of police may in certain circumstances prohibit processions in his district with the consent of his local authority and the Home Secretary. The major difference under the new Act however is that now the organisers of public processions must give advance notice in writing to the police not less than six clear days before the date of any procession which is intended to demonstrate support for or opposition to the views or actions of any person or body of persons; or publicises a cause or campaign; or which marks or commemorates an event.

Another new development under the 1986 Act is contained in s14 which confers a new power allowing a senior police officer to impose conditions in relation to public assemblies. Under this section, if the senior police officer, having regard to the time or place at which and the circumstances in which any public assembly is being held or is intended to be held, reasonably believes that (a) it may result in serious public disorder, serious damage to property or serious disruption to the life of the community, or (b) the purpose of the persons organising it is the intimidation of others with a view to compelling them not to do an act they have a right to do, or to do an act they have a right not to do, he may give directions imposing on the persons organising or taking part in the assembly such conditions as to the place at which the assembly may be (or continue to be) held, its maximum duration, or the maximum number of persons who may constitute it, as appear to him necessary to prevent such disorder, damage, disruption or intimidation. Section 16 defines 'public assembly' as an assembly of 20 or more persons in a public place which is wholly or partly open to the air.

Section 5A of the 1936 Act dealing with racial hatred has been restructured and amended to produce six new offences. Section 17 of the 1986 Act defines racial hatred as hatred against a group of persons in Great Britain defined by reference to colour, race, nationality (including citizenship) or ethnic or national origins. All six offences created by the Act require the consent of the Attorney-General to institute proceedings. All of these offences concern conduct which is threatening, abusive or insulting and which is intended or which is likely, having regard to all the circumstances, to stir up racial hatred. They are: (i) using such words or behaviour or displaying such materials; (ii) publishing or distributing such materials; (iii) presenting or directing a public play which involves such words or behaviour; (iv) distributing, showing or playing a recording of such visual images or sounds; (v) certain participation in a broadcast or cable programme service which includes such images or sounds; and (vi) possessing such material or recordings with a view to its being displayed, published, distributed, broadcast or included in a cable broadcast service.

Section 5 of the 1936 Act has also been repealed, and replaced by two new offences. Section 4 of the 1986 Act creates the offence of causing fear or provocation of violence. A person is guilty of an offence if he uses towards another person threatening, abusive or insulting words or behaviour, or distributes or displays to another person any writing, sign or other visible representation which is threatening,

CONSTITUTIONAL LAW

abusive or insulting, with intent to cause that person to believe that immediate unlawful violence will be used against him or another by any person, or to provoke the immediate use of unlawful violence by that person or another, or whereby that person is likely to believe that such violence will be used or it is likely that such violence will be provoked.

Section 5 of the 1986 Act creates the controversial offence of causing harassment, alarm or distress. A person is guilty of an offence if he uses threatening, abusive or insulting words or behaviour, or disorderly behaviour, or displays any writing, sign or other visible representation which is threatening, abusive or insulting, within the hearing or sight of a person likely to be caused harassment, alarm or distress thereby. Section 5 provides for three specific defences. First, that the defendant had no reason to believe that there was anyone within hearing or sight of his or her conduct who was likely to be harassed, alarmed or distressed; second, that he or she was inside a dwelling and had no reason to believe that the conduct would have been seen or heard by anyone outside; third, that his or her conduct was reasonable.

The 1986 Act also creates several miscellaneous offences. Under s30 a court by or before which a person is convicted or an offence connected with football may make an exclusion order prohibiting him from entering premises to attend a prescribed football match. Section 38 creates various offences connected with contamination of or interference with goods. Finally, s39 gives the most senior police officer present power to direct trespassers to leave land. The officer may arrest anyone who, knowing that such a direction has been given, fails to leave as soon as is reasonable practicable or, having left, re-enters within three months of the direction.

Note: The Criminal Justice and Public Order Act 1994 has amended the 1986 Act.

QUESTION TWO

The PRO organisation arrange a procession through the streets of London. They do not ask anyone for permission. The ANTI organisation arrange a counter demonstration, again without seeking official permission. When the two marches converge on the Strand, violence breaks out. Nobody in the PRO march uses force except in self defence. A police constable orders the PRO marchers to stop their procession and to disperse. They continue to march and are arrested. Pleased with their success the ANTI marchers disperse and make their way home. A dozen of them decide to have some 'fun' on the Underground platform. They surround an old lady and begin to chant 'euthanasia, euthanasia'. She is alarmed by this and collapses. The ANTI marchers later discover that she was of an unusually weak disposition and had previously suffered heart attacks. But at the time they panic and run away. One of them is intent on escape and has no intent of causing further trouble. The others take the opportunity of lashing out violently at passers-by.

Which offences, if any, have been committed against the Public Order Act 1986?

Written by the Editors

General Comment

A question which demands a comprehensive knowledge of public order offences but a well prepared student should have no problem if application is logical and thorough. Clearly a good grasp of the Public Order Act 1986 is essential.

11 PUBLIC ORDER

Skeleton Solution

- Introduction. Effect of the Public Order Act 1986.
- Powers of the police to impose conditions on processions – s12. Common law powers to prevent a breach of peace.
- Section 1 Riot.
- Section 2 Violent disorder.
- Section 3 Affray.
- Section 4 Provoking violence.
- Section 5 Disorderly conduct.
- Analyse and apply facts to above sections of the Act.

Suggested Solution

Regarding the problem for consideration, the PRO organisation have arranged a procession through the streets of London and have not asked for permission. While there is no requirement under the law that permission has to be obtained to hold a procession, under s11 of the Public Order Act 1986 the organisers of public processions must give advance notice in writing to the police not less than six clear days before the date of any procession which is intended to demonstrate support for or opposition to the views or actions of any person or body of persons; or publicise a cause or campaign; or which marks or commemorates an event. In not giving such notice the procession organisers therefore commit an offence. The same will be true of the organisers of the ANTI procession.

When the two groups converge violence, instigated by the ANTI marchers, breaks out and a police constable orders the PRO marchers to stop their procession and disperse. It is of course a fundamental principle of our law that one cannot be stopped from doing what one is lawfully entitled to do merely because others act unlawfully (*Beatty v Gillbanks* (1862)). However, s12 of the 1986 Act gives the police the power to impose conditions on certain processions if a senior police officer, having regard to the time or place at which and the circumstances in which, any public procession is being held or is intended to be held, reasonably believes that (a) it may result in serious public disorder, serious damage to property or serious disruption to the life of the community, or (b) the purpose of the persons organising it is the intimidation of others with a view to compelling them not to do an act they have a right to do, or to do an act they have a right not to do. Further, under s13 the chief officer of police may in certain circumstances prohibit processions in his district.

While the power therefore exists under the Public Order Act for the police to impose conditions on and even in some circumstances ban a lawful procession, it does not appear that the conditions for so doing apply in this particular case, and in any case they certainly may not be exercised by a mere constable. However, at common law a police officer has the power to take such steps as are reasonably necessary to prevent a breach of the peace and in so doing is acting in the execution of his duty so that a failure to obey would be an offence under s51(3) Police Act 1964 (*Duncan v Jones* (1936)) and if a breach of the peace is occurring or threatened there is a common law right to arrest preserved by the Police and Criminal Evidence Act 1984.

CONSTITUTIONAL LAW

As regards the violence which takes place in the Strand and the actions of the ANTI marchers on the Underground platform, various offences under the Public Order Act 1986 may have been committed.

The basis of these offences is fear for personal safety on the part of a person of reasonable firmness present at the scene. Section 1 redefines the offence of riot. Where 12 or more persons who are present together use or threaten unlawful violence and the conduct of them (taken together) is such as would cause a person of reasonable firmness present at the scene to fear for his personal safety, each of the persons using or threatening unlawful violence for the common purpose is guilty of riot.

The s2 offence of violent disorder has similarities with riot but the three persons (rather than 12) need not be acting for a common purpose. Note *R* v *Hebron* (1989) which established that mere threats suffice to support a conviction.

Section 3 defines the offence of affray. A person is guilty of affray if he uses or threatens unlawful violence towards another and his conduct is such as would cause a person of reasonable firmness present at the scene to fear for his personal safety.

Section 4 of the 1986 Act creates the offence of causing fear or provocation of violence. A person is guilty of an offence if he uses towards another person threatening, abusive or insulting words or behaviour, or distributes or displays to another person any writing, sign or other visible representation which is threatening, abusive or insulting, with intent to cause that person to believe that immediate unlawful violence will be used against him or another by any person, or to provoke the immediate use of unlawful violence by that person or another, or whereby that person is likely to believe that such violence will be used or it is likely that such violence will be provoked.

Section 5 of the 1986 Act creates the controversial offence of causing harassment, alarm or distress. A person is guilty of an offence if he uses threatening, abusive or insulting words or behaviour, or disorderly behaviour, or displays any writing, sign or other visible representation which is threatening, abusive or insulting, within the hearing or sight of a person likely to be caused harassment, alarm or distress thereby. Section 5 provides for three specific defences. First, that the defendant had no reason to believe that there was anyone within hearing or sight of his or her conduct who was likely to be harassed, alarmed or distressed; second, that he or she was inside a dwelling and had no reason to believe that the conduct would have been seen or heard by anyone outside; third, that his or her conduct was reasonable.

From the facts given in the problem it appears that the actions of the ANTI organisation in the Strand could amount to riot, violent disorder and affray since it appears that the violence was instigated by them. However, the PRO organisation acting only in self defence do not seem to fall within the definitions of ss1 and 2 since they acted only in self defence, ie no *unlawful* violence.

When the ANTI demonstrators gather on the underground platform it seems they simply surround the old lady and chant 'euthanasia, euthanasia'. From the facts given it would seem doubtful whether it would be possible to establish 'use or threats of unlawful violence' so as to sustain charges under ss1, 2 and 3 and s4 also depends upon the threat of 'immediate unlawful violence'. It would therefore seem that the actions in respect of the old lady would have to be prosecuted under s5, causing harassment, alarm or distress. The words 'euthanasia, euthanasia' could be classified as threatening and since an old lady has been singled out for the treatment none of the defences seem appropriate. It will of course be no defence that the ANTI group was not aware of her unusually weak disposition. In *Jordan* v *Burgoyne* (1963), a case dealing with similar provisions in the old s5, Public Order Act 1936, it was made clear that the person using threatening, abusive or insulting words cannot look at their effect on a hypothetical reasonable audience but must take note of the effect on the actual audience addressed.

The ANTI demonstrators then disperse, one on his own, leaving 11 who commit acts of violence on passers by. Since there are then only 11 people no offence of riot can be established but violent disorder and affray charges are available, under ss2 and 3 of the 1986 Act respectively.

Note: The Criminal Justice and Public Order Act 1994 has amended the 1986 Act.

QUESTION THREE

'The Public Order Act 1986 represents a failure on the part of Parliament to rationalise the law. Public order law remains a miscellany of disparate rules.'

Discuss.

University of London LLB Examination
(for External Students) Constitutional Law June 1991 Q4

General Comment

A question that requires a good knowledge of the central measures in the Public Order Act 1986, and also a knowledge of the related common law provisions. The theme of the solution is to pick out the salient provisions of the 1986 Act, and demonstrate the extent to which they overlap with other statutory and common law provisions.

Skeleton Solution

- Assemblies, Public Order Act 1986, other statutes, common law.
- Processions, Public Order Act 1986, other statutes, common law.
- Examples of other pieces of legislation and common law powers.
- Explain need for reform.

Suggested Solution

It is well known that under English law individuals are free to meet together in public in such groups and for such purposes as they see fit, subject only to the limitations imposed by the law. There is no right to march or demonstrate, but instead a variety of limitations imposed by common law and statute.

The Public Order Act 1986 (hereinafter referred to as the 1986 Act) represents an attempt to clarify certain points of law relating to public order, and to consolidate and update the law on a number of issues, but as the quotation under consideration

151

CONSTITUTIONAL LAW

suggests, it has only been partially successful in this respect. The problem remains that the term 'public order law' is necessarily vague. To ascertain the law relating to meetings both public and private, and marches on the highway, one still has to consult a variety of pieces of legislation, and some confusing and contradictory statements at common law.

Consider firstly the law relating to public assemblies. Section 14 of the 1986 Act allows a senior police officer to impose conditions in relation to such assemblies if, having regard to the time or place at which and the circumstances in which any public assembly is being held or is intended to be held, he reasonably believes that (a) it may result in serious public disorder, serious damage to property or serious disruption to the life of the community, or (b) the purpose of the persons organising it is the intimidation of others with a view to compelling them not to do an act they have a right to do, or to do an act they have a right not to do. He may give directions imposing on the persons organising or taking part in the assembly such conditions as to the place at which the assembly may be (or continue to be) held, its maximum duration, or the maximum number of persons who may constitute it, as appears to him necessary to prevent such disorder, damage, disruption or intimidation.

Section 16 defines 'public assembly' as an assembly of 20 or more persons in a public place which is wholly or partly open to the air. This may be thought to be a comprehensive measure governing such gatherings. But one would still have to have regard to other measures if the meeting takes place on the highway; see Highways Act 1980 s137(1), under which it is a criminal offence wilfully to obstruct the free passage along a highway. If the highway is obstructed then a constable can arrest those causing the obstruction. Obstruction, in this context, is a very flexible term. Special provisions apply to meetings in certain public places such as Hyde Park Corner or Trafalgar Square which are Crown property. For any meeting to take place the permission of the Secretary of State for the Environment is needed, and he can if he wishes impose restrictions on any meeting for which permission has been granted.

The 1986 Act also seeks to regulate the use of the highway for processions. Advance notice of public processions must be given in certain circumstances. Section 11 provides that proposals to hold a public procession must be notified to the police if it is a procession intended to demonstrate support for or opposition to the views or actions of any person or body of persons; or publicise a cause or campaign; or mark or commemorate an event. Written notice must be given to the police not less than six clear days before the date of the procession, or as soon as is practicable. The organisers commit an offence if they fail to satisfy these requirements or, if in general, the conduct of the procession differs from that indicated in the notice. The powers provided by the Act are directed to preventing serious public disorder rather than dealing with it when it has occurred. The framework of control has two stages. Marches can be allowed subject to conditions (s12) or banned outright (s13).

These provisions are tolerably clear in their scope and effect, but again they are not comprehensive. Other legislation needs to be consulted in certain cases. For example, Under s52 of the Metropolitan Police Act 1839, the Commissioner of Police of the Metropolis may make regulations for preventing obstruction of the streets within the vicinity of Parliament. Any contravention of those regulations is a criminal offence. The police also have the power to stop potential disorderly processions by bringing the possible demonstrators before the magistrates before the demonstration. They may

11 PUBLIC ORDER

then be bound over to keep the peace. Should they refuse to be bound over then they can be imprisoned for up to six months.

Those partaking in a procession along the highway could be dealt with under the common law if the procession goes beyond what is a reasonable use of the highway, since it may constitute a public nuisance. This offence is rare but it was used in the case of *R v Clarke (No 2)* (1964).

There remains the question of the offences that may be committed once disorder breaks out during a public meeting during a procession. The 1986 Act creates a range of new offences that can be used in such situations.

Section 1 redefines the offence of riot. Section 2 creates a new offence of violent disorder. Section 3 redefines the offence of affray. Section 4 largely replaces s5 of the Public Order Act 1936 with the new offence of causing fear or provocation of violence. Finally s5 introduces the controversial offence of causing harassment, alarm or distress.

All of these new offences co-exist, however, with long established offences such as breach of the peace, an offence drawn in such broad terms it allows the police the power to arrest in situations where the legality of their actions may be unclear.

A brief list will give a flavour of the other disparate offences touching upon 'public order law'. The Unlawful Drilling Act 1819, which prohibits assemblies for the purpose of training or drilling in the use of arms or practising military exercises without lawful authority. The Public Meeting Act 1908, makes it an offence to endeavour to break up a public meeting by acting in a disorderly manner for the purpose of preventing the transaction of the business for which the meeting was called together. The Representation of the People Act 1983 s97 makes it an offence to cause a disturbance at an election meeting. The Police Act 1964 s51(1) makes it an offence to assault a police officer in the execution of his duty. Section 51(3) makes it an offence to wilfully obstruct the police in the execution of their duty.

Finally, the Criminal Justice and Public Order Act 1994 adds further offences relating to the removal of trespassers, further powers to ban trespassory assemblies and powers to deal with squatters and 'raves'.

Not only does the 1986 Act co-exist alongside myriad other related offences, the Act itself was used by Parliament as an opportunity to enact measures which in some cases have only a tenuous link with public order. For example s38 creates various offences connected with contamination of or interference with goods.

In short it is submitted that the whole of the law relating to public order should be looked at again with a view to greater consolidation and rationalisation.

12 FREEDOM OF EXPRESSION

12.1 Introduction
12.2 Key points
12.3 Recent cases
12.4 Question analysis
12.5 Question

12.1 Introduction

English law relies on the principle that what is not prohibited is permitted and attempts are made to achieve a balance between one individual's right to express his opinions, another's right to be protected from the worst excesses of those views and the state's interest in ensuring that expressed opinions do not undermine either public order or state security. The result is a wide range of specific offences to provide remedies to either individuals or the state when views expressed go beyond what is considered tolerable. The area includes such diverse topics as theatre censorship and state security, contempt of court, obscene publications and the right to privacy.

While individual syllabuses may emphasise different facets of freedom of expression, the issue in each case is generally whether a balance between competing interests has been achieved.

12.2 Key points

a) *The protection of the State*

   i) Sedition

   This common law offence is now largely of historical interest as other offences have largely superseded the need to prosecute for sedition.

   The element of incitement to violence has been stressed. *R* v *Caunt* (1948) unreported.

   ii) Incitement to disaffection

   It is an offence to undermine the loyalty of:

   - a police officer: s53 Police Act 1964; or
   - a member of the armed forces: Incitement to Disaffection Act 1934. See *R* v *Arrowsmith* [1975] QB 678.

   iii) Incitement to racial hatred

   - Threats, abuse and insults which are likely to result in unlawful violence are criminal: Public Order Act 1986 s4.
   - Threats, abuse or insults which are intended or are likely to stir up racial

hatred are specifically dealt with by ss17–23 Public Order Act 1986. The offences are unlikely to be committed by those who use reasoned argument: *Jordan* v *Burgoyne* [1963] 2 QB 744.

Note the meaning of racial group – a group of persons defined by reference to colour, race, nationality or ethnic or national origins: *Mandla* v *Dowell Lee* [1983] 2 AC 548.

iv) Blasphemy

- Blasphemy is a common law offence committed through attacks on the Christian religion or the existence of God.

  The Law Commission has recommended that the offence be abolished and that any statutory alternative not be restricted to attacks upon Christianity.

- In *R* v *Lemon* [1979] AC 617 it was held that there was no need for an intention to blaspheme, publication was enough. Publication need not necessarily lead to a breach of the peace.

v) Criminal libel

Criminal libel covers cases of libel where there is considered to be some threat to the preservation of the peace. Prosecutions are rare and only with the order of a High Court judge: *Goldsmith* v *Pressdram Ltd* [1976] 3 WLR 191.

vi) Freedom of communication and information

- Government has a duty to preserve the security of the State. National security includes not only measures intended to protect the State from espionage but also all matters that are considered subversive. Governments are often seen as using the cloak of national security to 'gag' the communication of information which should be in the public domain.

- What is 'national security'?

  It is not clear exactly what is included in the concept of national security. Courts often accept the word of governments. National security interests have been invoked in a variety of instances, such as: defence of the realm and the prosecution of war (*The Zamora* [1916] 2 AC 77); the disposition of the armed forces (*Chandler* v *DPP* [1964] AC 763); nuclear weapons (*Secretary of State for Defence* v *Guardian Newspapers* [1984] 1 All ER 453); and the activities of intelligence services (*Attorney-General* v *Guardian Newspapers (No 2)* [1988] 3 All ER 545).

- Official Secrets Acts

  Section 1 of the Official Secrets Act 1911 creates offences of espionage. It is not restricted to spying but includes acts of sabotage: *Chandler* v *DPP* [1964] AC 763.

  Section 2 created some 2,000 offences directed at the misuse of information. It was criticised for being used to keep policy making free of outside scrutiny.

  In 1989, s2 was repealed by the Official Secrets Act 1989. The Act creates specific categories of information which is sensitive and should be controlled. These are: (i) security and intelligence; (ii) defence; (iii) international relations; and (iv) criminal investigations. The disclosure must be 'damaging'. This concept operates differently in respect of each of the four categories. There is no public interest defence or a defence of prior publication.

- 'D' Notices

  A form of extra legal censorship which depends on co-operation between governments and the press with the objective of achieving a ban on the publication of matters which are considered likely to jeopardise national security.

- Interception of Communications Act 1985

  Under the Act it is an offence to intercept communications (specifically telephone communications) unless authorised by the Secretary of State who may issue a warrant in the interests of national security or for the purpose of preventing serious crime or for the purpose of safeguarding the economic well being of the United Kingdom. See generally *Malone* v *United Kingdom* [1985] 7 EHRR 14.

- Breach of confidence

  An equitable doctrine to ensure that a person should not take unfair advantage of confidences obtained: *Argyll* v *Argyll* [1967] Ch 302; *Attorney-General* v *Jonathan Cape* [1976] QB 752.

  It is worth noting in this context because of the attempt made by the government in the 'Spycatcher' affair to assert that members of the security services owe a lifelong duty of confidentiality to the Crown: *Attorney-General* v *Guardian Newspapers (No 2)* [1988] 3 All ER 545.

  It seems that the courts are more willing to consider the issue of 'the public interest' and not to depend on the government's view: *Lord Advocate* v *Scotsman Publications* [1990] 1 AC 812.

- European Convention on Human Rights

  The three newspapers involved in the 'Spycatcher' case challenged the decision to grant an injunction against them as a breach of article 10: *The Observer and the Guardian* v *United Kingdom* [1992] 14 EHRR 153; *The Sunday Times* v *United Kingdom* [1992] 14 EHRR 229. The court found there had been a violation.

b) *Obscene publications*

  i) The trade in pornography is lucrative and the State seeks to limit publication to limit 'depravity'. There are statutory and common law offences.

  ii) Obscene Publications Act 1959

  An obscene article is one where the effect '... if taken as a whole, would tend to deprave and corrupt persons who are likely having regard to all the circumstances to read, see or hear the matter contained or embodied in it': s1.

12 FREEDOM OF EXPRESSION

- Article is defined widely and includes pictures, books and film negatives.
- The definition of obscene requires the jury to consider whether the article has a tendency to deprave and corrupt and this has caused inconsistency. It is not limited to sexual matters: *John Calder (Publishers)* v *Powell* [1965] 1 QB 509; *DPP* v *A and BC Chewing Gum Ltd* [1968] 1 QB 159.
- Policing the trade in pornography is difficult – 'an attempt to eradicate the ineradicable' (Robert Mark, ex Chief Commissioner for the Metropolis, in *Policing a Perplexed Society* (1977)). See *R* v *Metropolitan Police Commissioner, ex parte Blackburn* [1973] QB 241.
- Section 3 confers search, seizure and forfeiture powers.
- Section 4 makes it a defence if the material is 'for the public good on the grounds that it is in the interests of science, literature, art or learning ...'. Whether publication is for the public good is for the jury to decide.

See *Attorney-General's Reference (No 3 of 1977)* [1978] 3 All ER 1166; *R* v *Penguin Books* [1961] Crim LR 176.

iii) The Obscene Publications Act 1964 allows the police to seize material if the material was 'in possession for gain' thus it can be effective – material can be seized – before publication.

iv) Other legislation

This includes Customs Consolidation Act 1876, the Children and Young Persons (Harmful Publications) Act 1955, the Post Office Act 1953 and the Protection of Children Act 1978.

v) Common law offences

- Conspiracy to corrupt public morals: *Shaw* v *DPP* [1962] AC 220.
- Conspiracy to outrage public decency: *Knuller* v *DPP* [1973] AC 435.

vi) Cinema and theatre

There are general controls over films (Cinemas Act 1985 and Video Recordings Act 1984) and over live performances (Theatres Act 1968).

c) *Contempt of court*

i) Civil contempts

The breach of or disobedience to an order of the court: *Harman* v *Secretary of State for the Home Department* [1982] 2 WLR 338.

ii) Criminal contempts

The objective here is to ensure both the fairness of a trial and also that the judiciary is accorded respect.

iii) Contempt of Court Act 1981

The Act clarified the position regarding newspaper publication of matters of public interest which could prejudice the outcome of court proceedings by the following reforms.

See also *Attorney-General* v *Times Newspapers Ltd* [1974] AC 273, a case which went to the European Court of Human Rights.

CONSTITUTIONAL LAW

- It is an offence 'to interfere with the course of justice in particular legal proceedings regardless of intent' where the proceedings in question are active: s1.
- There is no offence if there was no reason to suspect that proceedings are active (s3) or that publication is a discussion in good faith of public affairs: *Attorney-General* v *English* [1982] 2 WLR 278.
- Section 10 gives limited protection to journalists of their sources unless disclosure is necessary in the interests of justice, national security or for the prevention of disorder or crime: *Secretary of State for Defence* v *Guardian Newspapers Ltd* [1984] 2 WLR 268.
- The prevention of crime exception in s10 encompasses the prevention of crime in general: *Re an Inquiry under the Company Securities (Insider Dealing) Act 1985* [1988] AC 660.

d) *Censorship*

i) Theatres are subject to the laws on obscenity, defamation and incitement to racial hatred.

ii) Cinemas are licensed by the local authority which attaches conditions and recommendations of the British Board of Film Censors are usually followed.

iii) Broadcasting

Both the BBC and IBA are under a duty to provide programmes which comply with good taste and decency and to preserve political impartiality. This last point has sometimes caused political controversy with governments.

e) *Defamation*

i) Publication of material which 'tends to lower a person in the estimation of right thinking members of society generally' (Lord Atkin in *Sim* v *Stretch* (1936) 52 TLR 669) is a tort and gives rise to a civil action for damages.

ii) Note the defences available.

f) *Prior restraint*

A person whose interests are likely to be affected by the publication of material or the Attorney-General in his role as guardian of the public interest can apply to the court for an injunction restraining such publication. The injunction is interim until such time as a full hearing of the issues can take place: see *Attorney-General* v *Guardian Newspapers* [1987] 3 All ER 316; *Attorney-General* v *Newspaper Publishing plc* [1987] 3 All ER 276. Note that some prior constraints are extra-legal, eg D notices.

12.3 Recent cases

X v *Morgan Grampian (Publishers) Ltd* [1991] 1 AC 1.

R v *Chief Metropolitan Stipendiary Magistrate, ex parte Choudhury* [1991] 1 QB 429.

R v *Secretary of State for the Home Department, ex parte Brind* [1991] 2 WLR 588.

12 FREEDOM OF EXPRESSION

12.4 Question analysis

London University has not questioned students directly on this topic in recent years. Other examiners may emphasise a particular area, for example State security, with a view to examining students' knowledge on that specific subject. The topic does lend itself to a general essay type question eg 'consider to what extent in your view a balance has been achieved between competing interests in the areas of ...' and an examiner could then identify the areas the student should focus on.

In any case a general knowledge of the topic is important in, for example, answering a question on a Bill of Rights.

12.5 Questions

QUESTION ONE

To what extent does the law successfully balance competing interests in the area of press freedom?

Written by the Editors

General Comment

An easy question requiring students to review the law on censorship.

Skeleton Solution

- Introduction – nature of freedom of speech in the United Kingdom – remedies available.
- Prior restraint – an evaluation of the effect of prior restraint on the media.
- Breach of confidence – its use particularly by government.
- Official Secrets Act 1989.
- Contempt of court.
- The individual and the press – remedies and contrasts with the above.

Suggested Solution

Freedom of speech is fundamental to a free society. It is protected by article 10 of the European Convention on Human Rights but of course the convention is not directly applicable in UK courts. The position in the United Kingdom is that individual members of the state are free to express views and opinions that are not against the numerous laws that restrict freedom of speech and to this extent the law attempts to balance competing rights. The press has a fundamental role to perform in informing the public, not least on government activities. However, individuals have a right not to be offended or abused and the state has a right to prevent the publication of sensitive material that could, for example, jeopardise national security. There is an inherent conflict here and some of the ways in which the law deals with that conflict in relation to press freedom will now be examined.

The major restrictions on press freedom are to be found in the laws on defamation, breach of confidence and contempt of court.

CONSTITUTIONAL LAW

It is important at the outset to draw a distinction between prior restraint and subsequent penalties. Blackstone (in his *Commentaries* (1765)) emphasised the importance in a free society of laying no prior restraints on publications – 'every free man has an undoubted right to lay what sentiments he pleases before the public; to forbid this is to destroy the freedom of the press ...' – and his sentiments were included in the first amendment to the American Constitution. It is arguable that prior restraint has become relatively easy to obtain in Britain either by the person whose interests are affected or by the Attorney-General as 'guardian of the public interest'. The injunction is interim and the applicant has to show that he has an arguable case, that the balance of convenience is against publishing and damages are not an adequate remedy. That balance of convenience is normally in favour of a ban and some writers (see G Robertson, *Freedom, the Individual and the Law*) argue that this can amount to political interference with free speech. In *Attorney-General* v *BBC* (1987) the government was successful in getting an interim injunction against a series entitled 'My Country Right or Wrong' on the grounds that ex-employees of the security services might have breached confidences during interviews.

Injunctions can also be granted to protect commercial interests when the courts balance the public's right to information against the private interest in ensuring that discussion should be prevented. In this context the private interest will be to protect trade secrets whilst the public interest may relate to the effect for example of a drug: *Schering Chemicals* v *Falkman Ltd* (1981). An injunction once granted binds third parties: *Attorney-General* v *Observer Newspapers Ltd* (1988). Whilst the nature of the injunction is limited to the period until trial, it may well be that the information may by then be no longer important.

Breach of confidence is a civil matter providing protection where information is given in circumstances of confidence. It can include intimate communications between husband and wife (*Duke of Argyll* v *Duchess of Argyll* (1967)), trade secrets (*Lion Laboratories* v *Evans* (1984)) and often arises from a contract of employment. Claims to confidentiality can be defeated if the claimed confidences relate to criminal activity or if the disclosure serves the public interest. A confidence ceases to be a confidence once it is in the public domain. In *Attorney-General* v *Guardian Newspapers (No 2)* (1988) the House of Lords held that given a government secret was in the public domain – in this case the information was obtainable in Australia and the USA – then the remedy should not be available to prevent British citizens reading it. Nevertheless, the court confirmed the lifelong duty of confidentiality owed by members of the security services. The public interest may continue to be served, however, where the revelations contain substantial allegations of wrongdoing.

Governments are concerned to limit information which is of a sensitive nature in terms of national security but also may be inclined to prevent publication where information is simply politically embarrassing. The use of the discredited s2 of the Official Secrets Act 1911 provides evidence of the preoccupation of governments with secrecy. In *R* v *Aitken* (1974) the government prosecuted under s2 for the publication of information already in the public domain and in the celebrated case of *R* v *Ponting* (1985) the jury found not guilty a civil servant who had 'leaked' information to an opposition MP which revealed that the government was attempting to deceive Parliament. Section 2 of the Act has been repealed by the Official Secrets Act 1989. Journalists and editors can be imprisoned if they encourage civil servants to make

12 FREEDOM OF EXPRESSION

disclosures or publish such disclosures. During the debate, attention focused on whether there should be a 'public interest' defence, but amendments to the Bill were successfully resisted. Under s5 members of the press can be successfully prosecuted if they publish information which they know is protected by the Act and they had reason to believe the publication would be damaging to the interests of the United Kingdom. If information is published from former or serving members of the security service the offence is one of strict liability. It is notable that the court in *Attorney-General* v *Guardian Newspapers (No 2)* (1988) accepted the principle of a public interest defence in breach of confidence actions which the government was anxious not to see in the Official Secrets Act 1989.

It is essential that court proceedings are not disrupted and justice is not impeded through press comment on cases in progress. In *Attorney-General* v *News Group Newspapers Ltd* (1987) an injunction to restrain further publication of allegedly defamatory material was refused because the trial was some months away and a substantial risk to proceedings would not result. Clearly if the press were to publish details of a person's previous convictions shortly before trial or publish a picture of someone involved in identification evidence there would be contempt. The Contempt of Court Act 1981 – legislation which followed the decision of the European Court of Human Rights involving the Sunday Times – limits contempt. There must be a substantial risk to proceedings – s2 and under s5 a discussion in the media in good faith where the risk to legal proceedings is incidental to the proceedings. This situation arose in *Attorney-General* v *English* (1983) where the discussion in the press fell under the protection of s5. Section 10 of the Act provides for the protection of journalistic sources unless 'it be established to the satisfaction of the court that disclosure is necessary in the interests of justice or national security or for the prevention of disorder or crime.' The courts have tended to order disclosure however eg *Secretary of State for Defence* v *Guardian Newspapers Ltd* (1984) and more recently in *X* v *Morgan Grampian (Publishers) Ltd* (1991).

While there are many remedies available to the government to restrict press freedom, the protections available to individuals are more limited. The action of defamation can be brought but the expense involved is often prohibitive. The private interests of individuals and the lack of a comprehensive law on privacy in this country all too often leave the individual with no remedy: *Re X (a minor)* (1975). The Press Council considers complaints against newspapers but in practice has little effect against newspapers which invade privacy in the interests of sensationalism.

QUESTION TWO

To what extent, if at all, have recent actual and proposed changes to the law relating to State security curtailed freedom of expression?

University of London LLB Examination
(for External Students) Constitutional Law June 1989 Q7

General Comment

A topical question on the Official Secrets Act 1989.

CONSTITUTIONAL LAW

Skeleton Solution

This answer could be very long. Important statutes to outline are the Official Secrets Acts and the Broadcasting Acts. Contempt of court is also important as is s159 Criminal Justice Act 1988.

Suggested Solution

The Official Secrets Acts 1911-1920 and 1989 are the major Acts protecting state security. Section 1 of the 1911 Act provides that it is an offence punishable with 14 years imprisonment if a person goes into or passes any prohibited place or makes any major sketch or collects records prejudicial to the safety or interest of the state. *Chandler* v *DPP* (1964) plainly shows that the 1911 Act is not restricted to spying, but includes acts of sabotage and acts of physical interference. Section 2 provided that it is an offence 'if any person having in his possession or control ... any document ... communicates the document' to any person other than a person to whom he should communicate it.' This section was the 'catch all' section and covered a vast area. The Franks Committee estimated that there were over 2,000 possible charges that could be brought under s2. It was also unclear if s2 required a guilty mind (mens rea). The section was repealed and the question arises as to whether or not the new Official Secrets Act 1989 expands freedom of expression or hinders it?

It is right that certain secrets must be kept in any state and vital secrets are protected in the Act. If we view, however, the function of the democratic state to be that of the efficient protection of information so that the country is run properly – not just refusal to disclose information – then the Act can be severely criticised. The test to be applied is the balance struck between access to information to citizens and protection to servants of the state so that they can in fact run the country properly.

Under the Official Secrets Act 1989 no new rights to information are provided for and ministers will continue to be able to withhold information embarrassing to their case. It is true that the vast bulk of information will no longer be protected by the criminal law but in the past civil servants were more likely to be disciplined or sacked for breaches of the Act rather than facing criminal prosecution (except in exceptional cases like Tisdall and Ponting). Many breaches of the 1911 statute went unpunished.

The 1989 Act makes it an offence for a member of the security and intelligence services or retired members to disclose any information relating to that work he has obtained while so employed. There is an offence relating to other Crown Servants or government contractors who make damaging disclosures of information they have obtained about the security services. Damaging disclosures in relation to defence and international relations are also offences by Crown Servants. A Crown servant also commits an offence if he discloses information he has received as such which results in the commission of an offence, facilitates an escape from custody or inhibits the detection of crime or arrest of offenders.

Where information is leaked from a foreign source and where information 'likely to be useful in the commission of a crime' is leaked it is outside the ambit of the Act. This is an improvement on the original Official Secrets Bill.

The concept of absolute offences is less strict. The areas covered have been reduced in the Act but there is no prior publication defence. Therefore it is of no avail to show

12 FREEDOM OF EXPRESSION

(i) no harm was done or (ii) that the matter was already widely published. This is particularly disturbing – an editor can be caught for repeating words forbidden today which had been widely published yesterday but not then forbidden.

Mr Douglas Hurd, the then Home Secretary, assured the public that this provision would be used sensibly, but there is still doubt about this especially in view of the 'Spycatcher' affair. No public interest defence will be allowed – so information revealing exceptional abuse of authority will not be a defence. Mr Hurd also said that a form of public interest defence would still exist because in some areas the prosecution would have to show a disclosure caused 'harm to the public interest'. The Act itself does not use the words 'public interest' so if a specific form of harm can be shown, a jury will have to convict. For more than a century a public interest defence has existed. In the 'Spycatcher' cases, Lord Griffiths continued to defend this principle – in exceptional circumstances a civil servant could be 'relieved of his duty of confidence' so that he could 'alert his fellow citizens to the impending danger'. A case can be made, therefore, that the 1989 Act should seek to uphold this principle because secrecy can be damaging in these 'exceptional circumstances'. (*Attorney-General* v *Guardian Newspapers (No 1)* (1987) and *(No 2)* (1988)).

The Government recently moved to prevent unnecessary secrecy rulings in Crown Courts and s159 of the Criminal Justice Act 1988 provides for the first time the right to question judges' decisions to close their doors to the public or impose reporting restrictions in criminal trials. This means that, for example, journalists would have the right to contest reporting restrictions.

It was journalists led by Jim Brooks which led to the recognition by the European Commission on Human Rights that the lack of method to appeal against a judge's secrecy order is a potential breach of human rights. As reported in *The Independent* (24 June 1989) it seems there is concern that draft rules accompanying s159 may lead to more secrecy and reporting restrictions. Do these new draft rules reflect Parliament's intention when it provided for an appeal system? These rules are drawn up by the Lord Chancellor's department in consultation with a committee of advisers including the Lord Chief Justice of England.

The rules seem to provide for appeals by way of written representation only when a justice closes his doors to the press. This, it is submitted, may negate the 'open justice' principle. The rules also provide for a new category of secrecy in relation to witnesses or 'any other person.' There is no provision for an expedited appeal. The Court of Appeal's decision is final and the matter cannot be tested in the House of Lords. The Lord Chancellor's department have said that the draft rules were designed for practicality, expediency and in the interests of national security. The paper appeal provides a quick method of appeal and nothing confidential is likely to leak out inadvertently (see *The Independent* 27 June 1989).

Contempt of court is another area where freedom of expression can be curtailed. The position is now governed by the Contempt of Court Act 1981. This Act was partly in response to an appeal made by the *Sunday Times* to the European Court of Human Rights. The European Court had said that the test was too widely drawn in the United Kingdom and had the effect of unlawfully silencing a newspaper's right to freedom of expression. Under the Act there can be contempt regardless of 'intent to do so', this is the 'strict liability rule', however, there are defences under s3, eg 'innocent publication ... etc' (see also *R* v *Griffiths* (1957)). Contemporaneous

163

CONSTITUTIONAL LAW

reporting and reporting a discussion 'in good faith of public affairs' are two further defences.

The protection of journalistic sources is given a limited defence only. (See *Secretary of State for Defence* v *Guardian Newspapers Ltd* (1984).) This limited defence is provided for in s10 Contempt of Court Act 1981. Disclosure will not be required 'unless it be established' (that disclosure) 'is in the interests of justice or national security or for the prevention of disorder or crime.'

The Death on the Rock programme screened by Thames Television on 28 April 1988, against the Government's wishes, illustrates a crisis with regard to freedom of expression.

This programme was 'a lightning conductor for the intense feelings that the Gibraltar shootings evoked in the minds of the British public ... The conflict was essentially one of divergent personal attitudes and value rather than of party political divisions (see the Windlesham/Rampton report on *Death on the Rock*). (All of the British public would understandably resent the IRA's brutal campaign of violence). Some people however, felt that the security forces were fully entitled to take such measures as were necessary to protect the people of Gibraltar and the Royal Anglian Regiment from planned assassination. Others, whilst abhorring the IRA's objectives and tactics, felt that the security force's actions (whether in Northern Ireland or elsewhere) fell outside the specific limitations of the rule of law by which they are bound. The question concerned the Broadcasting Act 1981 – did the programme 'Death on the Rock' offend against the due impartiality requirements? The Windlesham Rampton Report vindicated the objectivity of the television programme ('Whatever view is taken of the state of public opinion and the legitimacy of public opinion and the legitimacy of Government intervention, the making and screening of "Death on the Rock" proved that freedom of expression can prevail in the most extensive and the most immediate of all the means of mass communication.' (Windlesham Rampton Report).

It is true, therefore, that the human rights jurists may now look to television more than newspapers when allegations of contempt (or 'trial by television') are made.

The Broadcasting Act 1990 provides that where the Minister is of opinion that an item to be broadcast would promote or incite crime or undermine the authority of the state, he may order a person/company not to broadcast such item. The Home Secretary can issue an order under this Act requiring all television companies to refrain from broadcasting the forbidden item. This will include an interview or discussion of a person who appears or is heard on the particular programme and the person is representing or purports to represent a terrorist organisation or where the words support such an organisation.

To try to curtail terrorism is perfectly understandable in any civilised society. The Broadcasting Act 1990, however, has been subject to severe criticism. Since the Government's ban on broadcasting interviews etc with IRA members and sympathisers except during election campaigns, television companies have shown programmes with a particular person in view but whose words/voice is not broadcast. A television reporter may then report about the events. This is less than satisfactory and raises the question as to the usefulness of the Act. It might be more practical to leave the discretion in the hands of the directors of the various television companies.

12 FREEDOM OF EXPRESSION

The broadcasting restrictions were dropped after the initiation of the Northern Ireland peace process.

QUESTION THREE

'The security of the state is one of the most important functions of government.' To what extent does the law relating to national security reflect this importance?

University of London LLB Examination
(for External Students) Constitutional Law June 1991 Q8

General Comment

There is no 'right way' to tackle a question of this nature since its terms are open to such wide interpretation. Establish what you mean by the term national security law and proceed to cite relevant statutory and common law examples.

Skeleton Solution

- Explain difficulties of interpretation.
- Relate leading judicial review cases.
- Note judicial reluctance to question Ministers' views.
- Cite various statutory provisions concerned with national security.

Suggested Solution

The question refers to 'the law relating to national security', and asks to what extent that law reflects the importance of the Government's role in maintaining state security. An initial difficulty in answering such a question lies in ascertaining the area of law the question is referring to. Clearly national security is not a recognised discrete area of law such as contract or criminal law. If anything it is a concept that cuts across many different areas of law that is used to justify, action or inaction on the part of the Government of the day.

In proceedings for judicial review of administrative action the courts have, on occasion, refused to interfere with the decision of a Minister on the ground that he has cited 'acting in the interests of national security' to justify his actions.

R v *Secretary of State for the Home Department, ex parte Hosenball* (1977), concerned a challenge to the actions of the Secretary of State himself in refusing to give information about the reasons for making a deportation order against an alien. The Divisional Court and the Court of Appeal refused to grant an order of certiorari because the refusal had been based on grounds of national security. Note that if the refusal of reasons had occurred in what Lord Denning MR called an 'ordinary case', that is, one in which national security was not involved, the position would have been different. He stated:

'... if the body concerned, whether it be a Minister or advisers, has acted unfairly, then the courts can review their proceedings so as to ensure, as far as may be, that justice is done.'

Similarly in *Council of Civil Service Unions* v *Minister for the Civil Service* (1985), where the House of Lords had to consider a challenge to the validity of the Prime

Minister's oral direction prohibiting civil servants employed at GCHQ from membership of a trade union, Lord Fraser stated that:

'... whatever their source, powers which are defined, either by reference to their object or by reference to procedure for their exercise, or in some other way, and whether the definition is expressed or implied, are in my opinion normally subject to judicial control to ensure that they are not exceeded. By "normally" I mean provided that considerations of national security do not require otherwise.'

In that particular case, the House of Lords held that, had it not been for the issue of national security, (ie the need for the Prime Minister to pre-empt potentially damaging industrial action by unilaterally banning union membership), her actions would have been in breach of natural justice on the ground of her failure to consult the civil servants on an issue relating to their terms and conditions of employment.

The courts have always been careful to maintain the view that they will not accept an argument based on national security as being sufficient in itself to oust their jurisdiction, but in practice they have rarely if ever, rejected it. Some of the dicta in *Chandler* v *DPP* (1964) are instructive on this point. The House of Lords considered the appeal by CND members who claimed that they had not been planning to act in a manner prejudicial to the interests of the State by preventing planes carrying nuclear warheads from taking off. Lord Reid stated:

'Who then is to determine what is and is not prejudicial to the interests of the State? ... I do not subscribe to the view that the Government or a Minister must always or even as a general rule have the last word about that ... It is in my opinion clear that the disposition and armament of the armed forces are, and for centuries have been, within the exclusive discretion of the Crown, and that no one can seek a legal remedy on the ground that such discretion has been wrongly exercised.'

Lord Devlin concurred:

'.. there is no rule of the common law that whenever questions of national security are being considered by any court for any purpose, it is what the Crown thinks to be necessary or expedient that counts, and not what is necessary or expedient in fact ... In a case like the present, it may be presumed that it is contrary to the interests of the Crown to have one of its airfields immobilised ... but the presumption is not irrebuttable ... men can exaggerate the extent of their interests, and so can the Crown. The servants of the Crown, like other men animated by the highest motives, are capable of formulating a policy ad hoc so as to prevent the citizen from doing something that the Crown does not want him to do. It is the duty of the courts to be as alert now as they have always been to prevent any abuse of the prerogative. But in the present case there is nothing at all to suggest that the Crown's interests in the proper operation of its airfields is not what it may naturally be presumed to be, or that it was exaggerating the perils of interference with their effectiveness ...'

The judiciary, therefore, cannot be criticised for failing to give sufficient weight to the significance of the Government's responsibility in safeguarding national security.

Various statutes also recognise the importance of Ministers acting in the interests of national security.

In relation to broadcasting the Home Secretary can prevent television and radio programmes from being broadcast on the ground that damage would be done to

12 FREEDOM OF EXPRESSION

national security; see also the operation of the 'D' Notice committee (Defence, Press and Broadcasting Committee).

A further obvious example is provided by the Official Secrets Act 1989. Section 1 imposes a stringent duty on members or retired members of the security and intelligence services and those notified that they are subject to the section. It provides that such a person commits an offence if without lawful authority he discloses any information or document he has received in the course of such work or while such notification is in force.

Certain modern statutes expressly refer to the concept of 'national security' such as the Interception of Communications Act 1985, which was introduced to regulate 'phone tapping'. The Secretary of State may issue a warrant to intercept in this way if it is necessary in the interests of national security.

Similarly, s10 of the Contempt of Court Act 1981 which provides:

'No court may require a person to disclose, nor is any person guilty of contempt of court for refusing to disclose, the source of information contained in a publication for which he is responsible, unless it be established to the satisfaction of the court that disclosure is necessary in the interests of justice or national security or for the prevention of disorder or crime.'

The effect of this provision was considered in *Secretary of State for Defence* v *Guardian Newspapers Ltd* (1984), which concerned the refusal of the Guardian newspaper to reveal the source of leaked documents concerning the arrival of Cruise missiles at RAF Greenham Common. Regarding the construction of s10 of the 1981 Act, the House of Lords held that the disclosure of the document was needed in order to identify the servant of the Crown who in breach of his statutory duty had copied the document and supplied a copy to The Guardian. The real issue was that it had in its employment a servant or servants who had access to classified information and who were prepared, for reasons which seemed good to them, to betray the trust which was reposed in them. On that basis it was fully established that the exceptions to s10 applied, and that the Crown was entitled to discovery as an aid to pursuing its rights against its servant.

QUESTION FOUR

'When the security of the State is under threat the rights and freedoms of the individual must give way to the greater interests of society as a whole.'

Discuss in the light of recent changes in the law.

University of London LLB Examination
(for External Students) Constitutional Law June 1990 Q6

General Comment

A relatively easy question requiring students to assess whether the balance between state security and the freedom of the individual is achieved, or whether the state exercises excessive powers.

CONSTITUTIONAL LAW

Skeleton Solution

- Review procedures open to the State where national security is considered to be at risk:
  a) prerogative powers:
  b) Emergency Powers Act 1920;
  c) Public Order Act 1986;
  d) Prevention of Terrorism (Temporary Provisions) Act 1989.
- Conclude with question of justifiability.

Suggested Solution

In the modern world, threats to the security of some or all of the nation, may come in a large variety of forms, often considerably different from those experienced in the past. Principally, the development of systems that allow a complex society to function smoothly also make it vulnerable. From the terrorist's bomb on a plane to security considerations in defence establishments, law makers have been forced, by the circumstances of recent years, to curtail the freedoms that individuals have come to expect. Some prohibitions seldom have been placed 'across the board', but their effect has been felt in many areas of everyday life.

In extremis, it is conceivable that in circumstances of dire emergency, where civil authorities, due to internal or external disruption, abrogate their power in favour of military authorities, such a situation, although unlikely, would amount to the imposition of martial law. This term is something of a misnomer since it is a state where normal civil laws are in suspense in favour of the discretion of senior military commanders. Such a situation would certainly involve the individual's rights giving way to that of society. However, it is clear from such authorities as we have that the courts may still review whether the circumstances justify imposition of this extreme measure and may also exercise judicial review. Thus, in *Egan* v *Macready* (1921), a court felt able to declare that the prerogative purported to be exercised by military authorities had been superseded by statute. Furthermore, if Dicey is to be believed, liability would be incurred by military authorities for any unnecessary harm once civil law was restored. It is, however, more likely that the military would be indemnified by subsequent statute against legal actions arising out of the period of martial law.

A more common occurrence, relatively speaking, is the nation being forced onto a war footing, either where there is no official state of war in existence, or where there is actual hostility. Powers relating to the declaration and conduct of war are primarily matters of prerogative.

Since the prerogative allows for the internment and deportation of enemies and the requisition of their property, as well as the tactical destruction or confiscation of property generally, individual rights and freedoms may be curbed. Such powers were seen at work in the Persian Gulf, where sanctions prohibit the carrying on of all but humanitarian trade with Iraq and Britain retained for the military forces in the Gulf the right of interception of property and vessels. This directly interfered with the trading interests of individuals within this country. The crisis also saw the expulsion of diplomatic and other Iraqi nationals. Most of these prerogatives relate to the

12 FREEDOM OF EXPRESSION

conduct of affairs outside the United Kingdom or are exercised against those who are not British subjects. However, in other war situations, citizens might find their commercial and proprietary interests affected by such prerogative powers. Although, as in the case of the *Burmah Oil Co v Lord Advocate* (1965), the courts may review such actions and award compensation, indemnification of the Crown, in a similar manner to that effected by the War Damage Act 1965, would be likely to prevent redress from being made. Furthermore, it must be remembered that even where the exercise of prerogative is compensated, the rights of the individual still take a back seat to the immediate requirements of national security and as such are held in suspense until the immediate crisis has passed.

The immediacy of the crisis is largely the yard stick that the courts have used to determine the extent to which the Crown may set aside considerations of individual rights. In interpreting the Defence of the Realm Acts 1914–1915 and the Emergency Powers (Defence) Acts 1939–1940, the judiciary have given considerable weight to the degree of emergency at any given time. Under these statutes, wide discretionary powers are conferred on the Crown, enabling it to make regulations that it deems necessary for the safety of the nation, including the suspension of normal peace time courts. Such an order was not itself made, but regulations relating to the internment of British subjects were viewed by the courts with varying degrees of approval in various stages of the First and Second World Wars.

It is not only in times of war or military threat that wide legislative powers can be adopted by the Crown. In states of emergency the Emergency Powers Acts 1920 and 1964 provide for legislation by Orders in Council when the provision of essential services is disrupted. The breadth of the powers is such that a court might find it difficult to declare such Orders ultra vires. The necessity of positive affirmation by Parliament is intended to provide a constitutional safeguard, but this does not of itself guarantee the rights of individuals, except insofar as the Act prohibits excessive criminal sentencing, forced labour or military conscription and the outlawing of normally legitimate strike actions. However, the increased powers of the police and the stricter regulation of trade union activities has meant that in the last decade other methods have been used to ensure the supply of essential services, in contrast to the frequent use in the 1970s of these provisions.

These modern methods of control reflect what some writers, such as the late Professor De Smith, perceive as a change in the nature of the threats to the security of the state. The 1980s were marked by a sharp increase in public disorder, relating to industrial, political and leisure activities. Furthermore, there has been an increasing sensitivity to the dissemination of information both factually and subjectively generated. Whether such attitudes genuinely reflect a new form of threat to national security or the re-emergence of historical trends, accompanied by deepened insecurity amongst authorities, is open to debate. Nonetheless, in response to the changing situation, there has been a perceptible change in tactics. Instead of the sweeping invocation of emergency powers, the legislature has chosen to put into place more or less permanent structures that may be employed by subordinate authorities at their discretion. Although it is arguable whether violent disorders constitute serious threats to the security of the state, or at least the level of disorder that has prompted such measures, it is principally the police who now have wider powers in given circumstances to curtail the rights of the individual. Additionally, more and more activities are required to be performed only with authorisation and due compliance with regulatory stipulations. To enumerate the panoply of recent legislation that directly or indirectly tackle matters relating to the security of the state would be quite a considerable task. Therefore, our survey must confine itself to certain notable examples of the 'new tactics'.

The difficult area of the retention and security of official secrets and the consequence scrutiny, resulted in new legislation in 1989. It tightens the reign on the free dissemination of information, which will lead to a 'knock-on' effect for free speech. There can be no defence based on 'public interest' – that is to say that publication was done on the basis that the information should be in the public domain because it reveals government corruption and so on. Equally, the broadcasting reforms provide for a system of vetting material that is potentially harmful to the viewer, and as a result is certain to narrow the channels for more controversial forms of entertainment. The Public Order Act 1986, which regulates all manner of potential threats to the Queen's peace, prohibits, by virtue of s5, the use of communications and representations likely to cause harassment, alarm or distress to a person exposed to them. Similarly, material and communications that might induce racial conflict is liable to criminal sanction under ss17–23. To what extent these measures are intended to protect the state, rather than society, is debateable, but certainly the thinking behind such legislation is to prevent inflammatory situations from developing.

The Police and Criminal Evidence Act 1984 and the Public Order Act 1986 confer on the police significant powers with regard to freedom of movement and expression. The former allows for the use of road blocks and searches as a preventative measure, whilst the latter reforms and codifies public order laws imposing more coherent powers for the policing of demonstrations, processions and assemblies. Coupled with these measures are the requirements in most circumstances for due authorisation to organise these activities.

One must finally observe that other measures relating to the prevention of terrorism give rise to the prevention of the full exercise of certain public rights. Most recently, it has been announced that the free movement and free expression of persons in airport premises is to be restricted by the imposition of imprisonable sanctions for those who enter aircraft without authorisation or make misleading statements about the contents of baggage. Thus, it has been widely observed, a person exercising free speech by joking that he has a bomb in his suitcase might theoretically be convicted by virtue of these measures.

One is faced with a difficulty in these areas of relevance to the question. The security of the state is not seriously at risk by most of the activities that are envisaged by these statutes. The primary use of these laws is to protect society. However, since it is largely viewed by the courts that deciding what matters relate to state security is to be decided by central government, one must assume that the government's views on this matter must be conclusive.

The perceived change in tactics seems to confirm this view, since a shift in reliance on the concept of a transient national emergency to that of building safeguards into the everyday laws of the land must reflect a belief that the problem has changed. This might be an admission of the view that the Queen's peace is no longer prevalent throughout the land, which would indicate a siege mentality that requires individuals to relinquish their rights from day to day as new threats emerge. Alternatively, there might be a view that administrative convenience is better served by placing individual liberty in second place. This change must either signal the belief that the state has become more vulnerable or sensitive or that the democratic safeguards of using 'laws of last resort', which are brought out of the legislative armoury in times of dire emergency, are less important than they were. The fact that the Emergency Powers Act was used five times by the Heath government in the 1970s would appear to confirm the first synopsis. The complexities of the modern state make it more dependent and therefore more vulnerable and the facilities available to those who seek to threaten it have become equally sophisticated. As a result of such progress individual rights are placed between the rock of potential threats and the hard place that are the reinforced walls of the state.

13 POLICE POWERS

13.1 Introduction
13.2 Key points
13.3 Recent cases
13.4 Analysis of questions
13.5 Question

13.1 Introduction

This is an important constitutional law topic covering as it does the powers of the police to stop and search an individual on the street and enter his premises. It should be noted that some examination boards cover police powers on their English Legal System syllabuses. You should check your particular examination syllabus and past papers to establish whether this is a likely examination topic in your case. The University of Wolverhampton syllabus, for example, examines this topic in Constitutional and Administrative Law.

13.2 Key points

Virtually all police powers are now contained in the Police and Criminal Evidence Act 1984 – commonly referred to as PACE – and the codes of practice accompanying the Act.

You must know the following key sections of the 1984 Act.

a) *Sections 1–3*

These are the stop and search provisions.

They allow an officer to stop and search individuals and vehicles provided:

i) they are in public places, and

ii) the officer has reasonable grounds to suspect that he will find articles relating to:

- burglary
- theft
- joy riding
- obtaining property by deception

or that he will find an offensive weapon.

See *Harris* v *DPP*, *Fehmi* v *DPP* [1993] 1 All ER 562.

iii) An article searched for under s1 may be seized.

13 POLICE POWERS

b) *Section 4*

Road checks may be authorised to check whether a vehicle is carrying a person who has committed an offence, or intending to commit an offence, a person unlawfully at large or a witness to an offence. Note, in addition, the powers under s163 Road Traffic Act 1988.

c) *Sections 17–18 and 32*

Police powers to enter at common law are retained to deal with a breach of the peace: s17(6); *Thomas* v *Sawkins* [1935] 2 KB 249; *Lamb* v *DPP* [1990] Crim LR 58.

Police can enter to execute an arrest warrant or to arrest for any arrestable offence, to recapture someone unlawfully at large (*D'Souza* v *DPP* [1992] 1 WLR 1073), to save life and limb or to prevent serious damage to property.

Where a person has been arrested for an arrestable offence s18 gives a power of entry and search. The premises searched must be occupied or under the control of the person arrested, and there must be reasonable grounds for believing that there is evidence of the offence or of a connected or similar offence on the premises.

Section 32 confers powers to enter and search premises which the arrested person left immediately prior to the arrest and applies to any offence.

d) *Section 19*

This section gives a general right of seizure provided an officer is lawfully on the premises, ie:

i) he has a search warrant; or

ii) he has entered pursuant to the above sections.

e) *Protected material*

i) Legally privileged material – designed to protect the confidentiality of communications between client and legal adviser. Access cannot be obtained.

ii) Excluded material – defined in s11.

iii) Special procedure material – defined in s14.

Access to these categories of material cannot be obtained by means of an ordinary search warrant. Note that it may be seized if discovered in the course of a lawful search: s19.

f) *Section 24*

This section gives power to arrest anyone without a warrant provided it is an 'arrestable offence' as defined above.

The person making the arrest must inform the arrested person of the fact and reasons for arrest: s28. The reasons must be given as soon as is reasonably practicable: *DPP* v *Hawkins* [1988] 1 WLR 1166; *Lewis* v *Chief Constable of the South Wales Constabulary* [1991] 1 All ER 206. A person making the arrest may use reasonable force against the person arrested.

CONSTITUTIONAL LAW

g) *Section 56*

This section allows anyone who has been arrested and is at a police station the right to inform someone of his arrest as soon as is reasonably practicable.

h) *Section 58*

This gives an arrested person held in custody the right to consult a solicitor privately at any time.

This is an extremely important provision – in particular a person has a right by reason of this section to have his solicitor present before he is interviewed in relation to the offence for which he has been arrested.

i) *Section 76*

This is a most important evidential provision allowing a 'confession' to be given in evidence against an accused even though technically it would be hearsay evidence ie a statement made outside court by a person other than the one giving evidence and put forward to show the truth of what has been said.

Note the wide definition of a confession namely any statement wholly or partly adverse to the maker: s82.

Section 76, however, guards against the risk of confessions brought about by oppression by putting the onus of proof on the prosecution to show that it was not obtained by either:

i) oppression; or

ii) anything done or said which might render it unreliable.

Unless the prosecution can show this, the confession will not be admissable.

j) *Section 78*

This section goes hand in hand with s76 but is much wider because it applies to *any* evidence – not simply confessions.

It gives the court a discretion to exclude any evidence which, having regard to the circumstances in which it was obtained, would have such an adverse influence on the fairness of the proceedings that the court ought not to admit it.

This section is aimed at giving a court a discretion to exclude evidence obtained in breach of PACE eg an illegal search under s17 or an interview where access to a solicitor under s58 was denied.

A confession may not be excluded under s76 but may nevertheless be excluded under s78: *R* v *Mason* [1988] 1 WLR 139.

Furthermore, breaches of the Codes of Practice (see following section) may also lead to exclusion of evidence under s78.

k) *The Codes of Practice*

The major code provisions are:

i) once persons are suspected of a crime they should be cautioned;

13 POLICE POWERS

ii) basic comforts such as breaks for refreshment, proper rest, adequate heating and ventilation should be afforded whilst a person is in custody and being interviewed;

iii) consent to an identification parade is required. If a person is suspected it is wrong to show a witness photographs before asking that witness to pick someone out at an identification parade;

iv) if photographs are shown to a witness a minimum of 12 photographs ought to be shown.

l) *Recent developments*

The Codes of Practice have been recently revised and modified and the modified code came into operation on 1 April 1995. The major changes and improvements are as follows:

Once a person is detained at a police station he has to be informed not only that he has a right to have a solicitor present before he is interviewed but also that the services of a solicitor are free.

Interviews inside police stations should be made in the presence of a solicitor (if the detainee so wishes) but in any event shall be tape recorded.

Interviews outside police stations (which clearly cannot have the protection of being tape recorded or have the presence of a solicitor) are not permitted unless the following apply:

i) no decision has been reached as to whether the interviewee is to be arrested; or

ii) the questioning does not relate to the interviewee's involvement or suspected involvement in any crime; or

iii) delay in interviewing would result in:
- interference or harm to any evidence or potential witness;
- the alerting of others suspected of being involved in the crime;
- the hindering of the recovery of stolen property.

Where an ordinary identification parade is impracticable then identification by video is permissible (ie the witness may be shown a video containing the suspect and at least eight other persons of similar appearance to the suspect).

It is important to remember that a breach of the Codes of Practice is likely to result in the court exercising its discretion under s78 of the 1984 Act to exclude the admissibility of any evidence obtained as a result of a breach of a provision of the code.

m) *The Criminal Justice and Public Order Act 1994*

This Act effectively marks an end to the historic right of silence of the accused: see ss34–39 Criminal Justice and Public Order Act 1994. For other aspects of the Act see chapter 11.

CONSTITUTIONAL LAW

13.3 Recent cases

D'Souza v *DPP* [1992] 1 WLR 1073.

R v *Self* [1992] 1 WLR 476.

13.4 Analysis of questions

No questions on police powers have been set in recent years by some examination boards (although on the University of London LLB External programme the area is examined in English Legal System).

If this area is examined the likely examination question will be a problem solving exercise setting out a series of police actions eg entering premises, searching, seizing evidence, arresting an individual, and asking the candidate to comment on the legality or otherwise of the police actions.

13.5 Question

PC Black was called to the premises of Smiths (Jewellers) Limited following a report of a theft. When he arrived the owner, James Smith, told him that £450 had been stolen from his safe. There had been no sign of any break in or any damage to the safe itself. Smith told PC Black that he suspected an 'inside job' and named Terry Jones as a likely suspect. Terry Jones had only been employed by Smith for a few weeks and he knew the safe's combination.

PC Black went around to Terry Jones's house intending to arrest him. When he arrived no-one was in but the back door was not locked and PC Black entered the premises. Having established that Terry was not in PC Black proceeded to search the house and in an upstairs wardrobe he found £400 in cash wrapped in a pullover.

Just as he finished his search Terry Jones entered the house. PC Black asked Terry where he had been and whether he knew anything about the break in at Smiths Jewellers. Terry replied that he knew nothing about the theft. He was then searched by PC Black who found another £50 in cash in Terry's jacket pocket. Terry was asked where he got the money from and replied that it had 'nothing to do with' PC Black.

PC Black then arrested Terry and cautioned him. He took him to the police station where he was charged by the custody sergeant with theft.

PC Black then placed Terry in an interview room and asked him to make a statement. Terry asked whether he could speak to his solicitor before he answered any question but was told that was impossible. Terry refused to answer any questions and was kept in the interview room for a further six hours without being given any refreshments or being allowed to use the toilet.

Nevertheless, Terry still refused to answer any questions. However PC Black then told Terry that they were going to arrest and charge his eight months pregnant wife with receiving stolen money. However Terry was told that if he 'held his hands up' to the crime the police would not involve his wife.

Thereupon Terry signed a statement confessing to the theft.

Discuss the validity of PC Black's actions in this matter.

Written by the Editors

13 POLICE POWERS

General Comment

A question involving knowledge and application of the major aspects of the Police and Criminal Evidence Act 1984.

Skeleton Solution

- Was the entry lawful? Yes, because he had reason to believe Terry was guilty of an arrestable offence and might be at his house.
- Was the search legal? No, because he had no search warrant and had not arrested Terry when he searched the wardrobe.
- Was the search of Terry legal? No, because he had not been arrested when he was searched and it was not a public place therefore ss1–3 PACE not applicable.
- Was the initial questioning of Terry proper? No, because he suspected him immediately yet did not caution Terry before asking him any questions in breach of the Code of Guidance.
- The interview – in breach of Code of Guidance in way interview conducted. Wrong to deny access to solicitor: s58 PACE.
- The confession – oppressive/unreliable within meaning of s76 – *R v Fulling* (1987), *R v Samuel* (1988).
- Would evidence be admissible? Even though evidence obtained illegally court has discretion to allow its admissability. However strong argument that such illegally obtained evidence would be excluded because of s78.

Suggested Solution

This question demands a discussion of police powers and in particular, the limitations on such power laid down by the provisions of the Police and Criminal Evidence Act 1984 (PACE).

When PC Black went to Terry's house he did so with the intention of arresting him for the theft at the jewellers. Accordingly he had a right to enter the premises in order to arrest Terry – theft is an arrestable offence and Black had reason to believe that Terry would be at home: s17 PACE.

However Black did not have a search warrant. Whilst s18 of PACE allows the search of premises of an arrested person, when the wardrobe was searched Terry had not yet been arrested. The finding of the £400 was as a result of an illegal search; this may well lead a court to exclude evidence of this find pursuant to s78 PACE, a matter I return to later.

Furthermore, the search of Terry was illegal. He had not been arrested when he was searched and he was searched inside his house, that is to say a private place. The power to stop and search only applies to public places (see ss1–3 PACE).

Since Black suspected Terry immediately the Code of Guidance required that he caution Terry before asking him any questions. Accordingly evidence of Terry's refusal to give an explanation as to where he got the £50 from may, once again, be excluded under s78 PACE.

The interview at the station can be attacked on a number of grounds. Firstly s58

PACE gives a right to have a solicitor present on request of an accused. Black's refusal to allow access to a solicitor was a clear breach of s58.

Secondly in making Terry remain in the interview room for such a lengthy period without refreshment or being permitted to use the toilet, Black was in breach of the Code of Guidance.

The above two reasons would make any statement made by Terry liable to be excluded by reason of s78 in any event.

However, the confession is very likely to be excluded by reason of s76 PACE. Whilst this section allows a confession to be admitted in evidence it will not be allowed in unless the prosecution can prove that it was not made by reason of oppression or something said or done to make it unreliable.

Terry would argue that the way he was treated in the interview room amounted to oppression and, in any event, the threat about charging his wife was something said to make the confession unreliable. In *R v Fulling* (1987) Lord Lane included 'cruel treatment' under the heading of oppression. The treatment of Terry during the interview does appear to be 'cruel'. Furthermore in *R v Samuel* (1988) the refusal of access to a solicitor was deemed to be a matter making a confession unreliable.

It is most probable, therefore, that the confession would be excluded by reason of s76 but, in any event, it may well be excluded under s78. In *R v Mason* (1988) it was held that confessions could be caught by both s76 and s78.

I have referred to s78 a great deal in this answer. It provides, in effect, that unfairly obtained evidence may be excluded at the discretion of the court. The point to note here, therefore, is that while much of the evidence against Terry has been illegally obtained the court still has a discretion to admit it. However, equally it can exclude it under s78 which permits exclusion if it appears that, having regard to the way the evidence was obtained, its admission in evidence would have an adverse effect on the fairness of the trial. The tendency of courts is to use s78 in favour of defendants rather than against them ie evidence is normally excluded.

In summary, therefore, most of the evidence against Terry is likely to be excluded and Terry will probably not be convicted of this crime. The finding of the money was pursuant to illegal searches and is likely to be excluded under s78. The confession will be excluded under either s76 or s78.

14 UNIVERSITY OF LONDON LLB (EXTERNAL) 1994 QUESTIONS AND SUGGESTED SOLUTIONS

UNIVERSITY OF LONDON
LLB Examinations 1994
for External Students
INTERMEDIATE EXAMINATION (SCHEME A) and
FIRST AND SECOND YEAR EXAMINATIONS (SCHEME B)

CONSTITUTIONAL LAW

Wednesday, 15 June: 10.00 am to 1.00 pm

Answer *FOUR* of the following EIGHT questions

1 'The *Factortame* decision marks a significant constitutional departure from the traditionally accepted view of parliamentary sovereignty.'

   Critically assess this statement.

2 'Our unwritten constitution rests upon a separation of powers. It also rests upon a mutual recognition of those powers. It is for Parliament to make new laws and to amend old laws, including the common law. It is for the courts to interpret and enforce the law. It is for the government to govern within the law. Each in its own sphere is supreme.' (Lord Donaldson of Lymington MR, *M* v *Home Office and Another* (1992)).

   Discuss.

3 a) During the course of the 1992 general election Mr Smith, a political activist with no fixed party allegiance, published (at his own cost) and distributed 50,000 leaflets exhorting voters to express their dissatisfaction with the Conservative government's tax policies by abstaining from voting. On polling day the Conservative candidate lost the election, his previous majority of 30,000 votes being wiped out. The final result was Labour 15,000, Liberal Democratic Party 10,000, Conservative 5,000. 20,000 voters failed to vote.

   The Conservative Party candidate wishes to challenge the legality of the result of the election. Advise him.

   b) 'The detailed rules regulating constituency election campaigns are of little value given the absence of controls on national party campaigns.'

   Discuss.

4 'The increasing willingness of the House of Lords over the past 15 years to amend and delay Government Bills may be viewed either as an affront to democracy or a legitimate constitutional safeguard for the citizen.'

   Discuss.

5 'The uncertainties surrounding the scope and exercise of the Royal Prerogative give rise to serious constitutional questions concerning the rule of law in a democratic society.'

Critically assess this statement.

6 The (fictitious) University Complaints Commission was set up under the Education Act 1994 to receive and investigate complaints from students on 'academic matters'. In May 1994, Jane, a final-year student reading History at the New World University, was accused of removing legal articles from the library, contrary to university regulations. Following internal disciplinary proceedings, at which Jane was not represented, Jane was expelled from the University.

Jane complained to the UCC requesting an investigation. The Commission wrote to Jane stating that it did not have jurisdiction to investigate her complaint, as her expulsion from the University related to a disciplinary rather than academic matter.

Jane wishes to apply for judicial review of the decision of the University to expel her and the decision of the University Complaints Commission.

Advise her.

7 'For [Dicey] there was no need for any statement of fundamental principles operating as a kind of higher law because political freedom was adequately protected by the common law and by an independent Parliament acting as a watchdog against any excess of zeal by the executive.' (Wade and Bradley, 1993).

To what extent does Dicey's view require revision to meet the needs of today's society?

8 'One result of the legal reforms over the past fifteen years is that local government, once the most responsive form of democracy, is being relegated to the position of manager of local services with little or no residual autonomy.'

Critically assess this statement.

1994 QUESTIONS AND SUGGESTED SOLUTIONS

QUESTION ONE

'The *Factortame* decision marks a significant constitutional departure from the traditionally accepted view of parliamentary sovereignty.'

Critically assess this statement.

University of London LLB Examination
(for External Students) Constitutional Law June 1994 Q1

General Comment

A fairly straightforward question on the effect of membership of the European Union on the doctrine of parliamentary sovereignty. It is important to answer the question: that is, critically assess the statement. While it is possible to argue that *Factortame* either is or is not a significant departure, the approach taken here will be that it is not.

Skeleton Solution

- Dicey on sovereignty.
- Express repeal: *Macarthys Ltd* v *Smith*.
- Supremacy in EU law.
- European Communities Act 1972.
- Implied repeal: *Vauxhall Estates, Ellen Street Estates, Litster*.
- The *Factortame* litigation.
- Conclusion.

Suggested Solution

There is no doubt that the United Kingdom's membership of the European Union has had some effect on the traditionally accepted view of parliamentary sovereignty: in particular, the doctrine of implied repeal has been modified. To this extent the statement in the question is correct, although one might argue about the word 'significant'. In *R* v *Secretary of State for Transport, ex parte Factortame (No 2)* (1991), the House of Lords clearly accepted the doctrine of the supremacy of European Community law. But it is arguable that their Lordships did so by reference to the traditionally accepted view of parliamentary sovereignty; European Community law is supreme because Parliament has said so in the European Communities Act 1972.

Thus, the *Factortame* decision, far from departing in any significant way from the doctrine of parliamentary sovereignty, is in fact in accordance therewith. To explain this argument it is necessary to consider, first, Dicey's traditional view of parliamentary sovereignty; second, the doctrine of supremacy in European Union law; third, the European Communities Act 1972 and its effect on the doctrines of implied repeal and express repeal; fourth, the *Factortame* litigation itself. Finally, in conclusion, it will be suggested that that decision does not mark 'a significant constitutional departure from the traditionally accepted view of parliamentary sovereignty'.

CONSTITUTIONAL LAW

Dicey explained parliamentary sovereignty in terms of two propositions: in its positive sense, it meant that 'Parliament ... has ... the right to make or unmake any law whatever'; in the negative, that 'no person or body is recognised by the law of England as having a right to override or set aside the legislation of Parliament'. It is hard to see how European Union membership affects the former proposition; as Lawton LJ said in *Macarthys Ltd* v *Smith* (1979), 'Parliament's recognition of European Community law and of the jurisdiction of the European Court of Justice by one enactment can be withdrawn by another'. And, while the European Court of Justice can require that a national court set aside domestic legislation, the source of the power of an English court to do so lies in the European Communities Act – an Act of Parliament.

As a matter of European Community law, there can be few propositions clearer than the doctrine of supremacy as developed by the European Court of Justice; in the event of conflict between European Union law and domestic law, the former must prevail: *Costa* v *ENEL* (1964); *Amministrazione delle Finanze dello Stato* v *Simmenthal SpA* (1978). The supremacy of European Community law was accepted doctrine at the time the United Kingdom joined the European Community in 1972.

Apart from the incorporation of both past and future European Community law via s2(1), the European Communities Act 1972 s3 requires English courts to decide questions of European Community law in accordance with the principles laid down by the European Court of Justice – which include its jurisprudence on supremacy. Section 2(4) provides that the European Communities Act will have precedence over both pre-accession legislation and that, for Acts passed after 1973, these 'shall be construed and have effect' subject to European Community law; it is this latter which gives rise to arguments that membership has affected the Diceyan view of parliamentary sovereignty.

It seems clear that the courts have treated s2(4) as empowering them to depart from the doctrine of implied repeal (as laid down in *Vauxhall Estates* v *Liverpool Corporation* (1932) and *Ellen Street Estates Ltd* v *Minister of Health* (1934)), whereunder a later and conflicting Act impliedly repeals earlier legislation with which it is inconsistent: see, eg, *Garland* v *British Rail Engineering Ltd* (1983); *Litster* v *Forth Dry Dock and Engineering Co* (1990). But it is hard to find any statement in the dicta that express repeal has been abandoned; European Community law is supreme because English law says so, in the European Communities Act. This approach is exemplified in *Factortame* itself.

In *Factortame*, the applicants argued that the Merchant Shipping Act 1988 was in conflict with European Community law; the Divisional Court sought a ruling on the question of compatibility from the European Court of Justice and, pending its reply, ordered that parts of the 1988 Act should be disapplied. Its decision was reversed by both the Court of Appeal and the House of Lords on the grounds that English law did not permit the award of interim relief against the Crown (*R* v *Secretary of State for Transport, ex parte Factortame (No 1)* (1990)). Their Lordships referred a second question to the European Court of Justice: whether European Community law required that the Act be disapplied on an interim basis pending a final determination of the case on its merits. The European Court of Justice replied in the affirmative and the House of Lords complied.

But it is the reasoning of their Lordships that is most significant: as in the Divisional Court, where reliance was placed squarely on s2(4) of the European Communities Act 1972, Lord Bridge explained that such limitations as Parliament accepted on its sovereignty in 1972 were 'entirely voluntary'; the 1972 Act made it quite clear that United Kingdom courts were obliged to override any rule of national law found to be in conflict with European Community law; and there was 'nothing in any way novel in according supremacy' to European Community law.

In conclusion, there is little support for the view that *Factortame* marks a significant constitutional departure from the traditionally accepted view of parliamentary sovereignty; it accepts the supremacy of European Union law, but it does so because to do so is in conformity with the will of Parliament. There is nothing in *Factortame* to suggest that an English court would refuse to comply with an express repeal of the European Communities Act. Until such time, if ever, as that happens, the traditional Diceyan view of parliamentary sovereignty remains, modified no doubt, but largely intact.

QUESTION TWO

'Our unwritten constitution rests upon a separation of powers. It also rests upon a mutual recognition of those powers. It is for Parliament to make new laws and to amend old laws, including the common law. It is for the courts to interpret and enforce the law. It is for the government to govern within the law. Each in its own sphere is supreme.' (Lord Donaldson of Lymington MR, *M* v *Home Office and Another* (1992)).

Discuss.

University of London LLB Examination
(for External Students) Constitutional Law June 1994 Q2

General Comment

This is not simply a question requiring discussion of the doctrine of separation of powers; more is needed. It is essential to weave the basic discussion of separation of powers into an *analysis* of Lord Donaldson's quote. This involves application rather than mere repetition of knowledge.

Skeleton Solution

- Judicial and academic views: *Duport Steels* v *Sirs*; de Smith.
- Montesquieu's conception of separation of powers.
- British constitution as 'mixed' or 'balanced': the Crown.
- Position of Cabinet and the Lord Chancellor.
- Separation of powers in law: House of Commons Disqualification Act 1975; Act of Settlement 1700.
- The role of conventions.
- Functional overlaps: executive and legislature; executive and judiciary; judiciary and legislature.
- Conclusions.

CONSTITUTIONAL LAW

Suggested Solution

Lord Donaldson here repeats the familiar judicial learning on the doctrine of separation of powers; as Lord Diplock said in an earlier case, 'the British constitution, though largely unwritten, is firmly based on the separation of powers' (*Duport Steels* v *Sirs* (1980)). But it is important to note that not all agree. The late Stanley de Smith wrote that 'No writer of repute would claim that [the doctrine] is a central feature of the modern British system of government' (H Street and R Brazier, *Constitutional and Administrative Law* (5th edition, 1985), p31). It follows that the Master of the Rolls' dictum is based on an assumption: that 'our unwritten constitution rests upon a separation of powers'. It is thus necessary in discussing the quote to question whether this is a valid assumption.

The quote also posits two further assumptions: that legislature, executive and judiciary recognise the separation of powers; and that each organ of government concedes supremacy to the other in its proper sphere of operation. Parliament legislates, the judges judge, and the executive governs. These assumptions, too, are susceptible to challenge. This answer will attempt to challenge them.

The doctrine of the separation of powers as explained by the French jurist Montesquieu has it that 'All would be lost if ... the same body ... exercised these three powers, that of making laws, that of executing public decisions, and that of judging the crimes or the disputes of private persons' (*L'Esprit des Lois* (1748), Book XI, Ch 6). But the doctrine has never formally found a place in the British constitution, which is best described as a mixed or balanced constitution; ultimately, the Crown is present in all three organs of government – the Queen in Parliament, Her Majesty's ministers and Her Majesty's judges. Thus, for example, the Cabinet is chosen by and from the legislature; but the admixture is best exemplified by the Lord Chancellor who at one and the same time is head of the judiciary, member of the Cabinet and presides in the Upper Chamber of the legislature.

It is true that elements of a formal separation are to be found in legislation: the House of Commons Disqualification Act 1975 restricts the number of ministers who may sit in the Commons (House of Commons Disqualification Act 1975, s2), and disqualifies from membership holders of judicial office, as well as a significant number of members of the executive, including the police, civil service and armed forces (ibid, s1); the independence of the judiciary was confirmed in the Act of Settlement 1700 (see now Supreme Court Act 1981; Appellate Jurisdiction Act 1876). And true, too, that separation is effected informally through the operation of constitutional conventions. In the House of Lords, for example, lay peers do not participate in judicial business and the Law Lords do not participate generally in legislative business. But it is clear, as will be seen below, that there remain significant overlaps in function; it is thus hard to accept the Master of the Rolls' assertion that the constitution 'rests upon a separation of powers'.

It is in these functional overlaps that most difficulty arises in accepting Lord Donaldson's assumptions that each organ recognises and respects the exclusive competence, the 'supremacy' of 'each in its own sphere'. Thus, the executive enjoys significant legislative powers by way of delegated legislation; and, although formally Parliament retains control of powers delegated, the likelihood is that a government with a sufficient majority controls Parliament. Members of the executive are closely involved in the administration of justice: the Home Secretary in exercising the prerogative of mercy and the law officers of the Crown in civil and criminal proceedings.

The judges, in developing the common law, enjoy at least a quasi-legislative role (see, eg, *Shaw* v *DPP* (1962)) and regularly perform 'executive-type' functions chairing commissions or inquiries (see, eg, Lord Justice Scott and the Matrix-Churchill Affair). The functional division between legislature and executive is compromised, at least to the extent that government ministers must be members of one or other House of Parliament; and, as the High Court of Parliament, the legislature retains a judicial role in enforcing parliamentary privilege.

In conclusion, it would seem that Lord Donaldson's dictum paints too simplistic a picture. It is clear from the above discussion that the idea of the separation of powers is of importance in the British constitution and, to that extent, de Smith's view is also suspect. But to claim that the constitution 'rests upon a separation of powers' surely goes too far. Similarly, while there is certainly a degree of 'mutual recognition of those powers', the overlap in functions between executive, legislature and judiciary suggests that although each organ functions primarily within its own sphere, none is supreme therein. It is hard, therefore, to dissent from the view of the Donoughmore Committee (Report of the Committee on Ministers' Powers) in 1932 that the doctrine of separation of powers is no more than 'a rule of political wisdom which must give way when sound reasons of public policy so require'. It cannot be elevated, as Lord Donaldson seeks to do, to a fundamental of the constitution.

QUESTION THREE

a) During the course of the 1992 general election Mr Smith, a political activist with no fixed party allegiance, published (at his own cost) and distributed 50,000 leaflets exhorting voters to express their dissatisfaction with the Conservative government's tax policies by abstaining from voting. On polling day the Conservative candidate lost the election, his previous majority of 30,000 votes being wiped out. The final result was Labour 15,000, Liberal Democratic Party 10,000, Conservative 5,000. 20,000 voters failed to vote.

The Conservative Party candidate wishes to challenge the legality of the result of the election. Advise him.

b) 'The detailed rules regulating constituency election campaigns are of little value given the absence of controls on national party campaigns.'

Discuss.

University of London LLB Examination
(for External Students) Constitutional Law June 1994 Q3

General Comment

Although both parts to this question are straightforward, part (a) does require fairly detailed knowledge of a narrow area. One must always think carefully before attempting a two-part question; usually, single questions are easier. Be careful always to ensure that you answer both parts! Ensure, too, that the answer to (a) does

CONSTITUTIONAL LAW

constitute advice to the Conservative Party candidate and is not just a general essay; and that that to (b) comprises a discussion of the quote.

Skeleton Solution

a)
- Who may challenge: s121 Representation of the People Act 1983, and Conservative Party candidate.
- Grounds of challenge: corrupt and illegal practices (Representation of the People Act Part II); *R* v *Tronoh Mines Ltd*; *DPP* v *Luft*.
- Effect of challenge: void?

b)
- Comparison between local and national controls.
- Historical explanation: bribery and corruption.
- Modern law: expenditure (Representation of the People Act Part II); advertising (*R* v *Tronoh Mines*; *Meek* v *Lothian Regional Council*); broadcasting *(Grieve* v *Douglas-Home*; Broadcasting Act 1990); party funding (Trade Union legislation; Companies Act 1985).
- Conclusions.

Suggested Solution

a) Advice to the Conservative Party candidate falls conveniently into two parts: first, whether he can challenge the result; and, second, if so, the grounds of challenge. The conclusion will address the Conservative Party candidate's likely prospects of success.

Once an election has been held and the result declared, the only way to challenge that result is by way of a petition to the Election Court, comprising two judges of the Queen's Bench Division (s120 Representation of the People Act 1983). Under s121 Representation of the People Act 1983, petitions may be brought by voters, those claiming a 'right to be elected or returned at the election', or a candidate. Clearly, the Conservative Party candidate here falls within s121, probably under all or any of these headings. The petition itself is to be brought against the successful candidate, here the Labour Party candidate, as respondent or, if appropriate, the Returning Officers. The Election Court has power to determine that the respondent candidate was duly elected or that the election is void; it can order a recount or declare the runner-up elected.

The main grounds of challenge under the Representation of the People Act are that the successful candidate is disqualified, that the election has been conducted improperly by officials or that offences, such as corrupt or illegal practices, have been committed during the campaign. There is no indication on the facts either that the Labour Party candidate is disqualified from membership or that there have been any administrative irregularities in the conduct of the election. It follows that the Conservative Party candidate must rely in his petition on the commission of electoral offences.

The Representation of the People Act 1983 imposes strict controls on expenditure in the conduct of an election campaign. Under s75:

'No expenses shall, with a view to promoting or procuring the election of a candidate ... be incurred by any person other than the candidate, his election agent and persons authorised ... by the ... agent on account ... (b) of issuing advertisements, circulars or publications'.

Since the commission of corrupt or illegal election practices during the campaign may render an election void, the Conservative Party candidate will have to establish that Smith is in breach of this section.

While Smith's expenses fall within s75(1)(b), it is not clear whether Smith, a 'political activist' is himself a candidate, agent or authorised person. If he is not, there may be a breach of s75. (If he is, a further question will arise in respect of the limits imposed in s76). However, s75 applies at the local constituency and not the national level. In *R v Tronoh Mines* (1952), it was held that the prohibition applied to local constituencies, not national expenditure, and thus the defendant company's advertisement in *The Times* warning against the 'perils of socialism' was not in breach of the Representation of the People Act. Although not clear from the facts, it appears as if Smith's leaflet campaign is conducted in the local constituency and could therefore be in breach of s75.

Smith may argue that his expenses are not incurred 'with a view to promoting or procuring the election of a candidate' but were rather intended to prevent the election of the Conservative Party candidate. In *DPP v Luft* (1977) it was held that the offence was made out where, as on the facts here, unauthorised expenditure was incurred through a leaflet campaign designed to prevent the election of a candidate; the House of Lords accepted that expenditure designed to prevent the election of one candidate could indirectly promote the election of others.

In conclusion, the Conservative Party candidate may be able to challenge the result of the election on the grounds of the commission by Smith of electoral offences, although we are not given sufficient information to conclude definitively. If Smith has acted in breach of s75, the Election Court may declare the election void and a new election could be held. In the absence of any apparent link between Smith and the successful candidate, it might be doubted whether the Court would do so.

b) It is undeniably true that there is something of a contradiction between the rules regulating the conduct of elections at constituency as opposed to national level. The former are indeed quite detailed, particularly in the limits put on expenditure on the election. It is therefore somewhat anomalous that, despite these strict controls, there are few equivalent controls on national expenditure, for example on broadcasting or advertising in newspapers and billboards. However, to claim a total absence of controls goes too far: some control exists, both at national level and, more especially, when 'national' expenditure 'spills over' and directly affects the local campaign. Second, it does not follow that, even if there is a disparity between national and local control, local rules 'are of little value'.

The reason for this disparity is found, as so often in constitutional law, in history. Up until the beginning of the present century, bribery and corruption were rife during election campaigns; not until the Parliamentary and Municipal Elections Act 1872, introducing a secret ballot, and the Parliamentary Elections (Corrupt and Illegal Practices) Act 1883, imposing strict controls on expenditure, was it possible to establish an effective framework to stamp out such practices. This framework has remained largely in place in the Representation of the People Act Part II. In its inception, therefore, the system of local control was both necessary and justified.

Since then, however, the development of the party system and the growth in national campaigning has not been met with attempts to impose equivalent controls at a national level. It is true that the legislation makes 'no attempt to control the purchasing of victory on a national scale' (HF Rawlings, *Law & the Electoral Process* (1988), p137). However, it is important to appreciate that the paucity of national control does not, in itself, deny the validity of the local controls; these still perform an essential function in ensuring aspects of the fairness of elections by preventing (or limiting) corrupt and illegal practices.

Moreover, the detailed rules regulating local elections may impinge on national situations. In *R* v *Tronoh Mines Ltd*, although it was held that expenditure on national advertising was not caught by the prohibition on local expenditure, this was because the campaign was not intended to support a particular candidate in a particular constituency but rather a particular party generally. Clearly, where a national advertising campaign did have such an effect, it could fall within the detailed local rules. In *Meek* v *Lothian Regional Council* (1983) an advertising campaign by the council did fall within the local prohibitions since, geographically, it was 'local' (even though regional) and not 'general' political propaganda.

It is, however, clear from *Grieve* v *Douglas-Home* (1965) that national expenditure on party political broadcasts is not caught by the provisions of the Representation of the People Act and, to this extent, there is no real control on the levels of expenditure at the national level. The Election Court justified its decision on the grounds that broadcasts transmitted information of general public importance, and were not designed to procure the election of individual candidates. Again, a broadcast designed to procure an individual's election might yet be caught.

The absence of specific controls on the national campaign in the Representation of the People Act does not mean that the application of the general law is excluded. Thus, for example, controls on broadcasting exist under s6(1)(b) and (c) of the Broadcasting Act 1990, imposing a statutory duty of impartiality in broadcasting news and political programmes and, therefore, challenge may be brought for breach of this duty. Limited controls over advertising also exist in general law, for example under planning law regulating billboard advertising. It is true, though, that the effect of *Tronoh Mines* is largely to exclude national advertising from effective control. The most glaring area of disparity lies in the absence of rules regulating the financing of political parties at national levels, although even here there is some applicable legislation (see, eg, Trade Union and Labour Relations (Consolidation) Act 1992; Companies Act 1985).

In conclusion, although there is a significant lack of control over national election campaigns, legal controls are not wholly absent. Nor does absence necessarily cast doubt on the validity of local controls. That the detailed local rules do nothing to control national campaigns suggests not so much that these are of little value – they continue to play an important role – but rather that their value would be enhanced were a more comprehensive system of national control to be instituted.

1994 QUESTIONS AND SUGGESTED SOLUTIONS

QUESTION FOUR

'The increasing willingness of the House of Lords over the past 15 years to amend and delay Government Bills may be viewed either as an affront to democracy or a legitimate constitutional safeguard for the citizen.'

Discuss.

University of London LLB Examination
(for External Students) Constitutional Law June 1994 Q4

General Comment

Careful reading of this question is required: it is not a question on the House of Lords in isolation, but rather deals primarily with the relationship between the Lords and the Commons. As such, it admits of quite a general treatment and allows the candidate to discuss not merely the composition, functions and powers of the Lords, but also issues such as the electoral system, the 'elective dictatorship' and the inadequacy of scrutiny of government by the Commons. All these must, of course, be integrated into discussion of the specific quote. While it would be possible to argue that recent activism in the Lords is an affront to democracy, or that it is a legitimate constitutional safeguard, the approach taken here is that it is a bit of both.

Skeleton Solution

- Composition of Lords: hereditary and life peers.
- Electoral system: effect on composition of Commons.
- House of Lords' functions: scrutiny.
- Reform?

Suggested Solution

Figures suggest that the House of Lords has indeed been increasingly willing to amend government Bills: thus, while in the mid-1960s the average number of amendments per session was in the region of 500, by the mid-1980s there were well over 1,000, and between 1987 and 1993, this figure had risen to some 2,300 (see, generally, JAG Griffith and M Ryle, *Parliament: Functions, Practice and Procedures* (1989); DN Clarke & D Shell 'Revision and Amendment of Legislation by the House of Lords – A Case Study' [1994] PL 409). While it is important to realise that many of these amendments will be minor, technical, or moved by the government, there has been a consistent increase, during the period since 1979, in policy amendments, those dealing with the substance of the proposed legislation, and, moreover, in government defeats on policy issues. The effect of any increase in amendments will obviously have a delaying effect on the passage of legislation, but it is worth noting that the Lords attempted recently not merely to delay but to reject, on second reading, the War Crimes Bill. Only the eventual use of the Parliament Acts 1911–1949 – the first use of the 1949 Act and the first use of the procedures by a Conservative administration – ensured passage of the legislation.

If, then, we accept the statement in the quote for discussion, it is necessary to consider whether this recent tendency in the Lords to delay or amend Bills is either 'an affront to democracy' or a 'legitimate constitutional safeguard for the citizen'. Of course, the quote assumes that it is either one or the other. The approach taken here, however, will be to argue that it is more likely to be a bit of both.

Arguments that the role of the House of Lords in the legislative process is an 'affront to democracy' focus primarily on the composition of the Lords. As an unelected body, comprised largely of both hereditary peers, whose status as members of the legislature is derived from blood rather than the ballot box, and of life peers (Life Peerages Act 1958), who are political appointees, the House is fundamentally unrepresentative. As Lord Birkenhead once memorably said in debate to a member who annoyed him: 'The noble Lord represents no-one but himself – and I don't think much of his constituency!'

It is arguable, however, that the composition of the Commons, albeit that the members are directly elected by the people, is itself somewhat lacking in democratic foundations. The effect of the electoral system, when combined with the modern development of the party system, is to ensure 'strong government' – or, as Lord Hailsham has suggested, an 'elective dictatorship' – at the expense of representation of the electorate. The experience of the Alliance and, subsequently, the Social and Liberal Democratic parties since 1979, when a popular vote of roughly 25 per cent is regularly translated into a percentage of seats in the Commons in the region of 5 per cent, bears eloquent testimony to the inadequacies of the current electoral system in ensuring truly democratic representation in the House of Commons.

It follows that, while there is force in the assertion that the role of the Lords does constitute an affront to democracy, it does not tell the whole story. Concern, moreover, has been expressed of late that the powers of government are no longer subject to adequate scrutiny by the Commons; with the advent of the party system and party discipline, it is rare in modern times for a government not to enjoy a majority in the Commons. While rebellion by supporters of the government is less rare of late, it remains true that in the vast majority of cases scrutiny of the government is the function of the opposition; as, almost by definition, a minority, it is clear that such scrutiny can scarcely claim to be effective. Further, pressure on the parliamentary timetable has increased – as evidenced by the dramatic increase in the use of the guillotine in recent years – to such an extent that the adequate scrutiny of legislative proposals is often lacking.

It is in this context that it is possible to argue that the recent activism in the House of Lords can be seen as a 'legitimate constitutional safeguard for the citizen'. It is generally accepted that, particularly since the advent of life peers in 1958, the level of expertise and ability in the Lords has been significantly enhanced. This factor, when taken together with the lack of time in the Commons and the possibility of a 'strong' government inclining too much towards elective dictatorship, suggests that there is both merit in and justification for this increasing willingness to amend and delay government bills. It is also worth noting that while the Conservatives generally enjoy a majority in the Lords (albeit not over opposition and cross-benchers combined), it is paradoxically easier for the Lords to amend, delay and even defeat Bills proposed by a Conservative government than a Labour administration – for the simple reason that the latter is more likely to honour the promise in the preamble to the Parliament Act 1911 'to substitute for the House of Lords ... a Second Chamber constituted on a popular instead of hereditary basis'.

In conclusion, while it is undeniable that as an unelected and unrepresentative body it is certainly anomalous that the House of Lords should exercise so much influence, if not power, in the legislative process, it is going too far to describe its willingness to amend and delay government bills as an affront to democracy; ultimately, as the enactment of the War Crimes Act 1991 suggests, a government sufficiently determined will ensure it has its way. Equally, and for much the same reasons, it is hard to see how the House of Lords could be an effective constitutional safeguard for the citizen. Ultimately, the House will almost always respect the convention of deference to the will of the elected chamber; at best, the House can make the government think again. Rather, the true situation is that the House of Lords, undemocratic as it is, still has a useful role to play in the constitution in enhancing scrutiny of an increasingly powerful executive. Advocates of abolition or reform might better consider how an alternative electoral system, coupled with reform of the Commons and its procedures, allowing for more effective scrutiny and revision of Bills, could yet render the House of Lords superfluous.

QUESTION FIVE

'The uncertainties surrounding the scope and exercise of the Royal Prerogative give rise to serious constitutional questions concerning the rule of law in a democratic society.'

Critically assess this statement.

University of London LLB Examination
(for External Students) Constitutional Law June 1994 Q5

General Comment

A question that illustrates the dangers in question-spotting, since it requires knowledge of both the rule of law and of the Royal Prerogative. A tricky question, too, since both these areas must be discussed – and linked – in the context of the quote. However, given this overlap and that it is not an easy question, candidates familiar with the areas should not be dissuaded from an attempt; a good answer to a difficult question should gain a good mark. As ever, the success of the attempt depends largely on actually answering the question – critically assessing the statement; and to do this, the introduction is crucial.

Skeleton Solution

- Definitions of the rule of law, the Royal Prerogative and their relationship.
- Prerogative and statute: Bill of Rights 1688; *Attorney-General* v *De Keyser's Royal Hotel*; *Northumbria Police Authority*; *BBC* v *Johns*.
- Political control: ministerial responsibility.
- Judicial control: GCHQ case; *Everett*; *Binbasi*; *Bentley*.
- Conclusions.

Suggested Solution

It is doubtful whether Dicey's traditional exposition of the rule of law, focusing on government in accordance with law and equality before the law, remains wholly adequate. In a modern democratic society the rule of law means more: it requires, inter alia, clarity and certainty in law, so that individuals know what it is they can and cannot do. To the extent, therefore, that there are 'uncertainties surrounding the scope and exercise of the Royal Prerogative', it would be hard to disagree with the statement in the quote. But it will be argued below that the scope of the Prerogative today is relatively well-defined and that recent developments, particularly in judicial review of the Prerogative, have clarified many of the uncertainties surrounding its exercise.

Blackstone (in his *Commentaries*) defined the Prerogative in terms of the special pre-eminence enjoyed by the King over and above all others, so that prerogative powers were those enjoyed by the King alone and not shared with the ordinary subject. Such a definition does seem to offend the requirement of equality before the law, but it is important to recognise the justification for the existence of prerogative powers – that they are necessary to enable the Crown to perform its function of governing the country. Some inequality may thus be tolerable, provided adequate controls exist to prevent abuse of power. It is submitted that the controls available, both political and legal, are indeed adequate to ensure that the government, in exercising prerogative powers, is subject to the rule of law.

Certain propositions about the Prerogative are, in modern law, quite clear: it has been settled law since the Bill of Rights 1688 that the Prerogative is subordinate to statute; Parliament may thus abolish prerogative powers. Even when Parliament has not chosen to abolish a prerogative, *Attorney-General* v *De Keyser's Royal Hotel* (1920) establishes that, where prerogative and statutory powers co-exist, the Crown is precluded from relying on the former and must act under its statutory powers. While it is arguable that the *application* of this principle may give rise to some uncertainties – see, eg, *R* v *Home Secretary, ex parte Northumbria Police Authority* (1989) – the principle itself is clear. Similarly, prerogative powers are residual: in Diplock LJ's memorable phrase, 'It is 350 years and a civil war too late ... to broaden the prerogative'; its limits 'are now well settled and incapable of extension' (*BBC* v *Johns* (1965)).

That government is carried out in accordance with law is also ensured, at least in theory, through political controls; although in law prerogative powers vest in the Monarch, they are by convention exercised on her behalf by ministers of the Crown. Those ministers are, by convention, responsible to Parliament in respect of any exercise of prerogative powers. Should ministers abuse their powers, Parliament may remove those powers by statute. It is, however, arguable that the ability of Parliament adequately to control ministers is, at least in modern law, something of a fiction. To this extent it is true that the dominance of Parliament by the executive does pose serious questions concerning the rule of law in a democratic society – and not merely in the context of the Prerogative.

It is perhaps in recognition of this 'democratic deficit' that the past ten years have seen remarkable developments in judicial control of the Prerogative. The traditional rule was that the courts exercised jurisdiction to determine the existence of a prerogative power – they could thus decide that a claimed prerogative did not exist – but once its existence was established, they would not rule on the manner of its exercise. This traditional approach was abandoned in the GCHQ case (*Council for Civil Service Unions* v *Minister for the Civil Service* (1985)), where the House of

Lords held that, in principle, the exercise of prerogative powers was subject to judicial review, although their Lordships did add that not all prerogative powers were reviewable: in particular, where the exercise of the power gave rise to a 'non-justiciable issue', it would still be immune from review.

It is noteworthy, however, that in the recent case of *R v Secretary of State for the Home Department, ex parte Bentley* (1993), the Court of Appeal was willing to review the exercise of the prerogative of mercy, treating as obiter its inclusion in the list of non-justiciable issues given in GCHQ. Moreover, in *R v Secretary of State for Foreign and Commonwealth Affairs, ex parte Everett* (1989), the Court was prepared to review the prerogative power to issue passports on the basis that its exercise involved 'administrative decisions affecting individuals'; and in *R v Secretary of State for the Home Department, ex parte Binbasi* (1989) it was accepted that courts had jurisdiction to review the exercise of the Prerogative in refusing a grant of asylum.

In conclusion, it remains true to say that, in so far as the exercise of some prerogative powers remains unreviewable, primarily those that operate in the sphere of foreign affairs, serious constitutional questions concerning the rule of law do still arise – although it is, of course, always open to Parliament to intervene in case of abuse. It is however submitted that recent years have seen considerable clarification of the uncertainties surrounding the scope and exercise of the Prerogative and, while some do remain, the existence of the Royal Prerogative does not, in general, offend against the rule of law.

QUESTION SIX

The (fictitious) University Complaints Commission was set up under the Education Act 1994 to receive and investigate complaints from students on 'academic matters'. In May 1994, Jane, a final-year student reading History at the New World University, was accused of removing legal articles from the library, contrary to university regulations. Following internal disciplinary proceedings, at which Jane was not represented, Jane was expelled from the University.

Jane complained to the UCC requesting an investigation. The Commission wrote to Jane stating that it did not have jurisdiction to investigate her complaint, as her expulsion from the University related to a disciplinary rather than academic matter.

Jane wishes to apply for judicial review of the decision of the University to expel her and the decision of the University Complaints Commission.

Advise her.

University of London LLB Examination
(for External Students) Constitutional Law June 1994 Q6

General Comment

A reasonably straightforward problem question on judicial review. Such difficulty as there is lies in separating Jane's two possible challenges although there is a considerable overlap between the two. As ever, it is important in the answer to make it clear that Jane is actually being advised; do not, therefore, treat the question as a general essay. Structurally, the approach taken here is, it is submitted, appropriate for most problem questions on judicial review.

CONSTITUTIONAL LAW

Skeleton Solution

- Public law or private law?
- Procedural matters: leave, delay and sufficient interest.
- Grounds for challenge: GCHQ (illegality, irrationality and procedural impropriety).
- Remedies.
- Relevant case law: *Thomas* v *University of Bradford; ex parte Aga Khan; ex parte Datafin; ex parte Nolan; Page* v *Hull University Visitor; ex parte Brind*.

Suggested Solution

Jane has a number of hurdles to cross before she can apply for judicial review of the decisions of the New World University (NWU) and the University Complaints Commission (UCC). In the first place, she will need to establish that, in respect of both, her claim lies in public, rather than private, law. Second, assuming this requirement is satisfied, she will need to ensure that she satisfies the various procedural requirements. She will then have to establish the grounds on which she may challenge the decisions; and, finally, she will need to consider what remedies she seeks. It is proposed to examine each of these in their turn.

With respect, first, to the NWU, it might seem that Jane's relationship to the University is primarily contractual. Jane would have to consider whether the NWU is established by Royal Charter, rather than statute, in which case her claim would normally arise in private law under contract. If the charter provided for the resolution of disputes by a Visitor, these would probably fall within the Visitor's exclusive jurisdiction (*Thomas* v *University of Bradford* (1987)). There is insufficient information given in the problem to be certain, but on the assumption that the NWU and its disciplinary powers find their source in statute then, as a public body discharging public functions, this could be enough to establish that Jane's claim arose in public law. With respect to the UCC, established under statute, it seems clear that, whether one adopts a 'source of power' (see, eg, *R* v *Jockey Club, ex parte Aga Khan* (1993)) or functional test (see, eg, *R* v *Panel on Takeovers and Mergers, ex parte Datafin plc* (1987)), decisions of the UCC may be said to impact on the realm of public law. It would seem, therefore, that she may apply to challenge both decisions.

Jane must be advised of the importance of compliance with procedural requirements. Thus, Jane must act without delay, since a court can refuse to grant leave to apply for judicial review, or any relief sought, if there has been undue delay in making the application; the period is three months (Supreme Court Act 1981 s31(6); RSC Ord 53, r3(4)). There is no indication from the facts given that Jane falls outwith this period but, obviously, she must ensure she does not. Second, Jane must establish that she has locus standi to challenge either or both decisions since a

'court shall not grant leave to make ... an application [for judicial review] unless it considers that the applicant has a sufficient interest in the matter to which the application relates' (Supreme Court Act 1981 s31(3); RSC Ord 53, r3(7)).

Generally, whether the applicant does have sufficient interest is a matter of common sense – does the decision affect her? Some interests will be more sufficient than others – eg a financial interest in the decision taken, but no test is definitive, and it is always a matter of all the facts and circumstances. Here, it would seem that Jane clearly has the requisite sufficient interest. Finally, it is important to note that the court has a discretion whether to grant leave or not (Supreme Court Act 1981 s31(3); RSC Ord 53, r3(1)). Jane may yet fall foul of this requirement, though it would seem on the facts that her claim is not without merit.

The grounds on which a challenge to the decision of a public body may be made were conveniently laid down by Lord Diplock in the GCHQ case (*Council of Civil Service Unions* v *Minister for the Civil Service* (1985)): these are illegality, irrationality and procedural impropriety. It seems from the facts that Jane's grounds of challenge are different for the two bodies and it is thus necessary to consider them separately.

With respect to the decision of the NWU, there is a suggestion here of procedural impropriety, in the sense that Jane was not represented at the hearing of her case. Under the rules of natural justice, there is a right to a fair hearing (audi alteram partem). There is a variety of matters of which courts take account in deciding whether a hearing is fair, including adequate notice, oral hearings, a right to legal representation and the requirement of reasons. It always depends on all the facts and circumstances whether a hearing is fair. In *R* v *Manchester University, ex parte Nolan* (unreported) (see AJ Carroll: 'The abuse of academic disciplinary power' (1994) 144 NLJ 729 (May 27)), the Divisional Court suggested that the greater the gravity of the charge, the more appropriate a hearing would be. Given that we are told Jane was 'not represented' (which may mean either she was not actually present or, while present, she was denied legal representation), it would seem arguable that either constitutes a breach of the rules of natural justice. In *Page* v *Hull University Visitor* (1993) the House of Lords held that, even in the case of a university established under charter, a Visitor's decisions could be challenged by way of judicial review for procedural impropriety.

It is also possible that a challenge might lie in the sense that the punishment imposed – expulsion – was disproportionate to the nature of the alleged offence. While it is unlikely following the decision of the House of Lords in *R* v *Secretary of State for the Home Department, ex parte Brind* (1991) that proportionality is a separate head of review, it is still arguable that the decision could be categorised as irrational in the sense of *Wednesbury* (*Associated Provincial Picture Houses* v *Wednesbury Corporation* (1948)) unreasonableness.

A challenge to the decision of the UCC refusing to investigate Jane's claim could lie on the grounds that in misinterpreting the phrase 'academic matters' in the Education Act 1994, the UCC has made an error in law in deciding that it does not have jurisdiction. In *Page*, the House of Lords explained that, where Parliament has conferred a decision-making function on a public body, this could only have been done 'on the basis that it was to be exercised on the correct legal basis: a misdirection in law in making the decision therefore rendered the decision ultra vires'. Whether or not Jane may succeed on this ground will depend on whether or not disciplinary matters fall within the meaning of 'academic matters' in the Act. It is impossible to say what a court might decide here, but Jane has at least an arguable case.

Finally, it remains to consider the remedies that might be available to Jane. The most appropriate remedies would be certiorari to quash the decision of the NWU expelling Jane. Certiorari would also seem to be the most appropriate remedy vis-à-vis the UCC, requiring it to reconsider Jane's complaint.

In conclusion, Jane may well be able to challenge the decisions of both the NWU and the UCC. Whether or not she will be successful in her challenge will depend on all the facts and circumstances of her case. We do not have sufficient information here to reach a definitive conclusion.

QUESTION SEVEN

'For [Dicey] there was no need for any statement of fundamental principles operating as a kind of higher law because political freedom was adequately protected by the common law and by an independent Parliament acting as a watchdog against any excess of zeal by the executive.' (Wade and Bradley, 1993).

To what extent does Dicey's view require revision to meet the needs of today's society?

University of London LLB Examination
(for External Students) Constitutional Law June 1994 Q7

General Comment

A general question which, again, illustrates the dangers in question-spotting, since a good answer requires the adoption of an overall perspective. The question is sufficiently wide as to admit of an almost infinite number of approaches. Here, the intention is to concentrate on the protection of civil liberties (or human rights) in a system based on parliamentary sovereignty. Hence, the bill of rights debate is important to the answer.

Skeleton Solution

- Common law and civil liberties: general position; case law (*Dr Bonham's Case*; *Pickin* v *BRB*; *Malone* v *MPC*; *Malone* v *UK*; 'Spycatcher').
- Parliamentary sovereignty and civil liberties: scrutiny of executive.
- A bill of rights? The ECHR as a model.

Suggested Solution

It is submitted that Dicey's view does indeed require revision to meet the needs of today's society. It is questionable whether or not his statement was accurate when first made and mention will be made of this point below. Dicey based his assertion that there was 'no need for any statement of fundamental principles operating as a kind of higher law' on two propositions: the first, that common law provided adequate protection; the second, that Parliament was an effective check on the executive. It is proposed to discuss these propositions in their turn, pointing out the inadequacy of both in the light of contemporary society. It will be suggested in the conclusion that the most effective form of revision would be the incorporation of the European Convention on Human Rights as part of English law, as a prospective 'higher law'.

Whether or not common law has ever provided adequate protection for political freedom is a matter for debate. It may once have done so, in those days when, if an Act of Parliament was 'against common right and reason, or repugnant', the common law could 'control it and adjudge such Act to be void' (*Dr Bonham's Case* (1610)). But even when Dicey wrote, the doctrine of the sovereignty of Parliament was well-recognised. And, of course, in today's society, the idea that an Act of Parliament could be disregarded in so far as it was contrary to such fundamental principles as the 'the law of God or the law of nature or natural justice ... has become obsolete' (*Pickin* v *British Railways Board* (1974)).

The common law does, it is true, recognise fundamental principles, particularly in the area of civil liberties: 'England', it has been said, 'is not a country where everything is forbidden except what is expressly permitted: it is a country where everything is permitted except what is expressly forbidden' (*Malone* v *Metropolitan Police Commissioner* (1979)). And, thus, freedoms of speech, of assembly and of religion, for example, are inherent in the common law. But Sir Robert Megarry VC's dictum fails to inform us as to what restraints, if any, the common law can impose on prohibitions. Is there anything, any 'kind of higher law', to prevent everything being 'expressly forbidden'? It is suitably ironic that in *Malone* itself this principle of liberty was used to deny restraints on the powers of government to violate an individual's privacy: Mr Malone's only recourse lay outside the United Kingdom, before the European Court of Human Rights in Strasbourg (*Malone* v *UK* (1985)).

But these liberties are not necessarily protected from erosion, even by the common law itself. In 'Spycatcher' (*Attorney-General* v *Guardian Newspapers (No 1)* (1987)), for example, the House of Lords upheld an interlocutory injunction restraining freedom of expression because, on balance, the common law regarded the protection of confidential government secrets as a more worthy goal. Lord Bridge's famous dissent that the decision marked a 'significant step down that very dangerous road' to a totalitarian regime hardly suggests that the common law always guarantees adequate protection of political freedom.

Nor, more problematically, can the judiciary stand against the will of Parliament. Parliament can, and does, enact restrictions on civil liberties and, although the judiciary can apply presumptions such as those against alteration of the common law or in favour of individual liberty, ultimately, the concept of some 'kind of higher law' higher than an Act of Parliament has been alien to English constitutional thought since at least 1688. As Lord Scarman has argued, the common law is ultimately helpless 'in the face of the legislative sovereignty of Parliament which makes it difficult for the legal system to accommodate the concept of fundamental and inviolable human rights' (Lord Scarman, *English Law: The New Dimension* (1974), p15). This was also the theoretical position when Dicey wrote.

There was, however, more force in Dicey's second proposition, at least when he wrote. Parliament in the mid-nineteenth century enjoyed something of a golden age, when it truly did exercise a degree of control over any 'excess of zeal by the executive'. It was far from uncommon for governments to be forced to resign through loss of a vote of confidence. Since then, as Wade and Bradley point out, 'the inexorable growth of the party system and its attendant discipline has seen the executive increasingly gain control of the House of Commons' (AW Bradley & KD Ewing, *Constitutional and Administrative Law* (11th ed, 1993), p411); the House of Lords was effectively neutered in 1911 (Parliament Act 1911). While it would be an over-simplification to assume that Parliament could not restrain executive zeal in extremis, the practical likelihood of it doing so in the case of a gradual erosion of civil liberties is not great – one need only refer to the recent controversy over the enactment of the Criminal Justice and Public Order Act 1994.

Even if we accept that Dicey's view does require revision, and there is now a need for some 'statement of fundamental principles operating as a kind of higher law', the question remains how this need might be met. Proponents of this revisionist view rely strongly on the argument that Britain needs a new 'Bill of Rights' and usually look for it in the European Convention on Human Rights. Lord Lester has recently indicated his intent to introduce yet another Bill seeking to incorporate the Convention as part of English law but, at the time of writing, the prospects of it being enacted must be slim. Even if the European Convention on Human Rights were to be incorporated, while political considerations might influence a government seeking to legislate in an area impinging on rights contained in the enacted Convention and although a degree of entrenchment might be achieved on the model of s2(4) of the European Communities Act 1972, ultimately Parliament – for which read the executive – could not be prevented from repealing this purported 'higher law'.

There is, in conclusion, little doubt that Dicey's view is no longer adequate to explain away the absence of any fundamental higher law in the United Kingdom. At the very least, the ability of the common law to protect political freedom and of Parliament to control the executive has been significantly eroded. Although incorporation of the European Convention on Human Rights would, as explained above, be no panacea, it might nevertheless go some way to satisfy the need for a statement of fundamental principles operating as a kind of higher law. That need is as great today as it was when Dicey wrote; and it is submitted that he himself would have revised his views had he been writing on the needs of today's society.

QUESTION EIGHT

'One result of the legal reforms over the past fifteen years is that local government, once the most responsive form of democracy, is being relegated to the position of manager of local services with little or no residual autonomy.'

Critically assess this statement.

University of London LLB Examination
(for External Students) Constitutional Law June 1994 Q8

General Comment

As with all questions on the constitutional role and position of local government, a good answer requires a fairly detailed knowledge of rather a technical area. However, if the candidate has such knowledge, it should be possible to produce just such a good answer. But, as ever, the most important thing to do is to answer the question: by discussing the statement quoted.

Skeleton Solution

- Historical development.
- Local government: representative role.

- Financial control.
- Functional control: education; housing; police.

Suggested Solution

It is hard to deny that the past 15 years have seen considerable legislative activity by Parliament in the sphere of central-local government relations. No doubt, such is inevitable where the political complexion of central government has remained unchanged during that period, so that the almost inevitable tension between central and local government, where the two are of different political persuasions, has been exacerbated. However, the question in essence rests upon two assumptions: first, that local government was 'once the most responsive form of democracy' and, second, that the result of the recent reforms has been to relegate local government to the position of a 'manager of local services with little or no residual autonomy'. In discussing the quote, it is necessary to consider whether these are valid assumptions.

English law has long recognised a functional division of powers between local and central government, at least as long ago as the Justices of the Peace Act 1361; moreover, it is clear that a considerable degree of local autonomy was enjoyed by local officials such as sheriffs and constables prior to that date. The 1361 Act might well be seen as an early attempt at centralisation. By the seventeenth century, however, central control of the justices was much reduced. 'For the next 200 years', as Hood Phillips notes, 'local government was, subject to the legislative power of Parliament, almost autonomous' (O Hood Phillips and P Jackson, *Constitutional and Administrative Law* (7th ed) (1987), p583). Since the main reforms of the nineteenth century, establishing the modern framework of local government, the central-local relationship has been well-recognised as an essential part of the constitutional system in England.

It was in these nineteenth century reforms that local government first acquired its representative function. Starting with the Municipal Corporations Act 1835, several Acts were enacted to provide for locally elected councils (see, eg, Local Government Acts 1888 and 1894). Loughlin has pointed out that, at least until the advent of direct elections to the European Parliament, 'Local councils are the only governmental institutions outside of Parliament which are subject to direct periodic election' (M Loughlin, 'The Restructuring of Central-Local Government Relations' in J Jowell and D Oliver, *The Changing Constitution* (3rd ed, 1994), 261, at p264). The basic legal framework of local government elections is now contained in the Representation of the People Acts 1983 and 1985. As elected bodies, they thus enjoy a democratic legitimacy unmatched by any other institution of the constitution, save the House of Commons itself.

Indeed, it may be argued that in some respects local government enjoys more legitimacy than its central counterpart. Thus, unlike a prospective Westminister candidate, an intending councillor, to qualify as a candidate, must have some connection with the area in which the election is fought, either as an elector for the area, or as having resided, worked or occupied land there during the previous year (Local Government Act 1972, s79); similarly, a local authority's term of office is fixed by statute (the main statutory provisions, in the Local Government Act 1972, are rather complex; see, generally, HWR Wade: *Administrative Law* (7th ed, 1994), p122 et seq). In these senses, then, it is possible to argue that local authorities are a highly responsive form of democracy, where the links between represented and representative are much closer than at the national level. However, it should be pointed out that the turn-out of voters at local elections is generally far poorer than that for general elections, which tends to undermine their legitimacy and, hence, the claim that they are the 'most' responsive form of democracy.

Nevertheless, it might seem, given that they enjoy considerable democratic legitimacy, to be appropriate that they enjoy a degree of local autonomy in the conduct of those aspects of the executive function that may properly be carried out at local level. It is somewhat ironic, no doubt, that the current government should put such faith in the principle of subsidiarity (see the European Community Treaty, article 3(b) as the 'local' authority vis-à-vis the 'central' European Community, and yet be unwilling to concede a similar sphere of competence to local authorities in England. Yet it seems true that reforms in the last 15 years have tended to reduce local government to the status of a 'manager of local services with little or no residual autonomy'.

Central government has always exercised ultimate control over the structure of local government, culminating in the enactment of the 1972 Act. This process is certain to continue under the Local Government Act 1992 with the establishment of the Local Government Commission empowered to make recommendations to the Secretary of State for structural, boundary or electoral changes in local government (Local Government Act 1992, s13). In terms of finance, central government exerts the power of the purse-string, since local government relies primarily on government grants for the revenue to carry out its tasks: it may not therefore be too surprising that central government might wish to exercise greater control over how this money is spent, but it is certainly arguable that party political considerations have been to the fore of late. Further, although the alterations in the system empowering local authorities to tax – the community charge and its replacement the council tax – were intended to make local government more responsive to its electors, they have instead proved highly controversial and led to considerable friction over the issue of central governmental controls 'capping' local expenditure. As Wade says, 'the Local Government Finance Acts 1982–92 have given the central government a stranglehold on local authority revenue and expenditure' (see Wade (above) at p139).

The period since 1979 has also seen considerable legislative action by central government encroaching on the functions of local government. In matters such as education and housing, for example, historically typical areas of local control, recent changes have seen further centralisation. The Education Reform Act 1988 permits schools to 'opt out' of local authority control. The establishment of Housing Action Trusts under the Housing Act 1988 has removed council house ownership from local authority control. That this process is still continuing is evidenced by the Police and Magistrates' Courts Act 1994, which further reduces the role of local government in the provision of policing services.

In conclusion, there is much force in the assertion in the quote that local government, a responsive form of democracy, has been reduced to the status of agent of central government, deprived of much of the autonomy that it enjoyed in practice, if not strict law, in earlier years.

HLT Publications

HLT books are specially planned and written to help you in every stage of your studies. Each of the wide range of textbooks is brought up-to-date annually, and the companion volumes of our Law Series are all designed to work together.

You can buy HLT books from your local bookshop, or in case of difficulty, order direct using this form.

The Law Series covers the following modules:

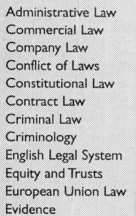

- Administrative Law
- Commercial Law
- Company Law
- Conflict of Laws
- Constitutional Law
- Contract Law
- Criminal Law
- Criminology
- English Legal System
- Equity and Trusts
- European Union Law
- Evidence
- Family Law
- Jurisprudence
- Land Law
- Law of International Trade
- Legal Skills and System
- Public International Law
- Revenue Law*
- Succession
- Tort

*No Textbook or Casebook available for this title

The HLT Law Series:

A comprehensive range of books for your law course, and the legal aspects of business and commercial studies.

Each module is covered by a comprehensive six-part set of books

- Textbook
- Casebook
- Revision Workbook
- Suggested Solutions, for:
  - 1985-90
  - 1991-94
  - 1995

Module	Books required	Cost

To complete your order, please fill in the form overleaf

	Postage	
	TOTAL	

Prices (including postage and packing in the UK): Textbooks £19.00; Casebooks £19.00; Revision Workbooks £10.00; Suggested Solutions (1985-90) £9.00, Suggested Solutions (1991-94) £6.00, Suggested Solutions (1995) £3.00.

For Europe, add 15% postage and packing (£20 maximum). For the rest of the world, add 40% for airmail (£35 maximum).

ORDERING

By telephone to 01892 724371, with your credit card to hand
By fax to 01892 724206 (giving your credit card details).
By post to:
HLT Publications,
The Gatehouse, Ruck Lane, Horsmonden, Tonbridge, Kent TN12 8EA

When ordering by post, please enclose full payment by cheque or banker's draft, or complete the credit card details below.

We aim to despatch your books within 3 working days of receiving your order.

Name

Address

Postcode

Telephone

Total value of order, including postage: £ ☐
I enclose a cheque/banker's draft for the above sum, or

charge my   ☐ Access/Mastercard   ☐ Visa   ☐ American Express

Card number
☐☐☐☐ ☐☐☐☐ ☐☐☐☐ ☐☐☐☐

Expiry date
☐☐☐☐

Signature

Date

Publications from **The Old Bailey Press**

Cracknell's Statutes

A full understanding of statute law is vital for any student, and this series presents the original wording of legislation, together with any amendments and substitutions and the sources of these changes.

Cracknell's Companions

Recognised as invaluable study aids since their introduction in 1961, this series summarises all the most important court decisions and acts, and features a glossary of Latin words, as well as full indexing.

Please telephone our Order Hotline on 01892 724371, or write to our order department, for full details of these series.